THE UNKNOWN BATTLE
Metz, 1944

THE UNKNOWN BATTLE

Metz, 1944

Anthony Kemp

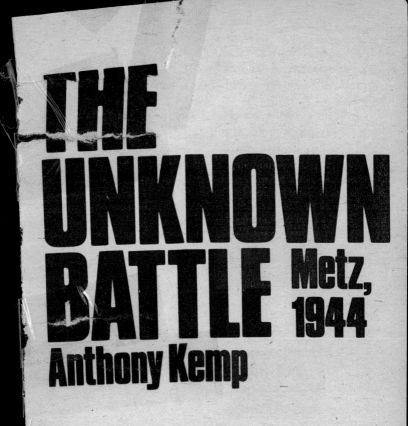

STEIN AND DAY / *Publishers* / New York

FIRST STEIN AND DAY PAPERBACK EDITION 100~
The Unknown Battle was originally published
in hardcover by Stein and Day / *Publishers*
in 1981.
Copyright © 1981 by Anthony Kemp
All rights reserved Stein and Day, Incorporated
Designed by Louis Ditizio
Printed in the United States of America
Stein and Day / *Publishers* / Scarborough House,
Briarcliff Manor, N.Y. 10510
ISBN 0-8128-8209-1

Maps printed by Defense Mapping Agency Topo-
graphic Center reprinted from Hugh M. Cole's *The
Lorraine Campaign* published by the U.S. Army
Historical Division, Washington, D.C., 1950.

"If you entrench yourself behind strong fortifications, you compel the enemy to seek a solution elsewhere."

—*Clausewitz*

"Les places fortes de votre Majesté défendent chacune une province. Metz défend l'Etat." (Each of Your Majesty's fortresses defends a province. Metz defends the State.)

—*Vauban to Louis XIV*

CONTENTS

Maps and Photos between pages 126 and 127

Map list

Diagram list

Introduction

The latter stages of the Second World War have been exhaustively chronicled in books and on film, and most of those involved in high command have given us the benefit of their memoirs. Among those officers, one of the most dashing was General Patton, who became a legend during his own lifetime and was a great believer in the public relations value of war correspondents. Indeed, the period June 1944 to May 1945 could well be described as campaigning by headline.

Patton's Third U.S. Army came to prominence during the breakout from Normandy and the headlong pursuit across France, after which it faded from the scene, only to reappear in the headlines during the Ardennes offensive in December 1944. This book is concerned with the period of stalemate between September and November 1944, when the Third Army was stalled on the Moselle and starved of headlines. Apart from the official history, the story of the struggle on the Moselle and the battle to capture the fortress city of Metz has never been detailed. Generals Bradley and Patton gave it scant notice in their memoirs, and it is almost as if a discreet veil of silence had been drawn over the whole affair—which is an injustice to those who fought and died there. It was certainly not an episode of which those responsible for the direction of the campaign could be particularly proud, as the only glory going was won by the junior officers and enlisted men of both sides.

For the historian, the Battle of Metz is full of ironies. For a start, it would seem to be the only instance in comparatively modern times of two battles having been fought over the same ground and with the same tactical problems—in 1870 and 1944. In addition, there nearly was another Battle of Metz in November 1918, which was avoided only when the German High Command requested an armistice—a battle which would also have involved American troops.

In 1870, a German army attacking a French force entrenched on the high ground to the west of the city, after suffering appalling casualties in frontal assaults, was content to conduct a leisurely siege. In 1944, it was the turn of the Germans to defend that same high ground, and the attacking Americans also suffered correspondingly in frontal assaults until they finally managed to turn the flanks.

Another oddity is that in 1944, the Germans were making good use of fortifications which their predecessors had constructed between 1870 and 1914. After handing the fortifications back to France in 1918, Germany reoccupied them again in 1940, without firing a shot.

The course of the battle was largely determined by chance. Had there not been supply problems, it is probable that the Germans would have been bounced back over the Moselle and would have made their stand in the Siegfried Line. The halt enforced on Patton by the fuel shortage at the beginning of September enabled them to rally and build up a front that was stiffened by the fortuitous presence of crack troops from the Metz military schools. Thus it was that Patton found himself involved in an unplanned battle and was forced to wage a type of warfare for which he had neither the talent nor the temperament.

The actual fighting was mainly a matter for the infantry of both sides. The terrain was unsuitable for armor, and the poor weather negated the advantage of air superiority possessed by the Allies. The battle represents the last time in which extensive use was made of permanent fortifications to fulfill their traditional purpose of delaying a superior force. Had the Germans been able to hold out just a few weeks longer, Patton would have been unable to respond flexibly to the threat posed by the Ardennes offensive. Hitler has been justly criticized for his tactical doctrine of holding on to territory at all costs, but in this instance, for the loss of some weak formations, he was able to impose a valuable check on the Allies and win a temporary propaganda victory.

The story of the battle, however, is not one of grand strategy, but an account of small, bitterly contested engagements at a time when the whole Allied line was threatened with winter stalemate. It is more a story of heroism on both sides, and a classic example of the unpleasant face of warfare. Suffering from the appalling weather conditions, the infantryman reverted to his primeval role as a one-man fighting unit, robbed of much of his twentieth century technical support.

Acknowledgments

A book of this sort can seldom be produced without the help of others who so often remain anonymous. Over a period of some five years I have written a vast number of letters to people who generously gave their time to answer my queries. The following authorities and private persons materially helped me in my research. To them I offer my thanks as well as to all the others, too numerous to list.

Susan Lemke of the library staff at the United States Military Academy at West Point took endless trouble on my behalf and made certain books available on long-term loan. Herr Gunther Fischer provided me with much of my knowledge of the Metz forts and loaned me an invaluable collection of maps. General Robert Nicolas also gave me plans of the forts as well as the benefit of his personal experience. Others who kindly gave or lent me books were Eversley Belfield, Robert (Hank) Williams, Prof. William McConahey, and Col. James Newton. The secretaries of the 5th, 90th, and 95th Divisional Associations put me in touch with veterans of the campaign, and Hans Stober, historian of the *17th SS Panzergrenadier Division,* gave me useful information. Lt. Cdr. Charles Robbins, USN, acted as my unpaid research assistant and produced copies of much of the documentary evidence on which this work is based. Others who corresponded include Phillipe Truttmann, Cletus Hollenbeck, Charles Bryan, Maj. Gen. Autry Maroun, Robert Ross, and Lt. Gen. John Kelly. Raun Kristensen and O. Andersen made a number of photographs available to me. Official bodies that provided help and opened otherwise closed doors include the *Verband Deutscher Soldaten,* The Office of the Military Governor of Metz, and the U.S. Army Military History Institute.

Finally I must mention my wife, who, in the cause of research has had to spend a number of "holidays" in one of the less popular corners of France. My thanks are due to her for her understanding, forbearance, and tolerance of "Metz mud."

Southampton, England

THE UNKNOWN BATTLE Metz, 1944

1. The General Situation:

Late August 1944

It is difficult to study a particular battle in isolation, since its origins and course are largely determined by the framework of the campaign during which it occurs. Earlier limited wars were often fought by two opposing armies on one particular front, but the very scale of modern warfare has meant that any theater of operations has become vastly extended. The subject of this book, the Battle of Metz, is but one episode in what is commonly referred to as the Northwest Europe Campaign. The campaign really began on 25 July 1944, when the Allied armies broke out from the confines of the Normandy peninsula, and ended in May of the following year when the German army surrendered unconditionally. To reduce the scale somewhat further, the operations that made up the Battle of Metz, and which lasted from September through to December 1944, were a part of the Lorraine campaign, waged during the same period by the Third U.S. Army.

If not for questions of grand strategy, and for certain decisions taken, the Battle of Metz might well have not taken place, or its course might have been entirely different. Thus, to fully understand the subject of this book, it is necessary first to consider the overall strategic situation that brought it into being, since this in turn directly influenced the type and scale of warfare waged in Lorraine.

THE ALLIED SITUATION

Planning for the invasion of the continent of Europe started back in 1943, finally to emerge as the operation known as Overlord. The Supreme Commander, General Eisenhower, was directed by the Combined Chiefs of Staff "to enter the continent of Europe and, in conjunction with the other Allied nations, undertake operations aimed at the heart of Germany and the destruction of her armed forces."[1] Actual detailed planning went only as far as the liberation of France up to the line of the river Seine, which, it was calculated, would be reached by D+90 (90 days after the initial landings). In fact this line was reached on 15 August (D+74), and, on the following day, units of the Third Army had a bridgehead at Mantes.

In the Overlord plan it was assumed that, on reaching the Seine, the Allied forces would pause to regroup and build up supplies, before making an assault crossing against a determined enemy. In the event, the totality of the German defeat in Normandy caught the Allies by surprise in that they were able to get over the Seine against negligible opposition.

The question was, What then? Shortly before the landings in June, SHAEF (Supreme Headquarters Allied Expeditionary Forces) planners laid down the general strategy to be followed once the lodgement area had been secured. Although Berlin was recognized as the ultimate political goal, the immediate military target was defined as the Ruhr area, the heart of German industrial production. It was rightly felt that the enemy would be forced to defend this vital zone; and thus the Allies would have the opportunity to defeat their forces in battle.

The problem was, How to get there? This question, in turn, led to the strategic controversy known as the "great argument." First, we must bear in mind that the post-Overlord scheme thought in terms of a gradual advance and a series of actions that would push the Germans back to their own frontier in the Aachen area by May 1945. It was assumed that, in the south, the front line on that date would be somewhere between Verdun and Metz.[2] It was considered too dangerous to advance by a single route and thus be laid open to a flank attack. SHAEF advocated an advance on a broad front, north and south of the Ardennes, which would ensure flexibility and force the Germans to spread their reserves. The main emphasis would be placed on the northern thrust along the traditional invasion route into northern Germany, via Maubeuge and Liège. Once across the Rhine and with the Ruhr neutralized, the way to Berlin would be open across the North German Plain. This maneuver would be supported by a subsidiary thrust on the Verdun-Metz line.

This is the first mention of the city of Metz in Allied planning; and it did not appear simply by chance. Any army wishing to move toward the Rhine south of the Ardennes had to pass through the Metz gap between the Ardennes hills and the Vosges, a basic fact of military geography. There was sound reasoning behind the decision to make this thrust a subsidiary one. The shortest route—and the one best suited for modern warfare—lay to the north of the Ardennes, over flat, open country plentifully supplied with airfields, and adjacent to the Channel ports for the delivery of supplies. The advance via Metz would, admittedly, lead to the Rhine, but through far more difficult country, virtually devoid of airfields. Without fighter cover, armored spearheads could not operate safely. Once on the Rhine in the Frankfurt-Mannheim area, there was no valuable strategic objective, except that the iron and coal mines in the Saar basin would have been "liberated." To complete the envelopment of the Ruhr, the attacking forces would have to turn to the north and move along the extremely restricted Rhine valley. Many writers have claimed that the route via Metz was the shortest way to Germany, which is true. The point is, however, that it did not really lead anywhere.

The post-Overlord scheme was an outline, rather than a plan for a given set of circumstances. The success of the breakout was so overwhelming that the Allied leadership found itself on the horns of a dilemma. Indeed, in mid-August, the whole command system was being called into question, and lack of firm overall direction was to lead to fatal delays. General Eisenhower, as Supreme Allied Commander, had deputies for air and naval affairs, but no commander of ground forces. He delegated this responsibility to General Montgomery for the assault phase of the landings. In addition, the latter was in command of the 21st Army Group, which was composed of the First U.S. Army under General Omar Bradley, and General Dempsey's Second British Army. It was recognized that, when Third U.S. Army became operational, Bradley would step up to command the 12th Army Group (First and Third Armies), which would be an all-American outfit. Thus, at the beginning of August, Bradley was in charge of an army group equal to Montgomery's, but subject to overall tactical supervision by the latter. From then on, since the strain of the campaign would be increasingly borne by American personnel, it was a situation that could not be allowed to continue. Montgomery was to continue to plead for a ground commander in overall charge, preferably himself, although he did declare his willingness to serve under Bradley. This particular controversy was only settled by Eisenhower's decision to take charge of the land battle himself on 1 September.

Speaking of the situation in mid-August in his memoirs, Montgomery said, with some justification, "But what was now needed were quick decisions and above all, a plan. And so far as I was aware, we had no plan."[3] This very search for a plan was the breeding ground for the "great argument." The comparatively easy successes so far had led to euphoria in the Allied camp, akin to the sentiment in 1914 that "the war would be over by Christmas." On 25 August, the day following the fall of Paris, the SHAEF Intelligence Summary included the following definitive paragraph:

"Two and a half months of bitter fighting . . . have brought the end of the war in Europe within sight, almost within reach. The strength of the German armies in the West has been shattered . . . and the Allied armies are streaming towards the frontiers of the Reich."[4]

In spite of Montgomery's statement that there was no plan, he naturally had one up his sleeve, which he put to General Bradley on 17 August. He called this the "German Schlieffen Plan of 1914 in reverse." The proposal was for the two army groups to advance together as a solid mass of some 40 divisions in a northeasterly direction, the direct route to the Ruhr. This massive force would pivot on Paris, and the right flank would be guarded by an American force strung out between Rheims and the Loire. The aim was to cross the Rhine before winter and to occupy the Ruhr. Montgomery definitely states that, at the time, Bradley agreed with him "entirely."[5] Needless to say, Bradley's own memoirs make no mention of this fact.

Instead, the Americans produced a plan of their own. This placed the emphasis on a thrust by the First and Third Armies through the Saar and on to the Rhine in the vicinity of Frankfurt. Bradley justified this in that it would carry his forces "past the fortifications of Metz and through the Maginot Line," and "across the undefended front that stretched beyond the Third Army."[6] Bradley here was speaking with the benefit of hindsight, because, as we shall see, the Americans had no knowledge of the Metz fortifications when they blundered into them.

Both these plans were developed by experienced staff officers brought up on the classic military dictum of concentration of maximum force at the decisive point. Both, however, were in direct contradiction to the SHAEF strategic aims, and differed radically as to the decisive point. This is not the place to get involved in the merits and demerits of the component parts of the "great argument," except insofar as they have a direct bearing on the Battle of Metz. Part of the problem lay in nonmilitary matters—politics, personalities, and public opinion. Support of the Montgomery plan, however desirable it might have seemed, meant stopping Patton in his tracks, a decision that was clearly politically impossible. He was the hero of the moment, his exploits being served up in banner headlines by often partisan correspondents.

Eisenhower has often been criticized for his lack of strategic sense, but, in weighing up all the various factors, he had to make some sort of a decision. In a series of meetings during the third week in August, he laid down the broad basis for the future conduct of the campaign and announced that he would take direct command on 1 September. In producing a compromise, he was obviously influenced by the SHAEF broad-front policy, especially as he recognized the greater importance of the northern thrust. All compromises have inherent strengths and weaknesses, but it is difficult to see how Eisenhower could have decided differently, given his position as "umpire" between two strident factions.

General Montgomery was directed to advance into Belgium with the immediate aim of taking Antwerp and neutralizing the V-weapon bases in the Pas de Calais. To help in this, he was allotted two of the three corps from General Hodges' First Army. Patton was to continue his eastward move, at least as far as Rheims, and to link up with the Anvil/Dragoon forces advancing up the Rhône valley toward the Vosges. However, the bulk of Bradley's fuel tonnage was allocated to the First Army, so that, in the words of Chester Wilmot, Patton was given "enough petrol to join the battle but not to win it."[7]

It was this one vital factor that was to become the heart of the problem during the ensuing weeks and months. In spite of the optimism of the planners in setting distant targets, such as the Rhine and the Ruhr, the iron hand of logistics had imposed severe limitations on future movement until additional port facilities nearer to the front lines could be secured. The Allies, by their very success, had outrun their communications, and there was very little they could do about it, especially as the bulk of their supplies were still coming in over the open beaches in distant Normandy. (As the whole business of supply had a direct bearing on the Metz campaign, it will be dealt with in some detail in a later section.)

The advance agreed on by General Eisenhower finally got under way on 29 August—by which date Patton's spearheads were already approaching Rheims, having managed to storm across the Marne. Three days later his mobile columns would be across the Meuse, but stalled for lack of fuel. Only thirty miles ahead of them lay the Moselle, just one more river on the way to the Rhine.

A great victory had been won in France, and many who have written about this period criticize the Allied leadership in general for failing to exploit it. Both Montgomery and Patton have had their fans, all of the opinion that their protégé could have won the war single-handed in 1944. In theory they probably could have done so, either collectively or singly, but this simply ignores the fact that the requisite supplies were not available for either of them. Thus, in the circumstances, Eisenhower's politically dictated military decision was probably the right one.

THE GERMAN SITUATION

When considering the German situation it becomes immediately apparent that the Allies lost a golden opportunity to inflict an even greater defeat on the enemy than they did. However, as we have seen, they were unable to exploit the opportunity offered, much to the surprise of German officers who have written on the subject after the war.

Between Normandy and the Seine, the German forces in the west suffered a catastrophic reverse. They lost some half-million casualties, and only just over 100 tanks were brought back across the Seine.[8] The divisions in the German order of battle existed in name only. Minus virtually all their heavy weapons and equipment, their strength was little better than that of regimental battle groups.

The supreme command in the field Oberbefehlshaber West (OB West) was held by Field Marshal Model, who had succeeded to the position on 17 August following the suicide of von Kluge. In addition, he retained command of Army Group B, which included the bulk of the forces in contact with the Allies. A wide gap had opened between it and Army Group G under General Blaskowitz, which was retreating toward the Vosges in the face of the Anvil/Dragoon force. Model was one of Germany's ablest tacticians, who had often been selected to command in situations where the prospects were grim. Although a "party general," he was not afraid to stand up to Hitler when the occasion warranted.

The fact was that Model's high-sounding title was largely illusory, as was that of any German commander at the time. Even before the war, the army had lost most of its power to Hitler and his direct military entourage, and after the bomb plot on 20 July 1944, what little authority remained was removed. Only a couple of months later, Model's successor, Field Marshal Gerd von Rundstedt, was to quip that he needed permission from Berlin to change the sentries outside his headquarters. Thus, the campaign in the west was Hitler's; and his field commanders only exercised their duties within rigid limits laid down from above.

After the defeat in Normandy, and as a result of the terrible losses suffered during the Russian summer offensive, under a normal political system, Germany should logically have sued for peace. Several senior officers, including von Rundstedt, urged this course on Hitler. Nothing, however, was further from the mind of the Füehrer, who in mid-August was already considering a counteroffensive that was to emerge as the Ardennes attack in December.

Hitler's main interest had always been in Russia, where two million troops were deployed, compared to some 700,000 in the west. After the defeats that had been suffered, his overriding aim was to buy time until he could deploy his V-weapons or until such time as the Allies should fall out. Therefore, as little ground as possible was to be given up, and his forces were to retreat step by step back into the prepared defenses of the Westwall, known (erroneously) to the Allies as the Siegfried Line. In late 1944, however, this prepared position along the German border was largely a myth. Originally built to hold the French while Germany was gobbling up Poland and Czechoslovakia, its bunkers, largely unfinished, had been neglected since 1940, and many of the keys were missing. There was neither the personnel to man it nor weapons to equip it. Throughout August and September, the rear areas were being combed for the elderly and infirm to be formed into static fortress battalions for service in the defenses, which had to be hurriedly reactivated.

Model repeatedly brought the state of affairs to Hitler's attention.

On 24 August he asked for 30 to 35 infantry divisions and 12 panzer divisions, following this by a stream of similar requests—all of which remained unanswered. There were no troops available on that scale. At the beginning of September, shortly before he was relieved of his command, Model received a set of instructions that were indicative of German strategy.[9] These emphasized Hitler's "stand and hold" doctrine, which had led to the loss of so many troops in isolated pockets and had not succeeded in halting Allied advances. The enemy was to be held in a general defensive battle in front of the Westwall to gain time so that it could be made ready. According to Hitler, success here would mean that The Netherlands could be retained and German territory would not be occupied. Allied aircraft would be kept as far away as possible, and even if Antwerp were to be lost, German possession of the north bank of the Scheldt would render the approaches useless. Finally, the vital Ruhr and Saar industrial and mining areas would be retained.

This basically was the strategy employed in Lorraine. It could have been upset with comparative ease in view of Allied mobility and overwhelming superiority in the air. However, lack of supplies brought Patton to a halt, and the terrain favored the defense. The irony was that both sides at the end of August 1944 were laboring under distinct difficulties, which caused them both to forgo the initiative. Although the Allies made further spectacular gains, they had to a certain extent run out of steam. In an attempt to regain the initiative, Montgomery launched the brilliant Arnhem operation, but when this failed, the front lapsed into stalemate.

☰ *2* ☰

Third Army and Its Commander

Throughout history, soldiers have fought and died as members of armies. What raises those armies from the anonymity of mere numbers on an order of battle is the personality of the commanders with whom they are commonly identified—in fame or infamy. The Third U.S. Army in the Second World War was one of those, its destiny irrevocably intertwined with that of Gen. George S. Patton, Jr., its legendary leader. Although the Battle of Metz was fought by only one corps of that army, the course of operations was largely determined by Patton. It is therefore necessary to examine briefly the man and the weapon that he forged in order to understand the role that he would play, a role into which he was pressed by force of circumstances, and for which he had neither the talent nor the inclination.

Senior commanders in the First World War were godlike beings, impersonal and aloof, directing operations from miles behind the front line. Their activities were reported only in the rigidly-censored dispatches from General Headquarters. Between the wars, the power of public opinion and, thus, of the media, increased enormously, partly fed by the influence of motion pictures. During the Second World War, each army was followed by its quota of war correspondents, eager to produce news and to promote the virtues of "their" general. Such practices led inevitably to the creation of personality cults and to success in war being measured in headlines and column-inches. In this respect, the British had their "Monty" and the Americans their Patton. Both commanders were newsworthy, eminently quotable, and eccentric. Other men, no less talented, tended to operate perhaps more discreetly: nobody has ever made a film about Simpson or Bradley.

George Patton was born on 11 November 1885, into a wealthy California family. Thus, from the outset, his background was totally different from that of many of the other successful American generals, who so often tended to be poor boys who made good.

Until he was 12 years old, he had no formal education. When he was finally sent to school, he was to all intents and purposes illiterate, but his head was stuffed full of the classics that his father had taught him. He proved, however, to be capable of learning, although he was never able to spell properly.

From school he moved to West Point in 1904, where his career was not marked by great intellectual achievement. He did, however, excel as a sportsman. From the point of view of his later career, it is interesting to note that the sports he preferred were individual ones, riding, shooting, and the like. He would always find it difficult to be just one member of a team. Patton graduated in 1909 and joined the cavalry. Thanks to his social connections and marriage to a New England heiress, he immediately moved into the higher echelons of the army. As aide-de-camp to the chief of staff, he gained the friendship of Henry Stimson, who would eventually become Secretary of War—a connection that would stand him in good stead during the Second World War, when he was often sorely in need of allies in high places.

Patton's first taste of action came in 1916 when he took part in a punitive expedition against Pancho Villa, the Mexican bandit. This was real Hollywood U.S. Cavalry stuff, and another indicator of the future methods of warfare that would be employed by Patton. It was during this minor campaign that he came to the notice of General Pershing.

On Pershing's staff, Patton went to France in 1917. There he was but a small cog in a vast administrative organization. Eager to see some action, he requested a transfer, only to be confronted by a difficult choice—command of an infantry battalion or a post with the newly created Tank Corps. After some misgivings, he chose the latter, although it existed at the time largely on paper. While training his embryo tank unit, another of Patton's legendary attributes made its appearance, that of the martinet. His men and equipment gained the reputation of being the smartest in the army, but spit-and-polish apart, he made a very real contribution to the introduction of armored fighting vehicles into the U.S. Army.

His chance to fight the Germans came in the St. Mihiel battle in September 1918. The battle itself was relatively unimportant, but for Patton it was a formative experience. The performance of his tanks was more or less disastrous, but Patton himself was everywhere, walking more often than riding. His method of exercising command was, to say the least, distinctly personal. This trait was not popular with the hierarchy, who accused him of wanting to take on the German army single-handed, and he received the first of many notable "carpetings." Wounded at the end of September during the Meuse-Argonne battle, he ended the war as a full colonel—only to revert to his peacetime rank of captain. The salient point that emerges from his exploits in the First World War was his advocacy of light tanks for pursuit, a form of fighting that he was to perfect 26 years later.

During the interwar years, Patton's career was unspectacular. Seeing that the army was no longer interested in the tank as a weapon, he rejoined the horse cavalry. He might well have ended up on the scrap heap as a retired colonel had not George Marshall risen to a position of prominence in the army—from which he was able to save Patton's neck on a number of occasions.

It was in 1940, with the object lesson of the German blitzkrieg tactics plain for all to see, that Patton returned wholeheartedly to his advocacy of the tank as a weapon. As the U.S. Army was slowly put on a war footing he was taken off the shelf and given command of a brigade in the newly formed 2nd Armored Division. During this early training program he earned the nickname of "Ol Blood and Guts," in his own words, "the best Goddam butt kicker in the whole army." His reputation for profanity was legendary, although he was a deeply religious man—just one of the many paradoxes in a complex character. In spite of, or perhaps because of, his four-letter words, his men respected him and perhaps even loved him. Soldiers will hate a pure martinet, but they will adore one who is also a successful fighter.

His chance came in North Africa and Sicily, where he gained his reputation as a fighting soldier, but his whole future was called into question by the notorious slapping incident in Sicily. He struck a hospitalized soldier whom he suspected of malingering—an action of which, at the time, no notice, seemingly, was taken. However, the affair did leak out, with the result that Patton was relieved of his command and very nearly disgraced. He may have had a fine reputation as a general, but to many people he was little more than a publicity-hogging braggart. The problem was that his character was far too complex to be simply labelled one way or the other. So much of the outward performance, including the pearl-handled revolvers, was purely for show. Under the brash exterior, he was a deeply emotional man and easily moved to tears.

Back in England for the buildup to the invasion of Europe, he was again in trouble (this time over a speech that he made) and again his usefulness was questioned. Passed over for the command of the assault phase in favor of Bradley, his junior in the army, Patton was relegated to control of a paper headquarters known as the Third U.S. Army. This assignment was part of the general deception scheme to persuade the Germans that the landings would be made in the Pas de Calais and not in Normandy. Robbed of his chance for immediate glory, he spent his time criticizing the plans for Overlord, without being able to exert any influence.

He did not set foot in France until a month after D-day, and then only in command of a headquarters without troops. Now almost 59 years old, his great worry was that events would leave him on the sidelines. Indeed, it is possible that his later conduct of the war was prompted by a feeling of having nothing to lose. His chance came in the great breakout from Normandy, although the Third Army did not become officially operational until 1 August 1944. From then on it was all go, and when SHAEF finally relented and allowed his army to be identified by the press, he could gain the acclaim and the recognition that he desired. His name and that of his beloved army were emblazoned in banner headlines throughout the world. Indeed, so great was his reputation with the enemy, that at one stage the Germans credited him with command of an army group!

His army consisted of three corps, XX, XII, and VIII, although VIII Corps remained in Brittany to besiege the German garrisons left behind there. His headquarters staff was mainly made up of officers who had served under him in North Africa and Sicily, and many of them were cavalrymen imbued with his own ideals of speed and surprise. Admittedly, the staff were overshadowed by the mercurial temperament of their chief, but they functioned as a smooth team. Patton himself was little bothered with such mundane matters as logistics and administration, spending much of his time away from base, roving the battlefield alone, distributing praise, and "chewing butts." Thus an efficient staff was vital to such a system of command; and in spite of his hot temper, Patton managed to keep his close associates right through to the end of the war.

At the end of August, the Third Army consisted of 314,814 officers and men divided into nine divisions, two of which were armored. In addition there were numerous special troops and headquarters units. By that time, the Third Army was a close-knit fighting organization flushed with victory and eager for the kill. Throughout history, successful armies have been characterized by high morale, and the Third Army was no exception. It has even been said that Patton created his army in his own image, and his troops were proud to be able to say, "I'm with Patton."

As far as the Battle of Metz is concerned, we are really interested only in XX Corps. This unit, in the forefront of the pursuit across France, was commanded by General Walton H. Walker, like Patton, a veteran of the St. Mihiel battle. Walker looked rather like a bulldog with a short, squat frame and a broad face usually set in a ferocious scowl. Patton's biographer, Ladislas Farago, describes him irreverently as a "roly-poly tanker." It would seem that Patton was fond of him but did not always take him too seriously. In many ways, he was the shadow of the more illustrious master whom he idolized, sharing his passion for smart appearance, and his energy and drive. Unlike Patton, he was unostentatious, wearing GI shoes and an ordinary webbing belt. Walker was approachable but it seems that he was never really liked. There was no General Walker popularity cult, no legends, and no anecdotes. His virtue in Patton's eyes was that he did what he was told—which meant that he survived in command of his corps.

Like an army, an army corps is purely an operational and administrative headquarters. Its divisions can be swapped around with other corps, simply by being assigned or transferred to suit operational requirements. It does, however, have its own pool of special troops, which remain attached to it: engineers, artillery, medical facilities, etc. The division is the highest tactical formation that remains as an integral unit; during the Second World War it kept its assigned regiments throughout its life.

Like a corps, an American infantry division in the Second World War also had special troops which were at the operational disposal of the divisional commander. These would normally comprise:

A number of field artillery battalions
A medical battalion
An engineer battalion
A quartermaster company
A signal company
A reconnaissance troop
An ordnance company
An antiaircraft battalion
One or two tank battalions
One or more tank-destroyer battalions

The headquarters company of the division was responsible for miscellaneous service troops such as military police, the divisional band and the like.

The teeth of an infantry division were its three regiments, each usually commanded by a full colonel. These were then subdivided into three battalions, each with four rifle companies and a heavy weapons company. At regimental level there were also attached special troops—engineers, artillery, tanks, etc.—and when the regiment moved with them it formed what was known as the regimental combat team, an integrated fighting unit.

The organization of an American armored division was somewhat different. Instead of regiments, it was divided into three combat commands, each under a brigadier general or a full colonel. Each combat command was a fully mobile, integrated unit that could operate independently, made up of tanks, tank destroyers, motorized infantry, self-propelled artillery, and combat engineers.

While the German army of the period was still relying largely on horses for the movement of equipment, the American army was highly mechanized. This brought with it the inevitably adverse tooth-to-tail relationship, a vast number of rear echelon specialists being required to keep one man in the front line firing a rifle.

At the end of August 1944, XX Corps consisted of three divisions: the 5th and 90th Infantry, and the 7th Armored. The 5th Infantry Division was a regular unit, which had spent the earlier part of the war guarding Iceland, and was commanded by Maj. Gen. LeRoy Irwin. After an unfortunate start in Normandy, the 90th Infantry had settled down under the command of Brigadier General Raymond McClain. Major General Silvester's 7th Armored had also been in combat in Normandy. None of the three divisions had suffered excessive casualties during the pursuit of the Germans across France.

Finally, a word about air support, a vital component of successful mobile warfare. The XIX Tactical Air Command (TAC) was assigned to cooperate with the Third Army, and by the end of August, a tightly knit system of air-ground coordination had been established. Under the command of Brig. Gen. Otto Weyland, the XIX TAC had two fighter-bomber wings, whose 600 aircraft were deployed mainly between Brittany and the Le Mans area. During August they had had to cover a number of missions, which had led to inevitable dispersion. Besides direct cover for the ground troops, they had to seal off the battlefield by attacking German reinforcements and protect the exposed long left flank of the Third Army, which meant flying missions as far apart as Brest and Metz. Although opposition from the Luftwaffe was negligible, the amount of support rendered during the Metz campaign was to be severely restricted by the terrible weather conditions.

This, then, was the Third Army and General Patton, who together would have smashed their way through to the Rhine and won the war on their own, had not certain adverse circumstances intervened.

$$\equiv 3 \equiv$$

The Situation in Lorraine:

End of August, Early September

THE SUPPLY PROBLEM

On 1 September 1944, the Third Army suffered the humiliation of running out of fuel. This may sound strange in view of the efficiency we have come to expect from modern armies and their logistics facilities, but this is exactly what happened. Prejudiced commentators have since made a number of wild accusations and hinted at treachery in high places. Patton, however, was simply a victim of circumstances, which have been outlined in Chapter 1. The fuel shortage was not something that happened out of the blue, as the staff had known some days previously that they would eventually grind to a halt.

The whole question of logistics is worth considering at this stage, since it preconditioned the events in Lorraine between September and December 1944. At this stage in the fighting in Europe, it was no longer the commanding generals who determined the extent of operations, but their G-4's (assistant chiefs of staff for supply). The growth of mechanization had led to great changes in warfare. The armies of the First World War, despite their vast size, had consisted mainly of infantry with a limited range of fairly standard weapons. Their logistical needs could be mainly met by railways and a shuttle service (largely horse drawn) from the railheads to the more or less static front lines. Just over 20 years after the end of that conflict, the armored division, airborne forces, and amphibious units had arrived on the scene. Even the ordinary infantry division had become fully motorized and was equipped with a variety of complex weapons: antitank guns, light howitzers, and other crew-served weapons. This, in turn, meant that during the Second World War, the number of support troops per fighting man had increased greatly. Another factor to be borne in mind is that, between 1914 and 1918, the Allied armies in France were fighting in a country with an intact political system and firmly committed to winning the war. They had the support of the French manufacturing resources, the railways, the police, and all the normal governmental functions of a developed nation.

In 1944, this was not the case. France was enemy territory that had to be invaded from the British Isles, which itself was unable to supply the vast American armies. The bulk of the Allied requirements had to be shipped across the Atlantic.

The disastrous Dieppe raid in 1942 had demonstrated to the planners the futility of trying to capture a defended port by storm. Hence the "Mulberry" harbors had to be developed for towing to the exposed Normandy beaches. At the end of August, the bulk of supplies was still being landed onto those same beaches, to meet the requirements of some 40 Allied divisions and the myriad headquarters, hospitals, and other special units. Only the port of Cherbourg was functioning. Brest, Calais, and Dunkirk were still in German hands, although Dieppe was liberated on 1 September. Hence Eisenhower's concern for the capture of the Channel ports and, above all, Antwerp.

The supreme irony was that, while Patton ranted about his shortages, there were enough supplies on shore in Normandy to go around. The lack was not of fuel, but of transport to bring it forward. As we have seen, the Allied strategy foresaw a halt on the Seine to build up stocks, followed by a systematic advance. The spectacular victory of the invading Allied forces threw all these careful considerations overboard, causing consternation among the staffs concerned. Prior to and after D-day, the Allied tactical bombers had roamed at will over northern France, smashing the railway network in order to isolate the battlefield and to hinder German reinforcements. Once they broke out from Normandy, the Allies were thus hoist with their own petard, and it was not until 30 August that the first train reached Paris by a circuitous route.[1]

Bradley's difficulties were enormous. His lines of communication were longer than Montgomery's, and every mile that Patton's tanks forged ahead added to the problem. Montgomery could at least hope for relief when Antwerp and the Channel ports were opened, but these would not greatly assist the Third Army in an eastward move through Lorraine. Without adequate railways, the only way to bring up supplies was by road; and this problem was partly solved by the American genius for improvization: A truck-convoy system running day and night, on roads that were closed to all other traffic—the famous "Red Ball Express"—was instituted. With headlights blazing, the trucks ferried supplies from the beaches to dumps northeast of Paris and any vehicle that broke down was ruthlessly bulldozed off the road. They managed to ferry 7,000 tons daily into the forward dumps, but the bulk of the vehicles used had to be taken from divisions who had been landed, but were not yet in the front line. Because the average round trip was three days, three trucks were needed in the system to deliver one daily load.

It was not until 6 September that the first train got through to the Third Army. A petroleum pipeline was laid as far as Alençon by 27 August, but could handle only relatively small quantities. One expedient tried was the establishment of an airlift for fuel and other supplies, but this could cope with only half the daily requirements. Starting on 23 August, the C-47's of Air Transport Command flew a daily shuttle into Orleans. By the end of the month, however, most of the aircraft had been withdrawn for use in a proposed airborne forces drop on Tournai scheduled for 3 September. What happened though, was that the First Army troops got there before the drop could be made, and it was cancelled. Bradley had tried to get the operation called off, but Eisenhower had been adamant.[2] An additional difficulty in the background was that Bradley was saddled with the responsibility of feeding Paris, another aspect which had not been forecast by the SHAEF planners.

Fuel was the key to the tonnage requirements. When the Germans were on the run, the ammunition requirements could be cut back, and the space thus saved used for fuel. When, however, the enemy stood and fought, the ammunition loads increased enormously. In addition, with the onset of the cold weather, items such as blankets, warm clothing, and shoes had to have priority.

Overall command of supply was in the hands of Services of Supply

(SOS), a part of the Communications Zone (Com Z) organization at SHAEF—presided over by General John Lee, who was cordially loathed by Patton. Indeed, Lee was one of those characters of whom nobody seems to have had anything good to say. Farago describes him as "a smooth-skinned, sharp eyed, balding, blond man with a face Hollywood usually typecasts in the role of a glad-handing suburban clergyman. Lee was a soldier of the old school with a reputation for being a martinet."[3] He had performed the same job in North Africa and Sicily, and it was rumored that he was behind the attempts to discredit Patton after the slapping incidents. In fact, SOS did the best they could with the available facilities, but to the soldier sitting in a tank with no fuel, this was simply not good enough. SOS became the whipping boy for all of the Third Army's troubles, for which there was unfortunately some justification. In spite of Eisenhower's direct order that the Paris area was out of bounds for the establishment of rear echelon headquarters, at the end of August, Lee moved his vast encampment from Normandy into a considerable number of the plushest hotels in the capital. To carry this out, 25,000 tons of vital fuel were consumed, and a vast number of trucks were taken out of circulation. According to Bradley, "When the infantry learned that Com Z's comforts had been multiplied by the charms of Paris, the injustice rankled all the deeper and festered there throughout the war."[4]

Patton's own supply at Third Army level was handled by his G-4, Col. Walter Muller, who had served him in that capacity since 1941. He became a legend as a scavenger, and complaints by outsiders about his activities were simply ignored. A good G-4 required the hoarding instincts of a hamster and the rapacity of a bird of prey. Muller successfully juggled with captured stocks, which he forgot to report to higher headquarters, and the limited amounts issued, to keep the army moving. Everything was fair, including the hijacking of supplies routed to other armies. Raiding parties made forays to the dumps of the First Army, apparently carrying off considerable quantities of booty. When Patton visited Bradley, he coasted in with his jeep almost empty of fuel to emphasize his plight, and asked permission to fill it at 12th Army Group motor pool.[5]

During August, the average requirements of the Third Army were some 6,000 tons daily, 1,500 of which were in the form of fuel and lubricants. In fact, the Third Army consumed some 400,000 gallons of fuel each day. Bradley reckoned that the tonnage lost through withdrawal of the airlift was the equivalent of one and a half million gallons, "enough to run Third Army four days nearer the Rhine."[6] On 28 August, deliveries were short 100,000 gallons, the amount used by an armored division in a day of cross-country fighting. Two days later, only 32,000 gallons arrived. Patton rushed off to see Bradley, in the knowledge that his troops were in Verdun and over the Meuse. "Dammit Brad," he begged, "just give me 400,000 gallons of gasoline and I'll put you inside Germany in two days."[7]

Indeed, without captured supplies, he would never have reached the Meuse. One hundred thousand gallons were discovered at Sens, which enabled him to move on to the Marne, and another similar quantity was found at Chalons by XII Corps, which carried them to the Meuse. In addition, large stocks of medical supplies and foodstuffs from German warehouses freed vehicle space for what little fuel was available.

There is, however, no evidence to support the later allegations made by members of Patton's staff that there was some sort of SHAEF plot to starve them of fuel for reasons of spite. The whole supply system was too large and full of checks and balances to permit a man such as Lee to pursue some sort of private vendetta. The decisions on allocation of supplies were made by Eisenhower acting on the strategic advice of his staff. The reasoning behind those decisions does not concern us here.

THE ADVANCE TO THE MEUSE

General Bradley visited General Patton on 28 August to pass on the Supreme Commander's decision and to discuss the supply situation. In the knowledge that the First Army was to have priority, Bradley had decided that the Third Army should come to a halt along the line of the river Marne, but was finally persuaded by Patton's eloquence, giving grudging agreement for an advance to the Meuse. Apprehensive that his superior might change his mind, Patton immediately issued his orders. Walker was told to get XX Corps moving toward Verdun, and Eddy's XII Corps was to try for a crossing at Commercy.

At this stage, Patton was still fired by optimism, in spite of a sober report prepared by his G-2 (assistant chief of staff for intelligence),

Colonel Koch, which pointed out the Germans were still not decisively beaten. Patton was inclined to dismiss this as a figment of imagination, but events were beginning to take the situation out of his hand. While he was with General Eddy, discussing the XII Corps move to the Meuse, he received a message that the daily fuel ration of 140,000 gallons had failed to arrive. A cautious commander, on receipt of such news, would have ordered an immediate halt until supplies could be built up. Not Patton, however. Convinced, with some justification, that the enemy was crumbling and their vaunted Westwail defenses were empty, he drove his units forward. Rigid fuel conservation measures were imposed, and with their vehicles partly supplied with captured fuel, the two corps pushed forward toward the Meuse against negligible opposition.

An irony was that Patton had been there before, in 1918. The Third Army was moving steadily over the battlefield known as the Meuse-Argonne and toward the St. Mihiel salient, places where so many of their predecessors had died in that earlier conflict. After her failure to join the League of Nations and the lapse into isolationism after the First World War, America was back in Europe, and her GI's once again fought on the threshold of Lorraine.

The immediate target for XX Corps was another emotive place, the ancient city and fortress of Verdun, which became immortal in 1916 when it withstood a formal siege for ten months. In 1940, it had been occupied by the Germans after a token resistance.

The spearhead of General Walker's corps was formed by the 7th Armored Division, which was closely followed by the men of the 5th Infantry Division. Indeed, their paths became frequently entangled as the infantry struggled forward along roads congested by tanks. They were moving across the plain of Champagne, open rolling country, and the scene of so many battles in history. On 28 August, however, some units were still to the south of the river Marne. The 5th Infantry Division's three regiments were the 2nd, 10th and 11th; and by that evening, the 2nd Infantry had established a bridge over the Marne near Epernay. From there it was only a few miles to Rheims, a major city and the traditional place where the kings of France had been crowned in its magnificent cathedral.

During the afternoon of 29 August, the 2nd Infantry Regimental Combat Team pushed into the suburbs of Rheims, encountering only light small-arms fire. The Germans retreated through the city as the three American battalions attempted to encircle them. By midnight, the heights to the east had been cleared; and, early in the morning of 30 August, the 2nd Infantry entered the city center, spending the rest of the day in mopping up snipers. A vast amount of food and medical supplies was captured, the former proving a welcome change to the inevitable combat rations that had been the troops' staple diet for so long. However, far more important from the men's point of view was the "liberation" of the contents of the champagne cellars in the area, much of which was marked "Reserved for the use of the German Armed Forces."

While the 2nd Infantry was busy taking inventory, the rest of the 5th Division was moved up into the Rheims area. General Walker's other division, the 90th Infantry, however, was still behind the Marne, stalled for lack of fuel to move forward. That day, instead of the required 140,000 gallons, only 32,000 were received. The withdrawal of the airlift was biting. Hearing that General Bull, Eisenhower's G-4, was going to be at Bradley's TAC HQ at Chartres, Patton flew off there to plead his case for an immediate eastward advance. Both Bradley and Bull were sympathetic, but Patton required more than sympathy. He was told quite bluntly by Bradley that he would get very little in the way of supplies.

Convinced that he had two battles to fight, one with the Germans and the other with his own high command, Patton stormed back to his command post. There he was informed by General Gaffey, his chief of staff, that General Eddy, whose XII Corps was supposedly on the way to the Meuse at Commercy, had called in to say that if he continued to advance, he would be out of fuel. In Patton's absence, Gaffey had authorized him to stop at St. Dizier. This apparently provoked one of the famous Patton explosions. Grabbing the telephone, Eddy was told "to get off his fanny" and to carry on until he ran dry.[8]

Although his troops were under orders to push on to the Rhine, Patton no longer had the wherewithal. Not only was he short of fuel, there were major shortages in such items as clothing, blankets, and vital spare parts. During the race across France, essential maintenance of vehicles had been skimped, and although nobody would have admitted it, the Third Army was tired.

In the meanwhile, during the afternoon of 31 August, the 11th Infantry Regiment Combat Team struggled forward through the 7th

Armored traffic jams toward Verdun. Traversing the Argonne battle-field without difficulty in spite of the broken nature of the terrain, by 1900 they were only six miles to the west of the city. Informed by their reconnaissance elements that there was a bridge over the Meuse still intact, the First Battalion drove on into Verdun without meeting any opposition. There they found that three tanks of Combat Command A of the 7th Armor had got there first and had seized the bridge, accompanied by a company from the 40th Armored Infantry.

Verdun lies on either side of the river, almost entirely surrounded by hills. To hinder any attempt at a counterattack, it was imperative for the Americans to move on through and occupy these, which they succeeded in doing by daybreak. Thus, the 11th Infantry had a secure bridgehead across the Meuse as a basis for an advance to the next obstacle, the Moselle. They were camping on the battlefield amid the debris left over from the First World War, an area that had been left as a shrine to French heroism. All through 1 September, XX Corps units moved into the bridgehead as extra bridges were thrown across the river. Tenth Infantry Regiment established their command post in the ruins of Fort Douaumont, the scene of some of the most bitter fighting in 1916. Corps artillery moved into Fort de Regret, the 11th Infantry into Fort Belrupt, and 5th Division quartered themselves in the Hôtel Bellevue. It also proved possible during the day to bring up the bulk of the 90th Division into the bridgehead. On reaching Verdun, XX Corps had marched 600 miles in 30 days, and the engineers had completed 16 major bridging missions, including the Eure, Marne, Seine, and Meuse.

In the city itself, more valuable stores fell into the hands of the victors, including a number of artillery pieces—soon to be in use against their former owners. Also captured intact were several ware-houses full of food and clothing, as well as the arsenal. These had been prepared for demolition, but some French civilians, members of the Resistance (FFI), had apparently cut the wires leading to the explo-sive charges.

That night, in an attempt to rectify their failure to blow the Verdun Bridge, a number of German aircraft dropped a load of bombs on the city center, repeating their sorties for two more nights. The bridge, however, remained in use, and although some damage was caused, casualties were light. At this stage, to all practical purposes, the advance of XX Corps came to a temporary but very definite halt.

Even reaching Verdun had been touch and go. Of the 17 tanks originally dispatched, 14 had run out of fuel on the way.[9] By 4 September, the entire 5th Infantry Division had only 2,000 gallons of fuel, half of which was required for daily cooking purposes.

However, while XX Corps fretted on the Meuse, Eisenhower held a conference at Chartres with Bradley and Patton on 2 September. The previous day, Bradley had ordered that 5,000 tons of stores should go to the First Army, engaged in supporting Montgomery's northward thrust, and only 2,000 tons to the Third Army. Patton was furious, already beginning to sense some sort of Machiavellian plot to rob him of the fruits of victory and headlines back home. Eisenhower justified the decision by pointing out once again the vital need for the Channel ports and Antwerp—until they were cleared, priority for supply would remain in the north. Patton claimed that his cavalry patrols had reached the Moselle and asserted (erroneously) that they had entered Metz, and that all he needed was fuel. "My men can eat their belts, but my tanks have gotta have gas."[10] If supplied, he claimed, he could break through to the Rhine, and in this he was supported by Bradley. As usual, Eisenhower gave way under pressure. He consented to a compromise, whereby Patton could secure crossings over the Moselle when he could get the fuel to move. Patton, naturally, failed to disclose that he had captured an additional 110,000 gallons, sufficient to get XII Corps as far as the river. These were all part of Patton's tactics at the time. By keeping moving until his troops ran out of fuel, he virtually forced Bradley to give him enough to get mobile again—he called it his "Rock Soup" method. This referred, of course, to the old tale about the tramp who went up to a house and asked for some water to boil a rock to make some soup. When he got the water, he then asked for a few odd vegetables to make it a bit more tasty, and then a pinch of salt, and finally ended up with some meat.

Although stalled, General Walker did manage some activity in an effort to fulfill his mission. The light vehicles of the cavalry (jeeps and armored cars) were able to make a number of sweeps toward the Moselle, but in spite of persistent rumors that they had done so, never actually entered Metz. That was pure wishful thinking on the part of the troops and those who later castigated the decision to cut off Patton's fuel. During the night of 31 August / 1 September, the 3rd Cavalry Group had penetrated out of the bridgehead as far as Étain, some twelve miles to the east. There they had managed to secure 4,000 gallons of fuel, enough to keep them moving on to the Moselle. Although their exploits during the next few days had all the dash of the Hollywood cavalry tradition, they were unable to accomplish anything decisive, except to spread alarm and despondency among the enemy.

One platoon, guided by a Frenchman, made a 70-mile sweep behind the German lines, and on the afternoon of 2 September, reached Thionville on the banks of the Moselle. Commanded by Lieutenant Jackson, this small force, comprising three armored cars and six jeeps, shot up the town and even succeeded in cutting the demolition leads under the main bridge. However, without force to back them up, they were finally driven off and returned to their unit. Twice wounded, Jackson was decorated with the Distinguished Service Cross. The 43rd Cavalry Reconnaissance Squadron was also active. One platoon roved northward to Longuyon, while another managed to establish an observation post on the heights overlooking the Moselle to the north of Thionville. They were able to radio back, "No enemy visible on the other side of the Moselle. Many good places for bridges, all undefended."[11]

Elsewhere, the cavalry was forced to curtail scouting on account of the fuel shortage. As they followed the retreating enemy, there was every indication that resistance was beginning to stiffen. One final effort at deception was tried out by General Walker in an endeavor to persuade the Germans that the main advance was to be made northward into Luxembourg. On 2 September he sent two task forces from the 7th Armored Division to advance on either side of the Meuse in a feint toward Sedan, but they ran dry before they got there. They had to wait until 4 September before they could be refuelled and retrieved.

In the words of the official historian, "During these days of enforced inactivity, the XX Corps commander and his staff were busy with plans for a drive that would reach Mainz, on the Rhine, 140 airline miles east of the XX Corps forward positions, before the German Westwall could be manned. . . . In the first days of September, however, there was little the XX Corps could do but commit ambitious plans to paper, wait, make a sterile record of the optimistic and pleading messages radioed in by the cavalry, put out daily periodic reports with the dour phrase, 'no change,' engage in gunnery practice when German planes came over at night in fruitless attempts to destroy the Verdun bridges, and hope that gasoline would soon arrive."[12]

General Patton called the decision to restrict his supplies "the most momentous error of the war."[13] The general assumption among his protagonists was that, if he had been given his head, he would simply have rolled through to the Rhine in a matter of days. After all, that river was only 100 miles to the east of the Moselle. However, in all the discussion of the "great argument," one element that is always ignored is the limiting one of geography. Patton's assumption was that he had the Germans on the run and should have been permitted to keep up the pace of his advance before they had time to organize themselves. This was correct tactics, but the terrain to the east of the Moselle was vastly different from that of northern France and was totally unsuitable for armor. There were few roads running toward the Saar and the Rhine, and the former river was to prove a formidable barrier to XX Corps the following December.

History is full of "might have beens" and considering them leads one into the realms of supposition. This book is concerned with the facts as they occurred, but in the conclusion there is room for some discussion of the oft repeated theme that the war could have been over in 1944—if only Patton had been given the supplies.

THE BATTLEFIELD AND THE CITY OF METZ

With the bulk of XX Corps established on the heights to the east of the Meuse, they were faced with an advance across the more or less level plain toward the Moselle, a distance of some 30 miles. Sparsely populated but well supplied with metalled roads, the ground rises gently as the river is approached, only to dip steeply into the valley. On the other side there is a further sharp rise, beyond which a plateau stretches out toward the Saar Valley, crossed by two lesser rivers, the Seille and the Nied. Between Metz and Thionville the river runs from south to north; and above the former, the valley stretches out into a broad flood plain. Below Metz, the Moselle runs in a restricted valley, the only access being via a number of narrow, winding ravines.

The river itself is slow running but fairly wide, having been canalized for barge traffic. The city of Metz is constructed on a number of islands in the stream, lying in a basin surrounded by the hills to the east and west. Those western hills were fortified strongly by the Germans just prior to 1914, to form an easily defended salient. (A detailed history of the fortress of Metz is given as an appendix.)

To the north, the area of the coming battle was limited by the fairly steep and rugged country leading into Luxembourg. Thus, the natural line of advance lay to the east along the old Roman road leading through Metz and onward to Saarbrücken and the Rhine at Mannheim. Because of the restrictions imposed by geography, this had been one of the favorite routes for armies throughout history, and the area around Metz and the Moselle crossings had long been a favorite battlefield. The city itself had never been taken by direct assault, and as late as 1870, the Chief of the German General Staff, von Moltke, reckoned its possession to be worth the equivalent of an army of 120,000 men.[14]

THE GERMAN SITUATION AT THE BEGINNING OF SEPTEMBER

It would appear that at least some of the senior German commanders shared the Allies' view of events already stated, to the extent of believing that the war was virtually over. Field Marshal von Rundstedt told Allied interrogators after the war, "As far as I was concerned, the war was ended in September." This cannot be dismissed as the wisdom of hindsight. At the end of June, when asked by Keitel what should be done, he had replied, "Make peace, you idiots."[15]

In spite of his frankness, von Rundstedt was called from honorable retirement and ordered to report to Hitler at Rastenburg, together with his chief of staff, General Westphal. There von Rundstedt was told that he was to take over his old job as OB West on 5 September. Model was quite happy to step down and return to the command of his Army Group B. Ostensibly, the reason for the recall of von Rundstedt was to alleviate a command situation that had become too complicated in that one man was the commander-in-chief and an army group commander at the same time. (Those who supported Montgomery's appointment as overall Allied ground commander should take note!) Model's probable fault was that he had tended to paint the situation too gloomily for Hitler's taste. Von Rundstedt was popular with the army, and backed by a young and able chief of staff, he was appointed to save the situation. The orders issued to the OB West on 3 September are a key to Hitler's strategic ideas for the campaign in the west and especially in Lorraine.[16] "On account of the weakness of our forces and the impossibility of introducing sufficient reinforcements, it is impossible at the moment to determine a line that can, and must, be held. It is therefore necessary to gain as much time as possible for the introduction of new units and the building up of the *West-Stellung* [West Position], and to destroy enemy forces by means of partial counterattacks." The main emphasis in the orders was placed on the reinforcement of the German First Army, the unit holding the Moselle line directly in front of the U.S. Third Army, and the assembly of mobile forces for a counterattack against Patton's unguarded southern flank. It is clear from this that Hitler had realized the danger threatened by a breakthrough in Lorraine and was determined to stop Patton at all costs. Although nothing was said in the orders about the planned offensive in the Ardennes, it was nevertheless implied. Two days earlier at a conference, Hitler had said "fog, night, and snow" would provide him with a great opportunity.[17]

Directly opposing Patton's forces was the German First Army, and there too was a change of command. On 6 September, General von der Chevallerie was retired on grounds of "ill health" and replaced by Gen. Otto von Knobelsdorf. The latter had had considerable experience as a corps commander in Russia and was known to be both a tough fighter and an optimist. His army, together with the Nineteenth Army immediately to the south, was placed under the command of Army Group G and General Blaskowitz.

During the last days of August, the German First Army had pulled back behind the Meuse with its forces totally shattered and on the run. It had been unable to impose any cohesive resistance to the Americans. Any counterattacks mounted had been local affairs of desperate men and were not coordinated as part of an overall plan. From the retreat, only nine battalions of infantry, two batteries of field artillery, ten tanks, and a number of antiaircraft and antitank guns had been retrieved. Reinforcements in the shape of elements of the 3rd and 5th Panzer Grenadier Divisions had arrived from Italy in time to see action in the Verdun-Commercy area, and the remaining troops of these units were in position along the Moselle by 2 September. In addition there was the exhausted 17th SS Panzer Grenadier Division (*Goetz von Berlichingen*), which was in the First Army area for refitting. Parts of this unit were thrown in to form an outpost line to the west of Metz, astride the main road from Verdun.

However, in pursuit of the "stop Patton" policy, the reinforcements that had been demanded by Model prior to his demotion were beginning to trickle in. During the lull before the American advance resumed on 5 September, four divisions and an armored brigade were moved in behind the Moselle. Although the First Army was only a collection of weak detachments at the end of August, by the first week in September "it was now the strongest of the German armies in the West."[18]

Directly facing General Walker's XX Corps, on the Moselle between Metz and Thionville, was the German LXXXII Corps, commanded by the artillery general, Johann Sinnhuber. However, apparent parity of forces was a delusion. Although lacking artillery, armor, and antitank weapons, the Germans were entrenched behind the excellent natural barrier of the river, and it is an ancient principle of warfare that an attacker requires a numerical superiority of at least three to one.

American intelligence had estimated that the enemy would not make a stand on the Moselle, but would retire to the prepared positions of the Westwall along the German frontier. This proved to be a false estimate, for as early as 24 August, Hitler had issued orders for the preparation of defenses in advance of the Westwall, the so-called *West-stellung*.[19] In the Moselle sector, Gauleiter Bürckel was empowered to call up the civilian population for the construction of defense works, and orders were also given for the reconditioning of the old fortifications of Metz and Thionville. A further order, issued on 1 September, was concerned with the rehabilitation of the Westwall.

In examining the German situation at local levels, one is confronted by the almost total lack of documentary evidence. Units on the run were not in a position to keep records and fill in their war diaries, and many groups were simply ad hoc formations filled out with stragglers. Thrown immediately into battle, the normal run of military paperwork was usually ignored, and little has survived in the archives below army-group level. Thus the following is a synthesis of the available but often contradictory evidence.

Writing after the war, General von Knobelsdorf painted a picture of chaos in his new command at the beginning of September.[20] He refers to an uncontrollable spread of rumors in the rear areas about alleged American successes, spread by escaping air force and noncombat units. As far as Metz was concerned, he stated that, ". . . panic had broken out. The party and civil authorities fled the town, which had then to be evacuated by the German population within a few hours. This panic spread to a number of military establishments, which set fire to ammunition and stocks of clothing without having received orders, and fled out of Metz taking with them the keys of the fortifications. When the engineers tried to prepare the fortifications for defense they met with considerable difficulties which caused loss of time. It took days for the personnel to be brought back. The burnt-out depôts could not be replaced."

The above is probably an exaggeration, but has a ring of truth about it. From another source we have a different tale, which may, however, contain a certain element of self-glorification. Standarten-füehrer Ernst Kemper was the commandant of the SS Signal School in Metz, and sometime at the end of July was appointed city commandant by Himmler (one of the many hats worn by Himmler at the time was commander of the replacement army). Shortly afterward, a meeting was held during which Metz was declared to be a fortress and was to be prepared for defense.[21]

Just what this term "fortress" meant to the Germans can be gathered from the text of Führer Order No. 11, issued on 8 March 1944, to define the duties of commanders of fortified areas. They "will fulfill the functions of fortresses in former times. They will ensure that the enemy does not occupy these areas of decisive operational importance. They will allow themselves to be surrounded, thereby holding down the largest possible number of enemy formations, and establish conditions favorable for successful counterattacks. . . . Each fortified area commander should be a specially selected, hardened soldier, preferably of general rank. . . . Fortified area commanders will pledge their honor as soldiers to carry out their duties to the last. Only the commander-in-chief of an army group in person, with my approval . . . will order the surrender of a fortress."[22]

In addition to the decision to defend the city, other steps were taken, according to Kemper. One of these, whereby elements of the population friendly to France were to be given the chance to leave, highlighted a problem that was to cause grave difficulties to the Germans, and was a direct result of their own political mistakes. When they annexed Alsace-Lorraine in 1870 after the Franco-Prussian War, they attempted to simply Germanify the area, but succeeded only in creating divided loyalties. Returned to the bosom of France in 1918, a resentful German minority remained—who were no doubt overjoyed in 1940 when their fellow countrymen returned. As far as Hitler was concerned, the two provinces were part of the German heritage, and he incorporated them into the Reich. This meant that they were not "occupied territory" in the strict sense of the word. Their inhabitants became liable for service in the German army and were subject to German law. This effectively prevented that same army from requisitioning supplies from the population and forced their quartermasters to go through normal legal channels, to the detriment of military "efficiency." In an endeavor to root out those who sympathized with France, a large number of peasants from the east were moved into the provinces and settled on former French farms. However, a sizeable potential fifth column remained, prepared to furnish the Americans with intelligence—much of which was of dubious accuracy.

A further measure apparently ordered by the Gauleiter was that city commandant Kemper was to take over the civilian administration together with a few key officials, and the rest of the civil servants were to retire to Saarbrücken. This idea, however, was quashed from above, with the result that the civilians "quietly crept back and resumed their duties."

Kemper goes on to say that toward the end of August the American advance became apparent when troops began to flood back through Metz. Immediate steps were taken to block off the roads leading into the city from the west. This enabled the collection of a large quantity of vehicles and ammunition, and 10,000 soldiers were redirected to units in the area, 2,000 of whom participated in the defense of the city. The airfield at Frescaty housed a large store of aircraft spare parts. These were shipped out of the city, together with much of the equipment belonging to the SS Signal School. The remarks of von Knobelsdorf, quoted above with reference to destructions, may well refer to a large clothing store which was housed in some of the forts. According to Kemper, the official in charge set the whole lot on fire rather than let it fall into the hands of the Americans. He also states that ammunition "no longer capable of being used" was destroyed, and admits that some desertions did occur.

There is, however, another version of events in Metz in early September, which is probably the most reliable.[23] Sometime toward the end of July 1944, Lieutenant General Walther Krause was appointed to command Division No. 462 in Metz. At the time, this unit was nothing more than a headquarters with a nominal staff, responsible for the various military schools and the training and replacement units in the Metz area. They were engaged in such matters as the reorientation of convalescents and the care of wounded prior to discharge. The officers and NCO's of the division were either unfit or overage, and none of the units were in any way ready for combat.

General Krause states that from about 22 August the defeats in France began to make themselves felt in Metz. He was made responsible, by the commander of Military District XII, which was based in Wiesbaden, for maintaining order in the city and the surrounding districts and for processing the refugees from the fighting. He makes it quite plain that the party and the state authorities under Gauleiter Bürckel "did not participate in defense activities in any way." Comparing the evidence of Kemper and Krause, we have the classic case of the quarrel between, on the one hand, the Schutzstaffel (SS) and the Nazi Party; and on the other, the German army. Looking for an average, one can probably say that at the end of August, some confusion reigned in Metz and that an excessive amount of equipment was prematurely destroyed. There is no evidence to support a wholesale exodus, although quite a number of civilians left, and there were some cases of desertion. By the beginning of September, the army, under General Krause, was firmly in control of the situation.

On 2 September, Krause was appointed fortress commander by General Sinnhuber (LXXXII Corps). However, on 7 September the higher command echelon changed to the XIII SS Panzer Corps (Lt. Gen. Priess), which assumed responsibility for the sector from Thionville to south of Metz. This was an SS Corps only in name as the bulk of the troops were normal army units.

General Krause took control of the roadblocks and set to work to assemble a fighting force capable of defending the city. His division had two infantry training battalions immediately available plus miscellaneous specialists, but by the beginning of September he managed to form a three-regiment division, which consisted of the Officer Candidate Regiment, the 1010th Security Regiment, and the NCO School of Military District XII.

The Officer Candidate Regiment (*Fahnenjunker Regiment,* sometimes referred to as the *Kampfgruppe von Siegroth*) was commanded by Colonel von Siegroth, and the unit was mainly composed of the cadets of an officer training school. They were not necessarily youngsters, as many of them were veteran soldiers from the Russian front who had been promoted from the ranks. They numbered some 1,800, most of whom had been commissioned as lieutenants on passing their examinations at the beginning of September. The regiment was filled out with some 1,500 sundry troops who had been gathered in from the retreating columns to give a total combat strength of 3,300 experienced men. It should be emphasized that this unit was purely a German army one and contained no members of the *Waffen SS*. American troops, when confronted by a hard-fighting German unit, often wrongly assumed that it was from the SS, which did not have a monopoly on toughness.

The 1010th Security Regiment, commanded by Lieutenant Colonel Richter, had retreated from France and consisted of two under-strength battalions (Krause gives a figure of between 500 and 600 men, minus heavy weapons). The personnel were mostly overage and their combat efficiency was low.

The NCO School of Military District XII (*Unterführerschule*), commanded by Colonel Wagner, was formed into a regiment of some 1,500 men who had been attending various courses. Krause rated their efficiency as high, although they had never before fought together as a combat unit.

In addition to the above three regiments, the two replacement battalions belonging to the division were stationed on the east bank of the Moselle to the south of the city. There they were joined by a battalion formed from the personnel of the SS Signal School—known as "Battalion Berg," after its commander. Initially, artillery was almost nonexistant, consisting of two battalions of a replacement unit armed with Russian 7.5cm cannon, and with no transport of its own. Krause said, "The horses for them had to be taken from the horse hospital and the harness from the supply depot. The adaptation of these animals to their new work was a difficult task." The only reinforcement received was a battery of four 10.5-cm guns.

Krause deployed the bulk of his forces around the western fortified salient. On the right, the 1010th Security Regiment held the line facing north between the Fèves Ridge and the Moselle. In the center, the NCO School was spread between St. Privat and Verneville. The area from there to the river at Ars-sur-Moselle was held by the Officer Candidate Regiment, to whom the bulk of the artillery was assigned.

As in all aspects of German activity in Metz, the record of their use of the already existing fortifications poses problems because of the lack of reliable sources. Between the wars, the forts had been allowed to decay. Those on the east bank had been largely disarmed, while those on the west bank had been used as command posts, stores, barracks, etc. When the Germans took over in 1940, they made use of some of the works to house underground factories, as well as stripping much portable equipment for use in the Atlantic Wall. An American legend often repeated in postwar unit histories was that the Germans had worked feverishly on the forts between 1940 and 1944. This is simply not true. Germany was a conquering nation and was not interested in spending money on outdated defenses in the interior of its territory.

In September 1944, German views on the value of the fortifications differed. Prior to this, on 24 August, within the framework of the general orders concerning the building of defensive positions in the west, Hitler had ordered that "in the fortress Metz-Thionville . . . the existing defenses are to be reconditioned and those not used are to be demolished."[24] However, there was neither time nor material and personnel available for anything to be done except on local initiative.

Standartenfuehrer Kemper states that it was possible to get one armored battery of four 100-mm turret guns into working order. The industrialist Hermann Röchling came from Saarbrücken with a number of mechanics, who succeeded in repairing the ventilation system, the ammunition hoists, and the lighting plant. The fortress telephone network was repaired and the ammunition, which was stored outside the forts in magazines, was brought in. It would seem that most of this was somewhat ancient, being either German of First World War Vintage or French from about 1918.

General Krause says that the garrison engineer commander told him that Metz "should be dismantled, as military defense with these fortifications was impossible." However, he goes on to say that this information was partly unreliable, as a detachment from the Officer Candidate School found a battery at Fort Driant that could be made to fire (this is probably the battery referred to by Kemper). In addition, a few 150-mm howitzers were brought into action at Fort Jean d'Arc. However, sighting devices for all the guns were missing, which thus had to be fired by direct observation.

What emerges from all this is that the Germans used the delay caused by the American supply shortage to put Metz and the Moselle line into a state of defense. Using what was readily available, a cohesive line was constructed and manned with troops of varying quality. Fourteen thousand men would be a reasonable estimate of the strength of 462nd Division in and around the city. When the fortress was originally constructed, it had a permanent peacetime garrison of 25,000 men; and in war, an entire army was to be stationed there. The larger forts each had a garrison of some 2,000 infantry, artillery, and engineers. Thus the defenders in 1944 were numerically weak, and instead of the original complement of over 90 turret guns, had but a handful of pieces and a grave lack of ammunition. To counterbalance this, they had all the advantages of terrain which they were to use to such good effect.

On 5 September, OB West estimated that there was the equivalent of four and a half divisions available for the Metz-Thionville sector. They were positioned on the eastern bank, except for the fortified salient to the west of Metz. The divisions were a mixture of odd battalions and burnt-out regiments, largely without vehicles, heavy weapons, and armor. Their state of training and efficiency varied considerably, from excellent to terrible. However, there was a front of sorts, as General Walker's men were to discover when they resumed their advance.

≡ 4 ≡

The Advance is Resumed

On 1 September, General Eisenhower assumed direct command of the land battle in northwest Europe, a factor which did nothing to diminish the backstage clamor over the "great argument." Indeed, in many ways, it aggravated the situation. General Essame wrote, "In the record of these first few days of September there is a fog, an arrest of action, a lack of clear direction which research does little to dispel."[1] As far as the Third Army was concerned, although they did not know it or want to realize it at the time, this date marked the end of the halcyon days of pursuit and the start of a totally different style of warfare.

The following day, a meeting was held at Bradley's headquarters near Chartres. In addition to General Eisenhower and the host, Patton and Hodges, the army commanders, and General Vandenberg from the Army Air Force were present. Patton naturally pleaded for supplies, but Eisenhower remained adamant on the principle of his broad-front policy. Stating quite rightly that he did not have the resources to back either thrust right to the hilt, he reaffirmed the priority of the northern sector. However, he did agree to a renewal of the eastward move toward the Rhine, which would be contingent on Montgomery's success in clearing the Calais area.

Thoroughly discouraged, Patton went off sightseeing to the areas where his small tank force had fought in 1918. All his plans seemed to have been stymied, and his visions of some sort of plot became more intense. Cornelius Ryan tells of a press conference somewhere about this time: "Patton's weekly press conferences were always news-worthy, but especially memorable for the General's off-the-record remarks—which, because of his colorful vocabulary, could never have been reported anyway. That first week of September, as a war correspondent . . . I was present, when in typical fashion, he expounded on his plans for the Germans. In his high-pitched voice, and pounding the map, Patton declared that 'Maybe there are 5,000, maybe 10,000 Nazi bastards in their concrete foxholes before the Third Army. Now, if Ike stops holding Monty's hand and gives me the supplies, I'll go through the Siegfried Line like shit through a goose.'"[2]

However, matters were slowly improving. Engineers managed to repair an airfield near Rheims so that heavy cargo planes could land, and by 4 September, enough fuel had arrived to restart cavalry patrols. Again the columns ranged out toward the Moselle both north and south of Metz. They reported that no bridges were intact and that opposition was stiffening. In one of these forays, the commanding officer of the 3rd Cavalry Group was ambushed and captured. They had avanced along the main road toward Gravelotte from Mars-la-Tour when they ran up against the advanced positions manned by the Officer Candidate Regiment. The Germans allowed the cavalry to pass through and then blew a bridge behind them. Brought to a halt, most of the force was destroyed or captured.

Headquarters of XX Corps, apart from assembling its scattered forces as and when the fuel situation permitted, was busy planning the advance to the Rhine. Two alternatives were considered during this waiting period, both of which aimed at seizing crossings over the Moselle. One favored the use of armor as a spearhead, in the hope of forcing a rapid decision, while the other proposed to use initially the two infantry divisions. In view of the difficult nature of the terrain to the south of Metz, it should have been obvious to the planners right from the start that armor there would have been highly unsuitable. The commander of 7th Armored Division and his officers were certainly in agreement on this.[3]

On 5 September, Bradley arrived at Patton's headquarters at Chalons-sur-Marne, whence the corps commanders were rapidly summoned to the meeting. Bradley again assigned the Rhine at Frankfurt as the Third Army objective as soon as the Westwall could be breached. Immediately as the conference was over, Patton issued his orders. General Walker with XX Corps was to attack eastward in two phases—first, to establish a bridgehead over the Moselle, and second, to cross the Rhine.[4] At no time was any mention made of expected German opposition. It was assumed that the enemy would make some sort of stand at the Westwall, which Patton thought could be breached easily by armor.

Armed with his orders, Walker rushed back to his headquarters and telephoned the glad tidings to his divisions—adding that the orders from General Patton "will take us all the way to the Rhine."[5] These verbal messages were followed the next morning by Field Order No. 10, upon which the first stage of the Metz battle was based (and its text is given in full as an appendix to the XX Corps operational report, *The Reduction of Fortress Metz*). This was a superbly optimistic document: "Third U.S. Army attacks to seize crossings of the Rhine River between Mannheim and Coblenz" was the stated intention. The mission of XX Corps was first to seize a crossing over the Moselle and then to capture Metz and Thionville. Second, they were to cross the Rhine in the vicinity of Mainz and prepare to advance to Frankfurt. The individual units were assigned missions as follows: The 3rd Cavalry Group was ordered to "reconnoiter to the Rhine without delay" and the 7th Armored Division was "to advance east in multiple columns; seize crossings over the Rhine." Cities and enemy strongpoints were to be bypassed and left to be mopped up by the following infantry. The 5th Infantry Division was to capture Metz and then continue to advance to the Rhine, while Thionville was assigned to the 90th Infantry.

Field Order No. 10 was truly a masterpiece of concise military staff work, but hopelessly vague. The crossing of the Moselle was only mentioned as a minor barrier on the way to the Rhine. The initial tasks were assigned to the armor, probably in the hope of grabbing a bridge; although, at the time that the order was issued, the cavalry had reported that all the bridges were down. The 7th Armored Division was ordered to advance in multiple columns, but whether they were to aim for one crossing site or to try for several on both sides of Metz was not clear.

Realistic intelligence about the enemy was almost nonexistent, except for the overoptimistic reports brought in by the cavalry. By 5 September, however, a note of caution was sounded by XX Corps G-2 when they estimated that there were 38,000 enemy troops in the area equipped with 160 tanks and self-propelled assault guns. In view of the already quoted figure of four and a half divisions estimated by OB West, the number of troops was a reasonable guess, but the total of armored fighting vehicles was very wide of the mark.

At this stage of the campaign, the American Army had run out of detailed maps and were using mostly 1:100,000 Michelin road maps. These were not bad for pursuit-type warfare where distances of thirty and forty miles per day were commonplace, but were totally unsuitable for static action. The reason for this map shortage lay in the SHAEF pre-Overlord estimates of the ground that would be covered by specific dates. The planners had been surprised by the speed of the advance and no provision had been made to supply maps of the terrain to the north of the Seine. The fortifications around Metz and Thionville were marked on some of the maps used by XX Corps, but nobody had any idea of the type, design, or actual sites of the forts. That may well sound incredible, but it is true. Due to the fact that the works were so well camouflaged by natural growth of vegetation, aerial photographs were of little help. In addition, the American army had never had any real experience of large-scale siege warfare, and thus there was no collection of background information about European fortifications in the archives.

In a letter written shortly after the war, Lt. Col. Howard Clark, who was XX Corps assistant engineer, gave the following summary of the situation: ". . . both the G-2 and the engineer at XX Corps had been concerned principally with the terrain and the Moselle River, both of which were known to be serious obstacles. Of the forts themselves almost nothing was known. Maps of 1:100,000 scale were the largest available, and these conveyed only a general idea of the location and number of forts. . . . Some apprehension was felt, but the general tendency was to hope for the best and to dismiss the forts as probably obsolete and incapable of offering determined resistance. The events of the next ten days . . . radically altered this view."[6]

However, before the advance could begin in earnest, General Walker had to shuffle his troops, which were still spread out between Rheims and Verdun. The 5th Infantry Division moved out of the Meuse bridgehead and advanced some 12 miles to take up a position between Étain and Vigneulles, roughly halfway between the Meuse and the Moselle. The other infantry division, the 90th, was still partly immobilized around Rheims, due to lack of transport and fuel. In fact, only enough fuel was available initially to move one regiment (357th Infantry Regimental Combat Team), which took up a position on the left flank of the 5th Infantry Division. Bridging equipment and heavy engineer stores were scattered in trucks that had run dry way back along the line of advance, mostly to the west of Rheims. These had to be refuelled from quartermaster trucks laden with jerry cans, a laborious and time-consuming process. It was not until 6 September that the bridging trains and the rest of the 90th Division were moved up into the assembly areas, together with the bulk of the corps artillery.

What followed was almost a case of the blind leading the blind. A powerfully equipped army corps of three combat-tested divisions stumbled blindly forward, buoyed up with optimism and with their sights firmly fixed on the distant Rhine. In retrospect, the impartial observer finds it hard to believe that such a major attack could be launched with so little planning, with such total lack of intelligence of the enemy, the terrain, and the defenses, and driving with the aid of ordinary road maps. This was the American genius for improvization at its very worst—improvization is only effective in a fluid tactical situation where the enemy is unable to organize. Patton was always a bitter critic of Montgomery, whom he regarded as a plodder. Monty's preference for set-piece battles may have wasted time in certain circumstances, but one cannot help but feel that in a situation similar to that which faced XX Corps, a few more days spent in planning would have been beneficial. A lot of American lives could well have been saved.

Just before dawn on 6 September, a strong reconnaissance force set out in four parallel columns toward Metz. Its mission was to reinforce the cavalry screens, who were beginning to find themselves in trouble, and to seize any bridges left standing. Some of the cavalry had succeeded in penetrating as far as the riverbank to the south of Metz, but had eventually been driven off. At about this time, the 17th SS Panzer Grenadier Division was in the process of withdrawing to the east bank, and it is probable that the cavalry met up with their rear guard. They had reported that all the bridges were destroyed, but had discovered a number of fording sites in the general area, Pagny, Ars-sur-Moselle, and Arnaville.

The four columns moved along the main road and hit the German outposts in the Mars-la-Tour area. This had been the scene of bitter fighting in August 1870 between the Prussians and the French, which had culminated in a series of engagements known as the Battle of Vionville-Mars-la-Tour. There they were stalled, and the reconnaissance commander, Lieutenant Colonel Boylan, sensibly decided to concentrate his widely spaced columns. Behind him, the bulk of the 7th Armored Division was also on the move, although there is confusion about its precise direction. It would seem that it had been left up to Colonel Boylan's force to determine the crossing site, although H. M. Cole cites a 7th Armored Division field order which assigned as mission a crossing to the north of the city.[7]

The armor also moved along the main east-west road with Combat Command CCA on the left and CCB on the right. They were followed by CCR in reserve, but the fuel shortage had forced them to leave behind the bulk of the 23rd Armored Infantry Battalion. The northern column, CCA, ran into German outposts in front of Ste.-Marie-aux-Chênes, where it was held up until the following morning.

It was CCB to the south that achieved the initial advantage. They found that the Germans had conducted a planned withdrawal from their positions around Mars-la-Tour. Moving eastward across the plateau, they encountered the first serious resistance from elements of the Officer Candidate Regiment, entrenched around Gravelotte. Again they were on the site of an 1870 battlefield, and it is perhaps an injustice that the whole area is littered with memorials to long-forgotten imperial German and French units, while nowhere is there any memorial to the dead of XX Corps. Small white crosses over individual graves from 1870 stand up haphazardly scattered in the grass, and one of the earliest war cemeteries in Europe can be seen at Gravelotte.

Brigadier General Thompson, commanding CCB, then received orders to swing south toward the riverbank, into the narrow ravines leading down that were totally unsuitable for armor. The roads were narrow and confined between rock walls overgrown with trees and bushes, perfect concealment for a group of enemy armed with panzerfausts. At the head of one of these ravines, up which the Prussians had come in 1870, lies the village of Gorze. There the armor ran into mines and antitank fire. With no room to deploy and bypass the obstruction, they were halted for the night. A company from the 23rd Armored Infantry Battalion did manage to get down to the riverbank on foot, but at daylight on 7 September were forced to retire by concentrated fire coming from the villages of Noveant and Arnaville.

Nevertheless, in a parallel action, CCB did succeed in establishing a weak presence at the edge of the Moselle. During the evening of 6 September, the rest of the 23rd Armored Infantry Battalion, commanded by Lieutenant Colonel Allison, arrived on the scene, having obtained fuel for their vehicles. They caught up with the left-flank column of CCB, which was stalled in front of Gravelotte—from where another ravine leads down to the river at Ars-sur-Moselle. This is the ravine in which runs a stream called the Mance, and where, in August 1870, thousands of General Steinmetz's troops were slaughtered in a vain attempt to cross it. In September 1944, it was mined and stoutly defended by the descendants of those Prussians, the Officer Candidate Regiment.

Allison's scouts, however, found a rough track leading through the Bois des Ognons, a wooded plateau between Gorze and the Mance ravine. This was unguarded, and during the night they passed along this, reaching the riverbank at dawn near a hamlet known as La Chêne. There they found themselves exposed to fire from both north and south, as well as from across the river. However, they hung on and during the afternoon they tried to put a patrol across. In view of the amount of fire encountered, this seems to have been a brave but perhaps unwise decision. The three boats were driven back by intense mortar and small-arms fire, and unfortunately this abortive attempt was to have serious repercussions almost immediately.

To the north of the city during the morning of 7 September, part of CCA managed to break free and reach the river at Mondelange. There they turned south on the main road leading toward Maizières-les-Metz, looking for a crossing site. Around midday they met up with the other column of the combat command, which had been held up at St. Privat. All three possible bridges in that sector were found to have been blown and the enemy had retired to the east bank. There was, however, a possible fording site at Hauconcourt. The armor then halted to wait for bridging equipment and for orders to tell them what to do. The divisional commander evidently still assumed that his unit would cross north of Metz, and he informed General Walker that he had a possible site.

Thus, on the first day of the resumed advance, XX Corps had run up against fairly stiff enemy opposition on the outpost lines—lines which would not have been there five days earlier, had the Americans been able to press home the advantage gained by crossing the Meuse. For the sake of clarity, the narrative must now be divided into a series of separate but often interconnected actions that took place up to the middle of September. These totally altered the Third Army situation. General Patton received his first bloody nose of the European Campaign, and XX Corps found their optimism rapidly evaporating in a type of fighting to which they were temperamentally unsuited.

THE DORNOT BRIDGEHEAD

This was a small and relatively minor action that normally would not have rated more than a few paragraphs in a newspaper report. It is, however, an important illustration of how the best-laid plans of generals can so easily go astray. Clausewitz, the eminent early nineteenth-century writer on military theory, introduced the human element into war by classifying it under the term "friction." The operations around Dornot, although marked by great personal courage, were a prime example of how shoddy staff work can put large numbers of ordinary soldiers at risk.

Major General Orlando Ward, one-time Chief of Military History of the U.S. Army, wrote the following in the foreword to a brilliant study of Dornot upon which much of what follows is based.[8] "This . . . pictures the difficulties of small-unit commanders and soldiers in executing missions assigned by higher headquarters. Such missions are based at best on educated guesses as to the enemy situation and probable reaction. Success, failure, confusion, outstanding behavior, as pictured here, illustrate battle as it did, and often can, take place. . . . We must remember that confusion, like fog, envelops the whole battlefield, including the enemy. Initiative, any clear-cut aggressive action, tends to dispel it."

On the evening of 5 September, General Walker had told Major General LeRoy Irwin, the commanding general of the 5th Infantry Division, to "pin onto" the tail of the armor and to follow up if the latter failed to secure a crossing. Irwin was unsure whether that meant he was to pass through the 7th Armored or to establish his bridgehead on the corps' right. Owing to the fact that corps had little idea of the progress made by CCB, he obtained no concrete information when he queried his orders. His division was somewhat dispersed anyway because there was no cohesive front line. On the left, the 2nd Infantry Regiment had advanced behind CCA on the northern thrust. On September 7 it collided head on with the German outposts in the vicinity of Amanvillers. With the 10th Infantry in division reserve, the 11th Infantry was strung out on the roads behind CCB. During the morning the 11th Infantry had at last managed to get past the opposition at the head of the ravine at Gorze. From there it moved down the narrow defile to join up with the armored infantry between Dornot and La Chêne. Without boats or bridging equipment, the armored column found itself hemmed in and unable to deploy. Its tail stretched back to Gorze, and without a bridge, it could not go anywhere or even turn around and withdraw. Most of the vehicles had bright cerise-colored air identification panels stretched over them that were plainly visible to the enemy on the high ground on the other side of the river. As opposed to the sector to the north of Metz, the Germans had not all withdrawn to the east bank, and the armor had simply broken through a thin part of their line. To the south the enemy was firmly entrenched around Arnaville, and to the north, at Ars-sur-Moselle. Completely unknown to the Americans, the guns of Fort Driant could also cover their position from the dominating high ground of the Bois des Ognons.

In an effort to dislodge the enemy from Ars, Brigadier General Thompson, commanding CCB, asked his divisional commander for the reserve unit, CCR, to launch an attack toward Ars. This was agreed to, but before they were anywhere near the river, their orders were countermanded, and they were ordered to make way on the roads for the infantry. The reason for the reversal is that during the morning, a rumor spread right back to corps that the 23rd Armored Infantry Battalion had managed to establish a bridgehead. The origin of the rumor lay in the abortive three-boat patrol.

At midday, General Irwin was ordered to force a crossing at Dornot, and he immediately sent forward the 11th Infantry, the commander of which, Colonel Yuill, had intended to cross further to the south. During the afternoon the regiment struggled toward the defile and then tried to pick their way through the armored traffic jam. In the early evening they received definite orders to cross the following morning and to use the 23rd Armored Infantry Battalion to increase their own forces. Colonel Yuill protested about this, as his 1st Battalion to the south was being virtually ignored by the enemy in the Arnaville region, but all to no avail. The 3rd Battalion therefore was deployed on the high ground to the north of Dornot, while the 2nd Battalion was ordered to make the actual crossing.

Incredible as it may seem, the first 11th Infantry troops to arrive at Dornot were astonished to find part of 7th Armored Division there, and the surprise was apparently mutual. "Neither had any idea of the other's presence or impending arrival."[9] The 2nd Battalion picked their way through the chaos to arrive during the night, and as the orders specified that a crossing was to be made before dawn, they would have to undertake the operation without even the benefit of a look at their objective.

At that time Dornot was a small village consisting of only one street, situated on the downward slope of the hills, some 500 meters west of the actual river. Between it and the Moselle was a main road and a railway, followed by a stretch of marshy ground partly occupied by a lagoon. On the opposite bank there was an irregular patch of woods, followed by another main road, beyond which the ground sloped upward to a range of low hills. On those hills, from which the Germans had an excellent view of the whole crossing site and into Dornot village, were two more of the pre-1914 forts—Forts Sommy and St. Blaise—which together made up the Verdun Fortified Group (see appendix for details). They were marked on the 11th Infantry's maps, but again, nothing was known about their construction or design. They were well camouflaged, and ultimately proved to be capable of withstanding anything in the way of bombs and shells that could be brought against them.

As far as the German opposition was concerned, their available forces were a mixed bag. On the west bank, the troops being contained to the north of Dornot by the 23rd Armored Infantry Battalion were from the Officer Candidate Regiment; they proved to be skilled and fanatical opponents. The far bank was held by a scratch replacement battalion (Battalion Voss) most of whom were elderly men suffering from stomach ailments, and the battalion formed from the SS Signals School (Battalion Berg). In addition, the bulk of the 17th SS Panzer Grenadier Division was in the area for refitting.

The paradox was that the very urgency of the situation and the need to exploit the supposed German disorganization forced the Americans to attempt to cross the river without sufficient preparation and against considerable odds. All chance of success from speed and surprise had long since vanished.

As dawn broke on the morning of 8 September, the situation in Dornot was chaotic. Armored vehicles and trucks crowded the only narrow road, and accurate enemy fire made movement dangerous. Heavy rain and even sleet turned the whole area into a morass, and difficulties were compounded when several trucks carrying ammunition were set on fire. The command situation on the spot was equally chaotic, as both the infantry and the armor had separate orders to establish a bridgehead. The commander of the 5th Infantry Division, General Irwin, had verbal orders placing him in command of all the troops in the area, but Brigadier General Thompson, CO of CCB, was not aware of this. As the highest-ranking officer in Dornot, he assumed that he was in charge of operations. The commander of the assault battalion, Lieutenant Colonel Lemmon, was most surprised to find that the armored units were also proposing to use the same crossing spot.

The early daylight hours were characterized by poor communication and confused orders. While division and corps argued, however, those whose job it was to carry out the operation reached agreement. Colonel Lemmon and Colonel Allison, whose armored infantry battalion had already suffered heavy casualties in the fighting to the north of Dornot, decided that their men would cross together near the lagoon and establish themselves in the small wood on the other side. The armored infantry would then swing north to attack in the direction of Jouey-les-Arches, while the 11th Infantry men would capture Fort St. Blaise. The 3rd Battalion, which was to cross later, would take Fort Sommy and protect the southern flank of the bridgehead.

By the time these matters were settled (about 0600 hours), it was obvious that the attack would have to be made in daylight. The surprising thing is that, in view of the determination to establish a bridgehead, there were hardly any boats available. On account of the traffic jam and the narrow approaches, the engineers attached to 11th Infantry had only managed to get a few down to the river, and it was not until 0800 that a few more appeared. The situation was a direct result of a lengthy tour of the rear areas made by Brigadier General Thompson during the night—after repeated requests for boats had been ignored. In one of the injustices of war, General Thompson was relieved of his command later that day. The reason for this drastic measure was that it was thought that CCB had established a bridge-head and then abandoned it. This was again the bogey of the abortive three-boat patrol rising up to haunt those involved, since, by that time, rumor had inflated it into a full-scale assault crossing. It was not until 1958 that the unfortunate Thompson was exonerated and rein-stated in rank.

Further delays were caused while the supporting artillery was positioned, and it was not until 1045 that the attack finally got underway—although oddly enough, the Germans were caught by surprise. Assisted by engineers, three rifle companies moved down to the riverbank by the lagoon, where they were subjected to small-arms and mortar fire. This was not excessive, but to avoid having to climb over the exposed railway embankment, the troops used an underpass which gave a certain amount of cover.

At 1115 the leading unit, F Company, started to cross in five assault boats, through a curtain of fire. Even loading the boats was extremely hazardous, and the waiting men had to take cover in a ditch some 20 yards from the edge of the water. When their turn came they had to scramble out, encumbered with their equipment, and make a rush for the boats.

Fire coming from the north on the same side of the river was so heavy that it became necessary to send a patrol along the river bank. This managed to wipe out much of the opposition, although a number of snipers remained to trouble the crossing site. One German gunner, who was concealed in a dugout, was able to fire directly across the lagoon. At night, he had the superb effrontery to sing German songs in a loud voice.

By early afternoon, F and G Companies plus a platoon each of heavy machine guns and 81-mm mortars were over the river. Artillery support for the crossing was severely limited by the shortage of ammunition for the howitzers. Valuable fire support, however, was given by the heavy weapons of the 3rd Battalion, which were posi-tioned on the high bluff to the south of Dornot, although they too had their ammunition problems. Cletus Hollenbeck was the instrument corporal for the machine guns and mortars of H Company. He wrote to the author as follows: "I was ordered to set up the 81's in position above the town and fire a round intermittently using 8 guns every fifteen seconds or so, as a protective cover for the men who were across, to stop enemy infiltrating into their position. For me this presented a problem. Where was the ammo coming from? We lost so many squad leaders that I had no one to order or organize a group to haul ammo, so I took it upon myself to do this. I got about 20 or so men, and we took off to the rear ammo dump and hauled in about 200 shells. Each man carried all he could handle, and when we got back to where I had made arrangements to position the guns, we were pretty bushed. I noticed the engineers were pulling out. I knew they had mortars on half-tracks, so I took about ten men into the town; and as I saw a half-track just across the road from the aid station, I asked the driver for any ammo he had. Fortunately he was loaded and said, 'Take it all if you want it.'"

With the two lead companies across, they were able to proudly claim that they were the Allied unit nearest the German frontier. They were followed by E Company and 38 men of the 23rd Armored Infantry Battalion, all that were left of the force that had been the first on the scene. The last element to enter the bridgehead was K Company from the 3rd Battalion of the 11th Infantry, who crossed at around 1700. Thus, by the evening of 8 September, four rifle companies and the few armored infantry were across the Moselle, supported by two heavy weapons platoons.

Confusion was not the prerogative of the Americans, who, quite by accident rather than design, had attacked right on the boundary between the two German battalions (Voss and Berg). The second sent in alarming and contradictory reports to the 37th SS Panzer Grenadier Regiment, which was the nearest larger unit. The 2nd Battalion of the 37th SS was supported by a number of antiaircraft tanks (*flakpanzer*), two assault guns, and one 75-mm self-propelled gun. They received a report that Battalion Voss had been routed. An NCO was sent to try to discover what was happening, and must have returned with reassuring news, because the original German orders for a counterattack specified only platoon-size assaults from north and south, to eliminate the enemy "if found." When the American landing was finally confirmed, the attack strength was upgraded to two companies supported by heavy weapons and armor.

The actual bridgehead was established in what became known to the defenders as Horseshoe Wood. During the late afternoon of 8 September, F and G Companies moved off on their mission to capture Fort St. Blaise. Owing to the small numbers of men available, the attack toward Jouey-les-Arches by the 23rd Armored Infantry

Battalion was cancelled. The two companies crossed the main road in front of their position; and with hardly any interference from the enemy, made their way uphill in open order, through fields and clumps of scrub. Indeed, the silence struck them as odd, and there were no casualties until they reached the outer defenses of the fort. There, the commander of F Company was shot and killed by a sniper as he bent over to question a wounded German.

Capturing the fort proved to be far too difficult a task. The attackers found themselves confronted by five rows of barbed wire through which they methodically cut a path, only to find themselves faced by an iron palisade 4 meters high. Beyond this was a dry ditch, some 15 meters wide and 5 meters deep, that surrounded the whole of the fort. A prisoner told them that there were 1,500 SS men inside, but in fact, the fort was unoccupied and its guns were not in operation at the time. However, faced by such obstacles, the battalion operations officer, Captain Church, ordered his men to pull back, and radioed for an artillery barrage. Unfortunately, when the shells arrived, three fell short, killing and wounding several men.

The Germans immediately retaliated with their own artillery, and at the same time, infantry attacked from both flanks. The two American companies were caught out on a limb on the exposed hillside, 2,000 yards away from their comrades in Horseshoe Wood and with their line of retreat about to be cut off. Captain Church radioed for E Company to move up in support, but by then it was too late. The flanks were swept by accurate machine-gun fire, and the broad main road had become a deathtrap.

Captain Church's only option was to order a retreat; although, in the circumstances, an orderly withdrawal proved to be impossible. The two companies separated and moved back down the hill in two ragged lines. Casualties were heavy and the survivors needed all of three hours to regain the shelter of the woods. Stragglers were still coming in during the night and the following morning, and the wounded had to be abandoned. Many of the casualties fell victims to a German subterfuge. One machine gun would fire tracer at roughly head height. Seeing this, the GI's would naturally crouch and run, only to be wounded by another gun firing ordinary ammunition just above ground level.

With the survivors of F and G Companies back in Horseshoe Wood, the real saga of the Dornot bridgehead began. The four companies dug a defensive perimeter enclosing an area of some 200 square yards. This minute foothold was all that had been achieved by evening and could only be held with the support of American artillery firing from the west bank. The handful of men crouching in their foxholes had to endure almost continuous bombardment and repeated counterattacks by a determined foe. Throughout the night of 8/9 September, wave after wave of Germans assembled on the far side of the main road and then charged toward the thin line of defenders, shouting "Yanks kaput!" Tanks cruised along the road spraying the woods with fire, hoping to provoke retaliation that would reveal the defenders' positions. Fire discipline, however, was excellent, the Americans waiting until the charging enemy were almost upon them before opening up.

Estimates of the number of Germans killed and wounded in these suicide attacks vary. The 11th Infantry men who were there at the time boasted of "hundreds," and it is safe to assume that casualties were heavy as a result of such primitive tactics. Captain Gerrie, CO of G Company, commented on the enemy in a message sent out of the bridgehead: "Watch out for these birds, they are plenty tough. I've never run across guys like these before, they are new, something you read about."

Such attacks, however, took an inevitable toll of the small number of defenders—who could not be reinforced. The woods were full of cries for medics, but First Sergeant Hembree, who was to be a tower of strength to the men in the bridgehead, passed around that the wounded were to stay quiet. "Top says not to yell if you get hit by a Jerry bullet because the bastards will know they've hurt us then." From then on, this advice was followed, an amazing example of self-discipline. There were plenty of heroes in the Dornot bridgehead—ordinary soldiers caught up in the tide of war, who, when called upon, performed above and beyond the normal call of duty. During the first night, two privates volunteered to man an advance post. Despite a subsequent order to withdraw, and armed only with rifles, they stuck to their positions. Although finally overwhelmed, their comrades found 22 dead Germans around their foxholes in the morning. Private Rex, who had only been in the army for 18 weeks, took over a machine gun whose gunner had been killed, and continued to operate it with great effect. He certainly accounted for a large number of the enemy casualties when the Germans charged in with fixed bayonets. Later, he gave his outer clothes to a wounded man and swam the river four times during the evacuation to help others to cross. The above are simply two examples of numerous incidents of personal heroism and of men who put their comrades before their own personal safety.

The original intention had been to establish the battalion command post in the bridgehead, but crossing difficulties forced Colonel Lemmon to remain in Dornot village where his headquarters was twice shelled, forcing the staff to move. During the night of 8/9 September, Captain Church returned to the west bank to report and to organize supplies. As a result of his advice, Colonel Lemmon requested permission to withdraw the battalion. Division, however, ordered that the tiny bridgehead be held "at all costs," as it was diverting German attention from another crossing that was to be attempted further south. The 2nd Battalion had become expendable.

Daylight movement across the river had become impossible. The only method of communication was by radio, and all thoughts of building a bridge were abandoned. Repeated requests for air strikes were in vain, as the available aircraft were needed elsewhere, thus depriving the defenders of that most effective weapon—the tactical fighter-bomber. During the night some engineers finally managed to bring up some more boats, which were used to evacuate the wounded and to ferry over supplies of water, rations, ammunition, and radio batteries. The main aid station was in Dornot, which meant that the wounded had to run the gauntlet of enemy fire between the riverbank and the safety of the railway underpass.

On the morning of 9 September, the general opinion above regimental level was that the bridgehead could be maintained and even expanded to the south. Those actively involved, however, realized just the opposite, and no further efforts were made to send in reinforcements. Frantic calls for air support remained unanswered as the enemy continued their mass attacks. Shells still poured into Dornot and the area of Horseshoe Wood. Oddly enough, the reason given by the 37th SS Panzer Grenadier Regiment to higher headquarters, for its failure to eliminate the bridgehead, was that the Americans were continually ferrying over fresh troops.

Certainly the Germans tried hard enough. A German officer employed a ruse by shouting in English, "Cease firing!" while at the same time his men formed up for a quick assault during the antici-

pated lull. This worked only once, and in the end to the attackers'
disadvantage. A platoon of E Company obeyed the supposed order,
but when it was repeated, recognized what they thought was a foreign
accent. Opening fire, the platoon killed some twenty Germans who
were caught in the open.

By midmorning of 9 September, most of the officers had been
either killed or wounded, and K Company was commanded by a
sergeant. The men later reported that their officers had apologized to
them when they became casualties. Because muzzle flash betrayed
their positions, the 81-mm mortars were abandoned and their crews
took up rifles from the dead. Although there were enough K-rations
and water available, most of the men had been without sleep for 24
hours or more.

During the night, the resupply mission was repeated and the day's
crop of wounded were evacuated. In spite of their reduced numbers,
the defenders even had the sublime cheek the following morning to
call upon the Germans to surrender—promising them that, if they
refused, they would deliver such a concentration of fire as the Germans had never seen before.

On 10 September, the new crossing further south at Arnaville was
well under way, and in view of this, the diversionary value of the
Dornot bridgehead was no longer vital. Therefore 5th Division finally
agreed to abandoning it. Because of radio silence, the order to withdraw was carried across to Captain Gerrie by two swimmers, both of
whom arrived safely. The evacuation was to commence that night at
2115. Unaware of this, the Germans issued orders for a final full-scale
attack to start at 2300.

To carry out the evacuation the engineers planned to use the few
remaining leaky assault boats and some rubber rafts for transporting
the wounded. Ropes stretched across the river and supported by
floats were to support the able-bodied men who were unable to swim.
Infantry were concentrated around the landing site to give covering
fire, and guides were posted to show the way up to the village where
hot drinks, food, and dry clothing were waiting. Once the evacuation
was completed, the artillery was to plaster the whole area with a
massive barrage in the hope of catching Germans moving into Horseshoe Wood. All portable equipment was to be thrown into the river.

The engineers carrying the boats, ropes, and other equipment were
delayed on their way to the riverbank by intense enemy shelling, but

the evacuation got under way with three leaky boats and one rope. Captain Gerrie supervised the loading of the wounded while the others made their way back by swimming or clinging to the rope. The water was cold and the current, swollen by rain, was swift. A number of men lost their lives by drowning, while several strong swimmers made repeated trips to help others. The only brief moment of panic was when Captain Gerrie left the water's edge to search the woods for wounded, but order was soon restored. When the engineers finally got their extra boats into operation around 2230, matters were greatly speeded up.

As the last boatloads left the east bank, an officer and an NCO crossed the river to see that nobody was left behind (many were so exhausted that they fell asleep while waiting for their turn in the boats). With them they had a green flare, which was to be the signal for the artillery to open fire. As they crouched alone on the river bank, two enemy tanks came out of the woods and fired across the river, hitting one of the last boats. This accounted for a number of men subsequently listed as "missing in action."

By coincidence, at that moment the Germans themselves fired a green flare. Knowing that the artillery would respond almost immediately, the two-man rear guard scrambled into their rubber boat and beat a hasty retreat. But in spite of all their precautions, one man was left behind; he had fallen asleep in his foxhole. Waking in the morning, he found himself alone and walked down to the river "across dead Germans from his foxhole to the riverbank." There, he pulled himself across on a rope that had been left in place to cater for such an eventuality.

The "butcher's bill" was heavy. The Germans certainly lost several hundred killed, and one can assume a corresponding number of wounded. As far as the Americans were concerned, K Company of the 3rd Battalion emerged with no officers and 50 men. The 2nd Battalion's three rifle companies which were engaged had only two officers left fit for duty and lost 200 casualties (50 percent of those committed). The 23rd Armored Infantry Battalion, which had been in action on both sides of the river, lost 200 men in four days. However, after the evacuation, large numbers of men were listed as nonbattle casualties on account of fatigue and exposure. The final total, given as an estimate in the official history, comes to 945 killed, wounded, and missing.[10]

The small handful of survivors was withdrawn for rest, and to all intents and purposes, the 2nd Battalion, 11th Infantry, temporarily ceased to exist. The Dornot operation, because it failed, tended to be overshadowed by the successful Arnaville action. However, without the diversionary aspect of the former, the latter might well have proved to be far more costly. The gallant defenders of Horseshoe Wood were victims of false optimism and poor planning on the part of their superiors, and their deeds have remained buried in the archives and little-read official publications. The great operations of war about which we read are made up of hundreds of Dornots—hasty, ill-conceived, improvised, but nevertheless heroic.

THE ARNAVILLE BRIDGEHEAD

Late on 8 September, the day of the crossing at Dornot, General Irwin came to the conclusion that the bridgehead there was far too contained to be capable of useful exploitation. Although the bulk of the 11th Infantry was engaged at Dornot and the 2nd Infantry was trying to batter the hard way into Metz against the forts in the west of the city, he still had a regiment, the 10th Infantry, available. Already the 3rd Battalion was on the high ground on either side of the defile that led down to the river at Arnaville, some three miles to the south of Dornot. He therefore ordered the commanding officer of the 10th, Colonel Bell, to carry out a crossing. In contrast to the haphazard scramble at Dornot, Colonel Bell was given a whole day to prepare the operation that was scheduled to begin on 10 September. Even more sensibly, the exact time and place were left for him to determine after a thorough reconnaissance.

The bulk of the regiment was at Chambley, fifteen miles west of the river, but while they were assembled to move up, Colonel Bell and a small party went forward to reconnoiter, although there were still some enemy on the west bank. Like Dornot, Arnaville lies somewhat back from the flood plain of the Moselle valley. An extra complication was that between the railway and the river itself was a further obstacle, a canal. However, a lock was discovered, the gates of which could be used as a crossing for infantry. Beyond that there was a level marshy area some 200 yards wide to be traversed. The high ground on either side of the Arnaville approach road provided an excellent base for covering fire and observation. On the far bank, there was a further marshy plain some 500 yards wide, but completely devoid of cover, between the river and the main north-south road. On the road itself was Voisage Farm, beyond which the ground sloped steeply upward into wooded hills. Hill 386 and the Côte de Faye (Hills 325, 370 and 369) seemed to offer good defensive positions, and became the individual battalion objectives. To the southeast the site was bounded by the village of Arry, while Corny lay to the north. This was not really an ideal site for a crossing because the only roads out of the area led from the villages at either end, and both of them were minor ones. Thus the infantry would have to fight their way over the hills in the center before armor could be deployed. However, a bad site was better than none.

On returning to his command post, Colonel Bell issued his orders at 1400 to the regiment and its usual combat-team support elements. The attack was to commence just after midnight, with the 1st Battalion leading off to capture and hold Hill 386. They would be followed by the 2nd Battalion at 0400 on 10 September, whose mission was to occupy the Côte de Faye. No less than 13 battalions of field artillery were to be in support, culled from corps and division, and as an innovation, a smoke generator company was on hand to provide a smoke screen. Without the smoke screen, the turret guns from Fort Driant in the north would have a field day. The plan was based on surprise and was to be mounted without preliminary bombardment. Finally, boats and engineer stores were on hand and ready for use, as opposed to the chaotic situation at Dornot. The 3rd Battalion was to remain on the high ground around Arnaville to protect the crossing site. They were to be supported by tank destroyers whose mission was to fire across the river and pick off any enemy armor that appeared. As soon as possible, antitank guns and 105-mm howitzers were to be ferried across into the bridgehead.

Thus, on paper, the planned attack was well supported; in addition, air strikes were promised. Early on 9 September, Ninth Air Force had turned down requests for strikes over the Moselle with the justification that corps artillery could provide adequate support. At that time their primary mission was still the bombing of Brest, which continued to hold out in the rear of the Allied forces. By the evening, however, 12th Army Group was convinced that the situation was deteriorating and gave orders for a number of fighter-bombers to be released to fly missions over the bridgehead.

Just as the Dornot attack had hit a battalion boundary, the Arnaville crossing was made (evidently fortuitously) against the boundary between the XIII SS Corps and the XLVII Panzer Corps to their south (the actual boundary was in Arry). In the area of the XIII SS Corps was the 282nd Infantry Battalion (one of the replacement battalions belonging to General Krause's 462nd Division), backed up by elements of the 17th SS Panzer Grenadier Division, while the southern flank was held by part of the 3rd Panzer Grenadier Division. Both these armored units were chronically short of armored vehicles; although by then, their personnel had been brought back up to strength.

At this stage it is worth quoting the estimate of the situation given by the chief of staff of XIII SS Panzer Corps, Col. Kurt von Einem (only one of its eight divisions was an SS unit).[11] "The enemy then tried to cross the Moselle to the north and south of Metz. . . . A continuation of his offensive on a large scale in the direction of the Saar could only be reckoned with after reinforcement with fresh troops and thorough material preparation." If that was what Einem really believed at the time, he must have been gifted with powers of prophecy. He goes on, "Local reserves had to be made ready to meet these crossing attempts although troops and materials were strictly limited. . . . A particular disadvantage was the fact that the enemy could make his preparations for crossing more or less undisturbed, as we had available neither our own air support nor sufficient artillery ammunition." Ask any American who was at Dornot or Arnaville and he will tell you that he did not notice that the Germans were short of ammunition. As we have seen, the crossing preparations were not exactly "undisturbed."

During the afternoon, as the assault battalions were moving up to the start line, their commanders and most of their other officers were able to go forward and personally observe the crossing site and their objectives across the river. They were even furnished with 1:25,000 maps, which were a distinct improvement on the commercial road maps that they had been using until then.

Met by guides, the leading company from the 1st Battalion moved down to the riverbank on schedule, each man laden with all the ammunition he could carry, three K-rations, and a full canteen. They crossed the lock gates over the canal, but when they arrived at the edge of the water, they found that the engineers were not yet ready. However, at 0115 they were loaded into twenty assault boats and slipped across, meeting only some scattered rounds of small-arms fire. However, when they had organized and began to move off across the flood plain toward the road, they were met with machine gun and mortar fire. Artillery did not really begin to harrass them until daylight, but this may well have been a result of poor communications. General Krause stated that it sometimes took several hours for a message to reach him from the Moselle valley.

In the meanwhile the engineers ferried over the bulk of the battalion, and their commanding officer realized that if they were caught in the open on the flood plain at dawn, they would be sitting targets. With the 2nd Battalion crowding in behind them, the only way was forward; but the various companies had gone to ground in face of the increasing enemy fire. A machine gun enfiladed the main road, making it a deathtrap.

The initiative was seized by Major Haughey, temporary commander of the 1st Battalion, who sent his S-2 forward to find a way up to the objective on Hill 386. This officer discovered a track in a ravine running upward from Voisage Farm; and, gathering a platoon each from A and C Companies, he charged up the hill. With fixed bayonets and firing from the hip in true textbook style, they reached the top at the rush and dislodged a small party of Germans.

As the rest of the battalion crossed the road and made their way into the hills, the deadlock of inertia was broken. The 2nd Battalion assembled and, in spite of heavy small-arms fire, made their way up toward the summit of Hill 310. Near the top they encountered a line of Germans in trenches. Again, bayonets were fixed, grenades were thrown, and the enemy was expelled. These instances of close fighting with bayonets, reminiscent of First World War tactics, are supported by the unit historians, although other sources do not mention the fact. The bayonet was not used much during the Second World War, except for opening bully beef cans; and in a note, Charles MacDonald describes the terms "fixed bayonets" and "marching fire" as a "bromide" or journalistic cliché.[12] However, it would seem in this case to have been true.

Thus, by the time dawn broke, the initial objectives had been secured, but as a foretaste of things to come, individual tanks appeared along the main road, coming from north and south. Indeed, the village of Arry was to be a thorn in the side of the bridgehead for some days until it was finally cleared. It housed a platoon of German tanks and a considerable number of infantry. Some of the latter made a first tentative counterattack against Hill 386 at around 0830 but were easily repulsed. The main opposition came from mortars and artillery, although some tanks were spotted cruising in the distance.

The first serious counterattack, again from Arry, started at 1230 with an artillery barrage directed at C Company positions on Hill 386. Several men were wounded, including the radio operator, and the shelling was followed by five tanks, three of which were said to be Tigers. Bazooka rockets simply bounced off the heavy armor. The infantry were caught out on the bare slopes, and when they attempted to withdraw to shelter in the woods, they were cut down by tree bursts. In the confusion, a number of men continued back down the reverse slope and the company commander was wounded.

However, the tanks were not followed up by infantry—luckily for the handful of defenders—and contented themselves with cruising along in front of the American positions. They finally withdrew when American artillery support arrived, which gave the executive officer of C Company a chance to reorganize. Part of the unit had retreated all the way back down to Voisage Farm and had to be coaxed back into position. However, the reoccupation of the bare summit tempted the tanks out once again. But, "in almost movielike tradition," a group of P-47 Thunderbolt fighter-bombers appeared and proceeded to bomb and strafe the enemy armor, which promptly withdrew.

This intervention was the first positive result of the promised air support, which would have done so much to help the tenacious defenders at Dornot. Before departing, the aircraft devoted their attentions to Arry, leaving the village a smoking ruin.

The seriousness of the counterattack persuaded the regimental commander to commit part of the 3rd Battalion, which had been left holding the crossing site on the west bank. He ordered I and K Companies to cross and to take Arry, in an attempt to anchor the right flank of the bridgehead. Counterbattery work was proving difficult as the German artillery was well concealed. Some of the incoming shells were from Fort Driant, but most were fired by mobile batteries. Fire control was by forward observers linked by radio to the guns on the west bank. We have heard that the Germans were apparently short of ammunition, although they were managing to keep up a pretty high rate of fire. The American artillery certainly was short of ammunition, as the preoccupation with fuel during the first week of September had led to lack of space for shells. On 9 and 10 September, Corps Artillery fired 10,000 rounds which ate severely into their stockpile. Unaware of the situation, the infantry complained bitterly on occasions when the required fire support failed to arrive.

During 10 September, the equipment from the 84th Chemical Company was positioned. This unit had previously been employed on trucking duties with the Red Ball Express, and the personnel were inexperienced in combat—which in turn led to complications. However, their contribution was to prove vital to the success of the Arnaville operation—without the smoke screen the enemy would have had perfect observation over the whole of the crossing site. Their activities continued until 8 November, the day of the final breakout toward the encirclement of Metz.

The engineers on the spot were initially concerned with ferry operations. General Irwin had ordered late on 10 September that a bridge must be in place over the Moselle by the morning, but compliance was not so easy. Bridging operations were complicated by the nature of the site itself, and the river, which at that point was some 80 yards wide and with a fairly fast current. In addition to the main stream, there was the canal and a smaller stream known as the Rupt de Mad. The area had been bridged by the French in 1940, and the tangled remains of their structures were still there in 1944. A further difficulty was present in the form of high dikes, which meant the provision of earth moving equipment. The first priority was for a vehicle bridge across the lock, and careful reconnaissance had discovered two possible sites across the main river. However, it was not until the night of 10/11 September that operations got under way.

In the meanwhile, during the afternoon, the two companies from 3rd Battalion crossed the river and advanced along the road from Voisage Farm to Arry, in the wake of the aircraft which had bombed the village. They entered Arry without much difficulty and ferreted out the remaining Germans, although three tanks managed to escape to the east. By 2130 the place was reported clear, but the infantry were ordered to withdraw to the farm. This would seem to have been self-defeating since the object of bringing over the reinforcements was to capture and hold Arry. The problem was that there were too few men available, and some sort of bridgehead reserve was necessary. To understand this dilemma one has to look briefly at the broader situation. Although General Walker's orders had called for an advance to the Rhine, by 10 September his corps was holding a front of 40 miles with two infantry divisions. His armored division could not really achieve much in such difficult country and part of the front was held by miscellaneous cavalry units which were not equipped for static warfare. To reinforce his bridgehead he would have to strip his line or shorten it. The Third Army had no reserves that could be brought up, and there were no signs of a German collapse.

It would seem that Colonel Bell had intended that Arry should be held by C Company of the 1st Battalion, stiffened by a few antitank guns—which could only be ferried over during the evening. It was not until 0300 that C Company moved back into the village, only to find that the enemy had reestablished themselves there. In a fire fight in the main street, the company commander and a platoon commander were put out of action. This resulted in a "mad scramble to escape"[13] on the part of the rest of the men. Another platoon commander managed to restore order, and the company dug in on the outskirts of the village. Having suffered heavy casualties from shelling and only 43 strong, they were withdrawn the following morning. The rest of the 3rd Battalion was brought over in the evening to form a reserve strongpoint around Voisage Farm, where the aid posts were situated.

To try to alleviate the shortage of infantry, 5th Division decided to commit as much of the 11th Infantry Regiment as could be withdrawn from the Dornot area. The 3rd Battalion was ordered to cross and take Corny, the village to the north of the bridgehead. Only L and M Companies were available, as K Company had been depleted in the Dornot operation and I Company was left behind to guard the former crossing site. After the inevitable delays with boats, it was decided to send them over as near to their objective as possible. A site was chosen further north at Noveant, and L Company went over first, trailing a telephone wire behind them. When the engineers had returned to the west bank with the boats, the telephone rang. It was L Company informing them that they had been landed on an island in the river! Reconnaissance had not shown this and many units still had unsatisfactory maps. As a result, the company had to be retrieved; and, finally, the battalion was taken over the main 10th Infantry crossing site.

However, in the meanwhile their antitank platoon had crossed at Arnaville, and naturally assumed that the rifle companies were on their way to Corny. They moved on up the road toward the northern end of the bridgehead, where they blundered into the enemy-held village. There they encountered heavy fire and were forced to withdraw, abandoning the guns. Most of the men made their way to safety, although many of them had to swim back across the river. When the two infantry companies finally reached Corny, they were able to establish themselves in some buildings in the southern outskirts and set up the antitank guns. As the village itself was heavily mined and booby-trapped, and as the enemy could see into it from the surrounding heights, no attempt was made to occupy it fully.

Thus, by the morning of 11 September, 5th Division had the bulk of three infantry battalions across the Moselle, occupying an area 3,500 by 1,500 yards. Supply was by raft and assault boat, although preparations for permanent bridging were under way. Some antitank guns and mortars had been ferried across, but the villages at both ends of the bridgehead had not been secured. As Dornot had been evacuated during the night, Arnaville was the only XX Corps foothold across the river. (To the south, XII Corps had a small foothold at Pont-à-Mousson.)

At dawn, a strong counterattack was launched, initially against the 2nd Battalion positions. A company of infantry and a platoon of tanks closed in on the American positions and almost succeeded in penetrating the thin line of foxholes. They were only beaten off by concentrated fire from heavy machine guns and the 81-mm mortars. Communication snafus led to a delay in bringing in artillery support, but when the guns on the west bank finally opened up, they caught the Germans in the act of retreating. The victory, however, was a Pyrrhic one, as it cost the battalion 102 casualties that it could ill afford. Just after this, another composite tank-infantry force hit the 1st Battalion, but was beaten off by accurate fire from the artillery and the tank destroyers emplaced above the village of Arnaville. The tanks retreated back into Arry, where they were bombed by P-47's during the course of the afternoon. These enemy units came from the 3rd and 17th SS Panzer Grenadier Divisions. The 5th Division historian insists that there were members of the Officer Candidate Regiment fighting in the Arnaville bridgehead, but this is untrue—that unit was only involved in the Metz perimeter. Their fighting abilities, however, became legendary; and wherever stiff opposition was encountered, the Americans tended to assume that the enemy were "fanatical Nazi officer candidates."

After these two attacks, fighting in the bridgehead died down, and attention was concentrated on efforts to bridge the Moselle. During 11 September, the engineers put in a number of bridges over the approaches: a Bailey bridge over the Rupt de Mad at Arnaville, a double treadway over the canal lock, and a treadway over the Rupt de Mad between the canal and the river. Only after this work had been completed was it possible to assemble material at the two possible crossing sites over the river that had been selected. During the morning, an order was given to stop making smoke as it was hindering the work of the engineers.[14] This had the unfortunate effect of provoking an immediate German response. The artillery from Fort Driant and the field batteries opened up with gusto, damaging equipment and killing and wounding some of the engineer personnel. During the afternoon work was resumed at the southern of the two sites, and with the aid of the resumed smoke screen and the evening dusk, one third of a bridge had by then been constructed.

During the day, however, there was another development: a fording site was discovered. The basic engineering work was completed by 1030, but one part of the river bed was found to be 4½ feet deep—critical for armored fighting vehicles. In the hope of lowering the water level, efforts were made by artillery to break down a dam that was further downstream near Ars-sur-Moselle. These attempts failed, but a direct hit was scored during the early evening by fighter-bombers, causing a 7-inch drop in level. In the meanwhile, the engineers managed to fill part of the deep channel with sections from a treadway bridge. Two platoons of tank destroyers took the risk of crossing during the afternoon. Progress was slow as each vehicle dislodged the bridge sections, which had to be replaced. At one stage, enemy artillery managed to blast the bridge sections out of the water. In spite of these difficulties, six tank destroyers got across, followed by nine tanks, and the following morning, the rest of the supporting armor moved into an assembly area to the east of the main road.

The difficulties encountered in bridging so many obstacles were not really appreciated at the time and there was some criticism voiced against the engineers. General Irwin noted in his diary that "engineers at bridge [were] not well coordinated." Such critical comment forgets that much vital equipment was destroyed by the constant shelling and that a number of the bridge builders became casualties. The lot of the engineers in combat is an unenviable one. Being unarmed and unable to fight back, they have to get on with the job without being able to take cover or any form of evasive action. The combat soldier is trained to cope directly with the enemy, but it takes a brave man to cling to steel girders edging their way across the river, equally at the mercy of the elements and enemy gunfire. The men working at the fording site spent hours on end up to their waists in the bitter cold waters of the Moselle.

A far greater problem than the lack of a bridge was the vexing shortage of manpower. The only forces immediately available were the men and vehicles of CCB of the 7th Armored Division, who were still on the west bank waiting for a place to cross. However, unless sufficient infantry were available to expand the bridgehead, there was nowhere for the armor to go. Packed into a confined space, they would be sitting targets for the German artillery. The only spare infantry was the shattered 2nd Battalion of the 11th Regiment, and the division as a whole was short 60 officers and 1,600 men. Although replacements were coming in, in batches, most of them were untried in combat. Generally, experience has shown that green replacements, thrust into a combat situation without a preliminary shake down period, become the first casualties. A fighting unit is a team, and the basis of its morale is mutual trust. Replacements have to be absorbed before they become members of that team.

After the temporary lull in construction caused by enemy shelling, work recommenced; and at 1230 on 12 September, the Moselle was spanned by a treadway bridge at the northern site. This was supplemented by a raft footbridge which was used for the evacuation of walking wounded. Immediately CCB started to cross, and by the evening, five medium-tank companies and seven tank destroyer platoons were in the bridgehead. There they had to park on the floodplain below the hills, where some were knocked out by enemy artillery. The bridging work progressed on into 14 September. The first bridge was damaged but speedily repaired, and by 1700 on the 14th, a second main bridge was ready for use. Throughout the Arnaville operation, the 1103rd Engineer Combat Group constructed a total of six bridges, losing in the process six men killed and some 100 wounded.

In the bridgehead itself, rain fell during the night 12/13 September, producing a sea of mud on the low-lying marshy area, which effectively bogged the massed armor. However, it also seemed to impede the enemy, which was a lucky circumstance from the point of view of the GI's crouching in their waterlogged foxholes. Most of them had had little sleep and no hot food in three days of constant alert. Both the 1st and 2nd Battalions of the 10th Infantry had been reduced to 50 percent of their normal strength, and fatigue was a major problem. The 3rd Battalion of the 11th Infantry was still in the outskirts of Corny, while the 3rd Battalion, 10th Infantry, was in reserve at Voisage Farm.

Later on 13 September, a patrol again moved into Arry, only to find the place once more abandoned by the enemy. Oddly enough, the same mistake was repeated, as no effort was made to garrison the village after the patrol had withdrawn. Apart from that there was little or no action in the bridgehead that day, as higher headquarters busily searched for more manpower. At corps level, plans were made for a general reshuffling along their 40-mile front line. They decided that the 90th Division then in the Thionville area would move south to take up the burden of fighting in the Metz perimeter. This in turn would release CCA of the 7th Armored Division and the 2nd Infantry Regiment Combat Team for action in the bridgehead. General Irwin finally ordered another battalion of the depleted 11th Infantry to cross the river and issued plans for a twofold attack. CCB was to advance southeast to capture Mardigny, and the infantry was to seize Hill 396, the dominant feature in the area.

The following day, the cold sweeping rain continued. Proposals for expansion were cancelled, although XX Corps was still issuing optimistic orders. A new field order on that date called for the 5th Division to expand its bridgehead and continue to attack and capture Metz. The whole of 7th Armored Division was to cross the Moselle and hook around the city from the southeast. Replacements continued to trickle in, including the battle-weary remnants of the 23rd Armored Infantry Battalion.

The postponed attack was rescheduled for 15 September, regardless of the state of the weather. It consisted of two separate actions as outlined above. The armor was divided into two task forces. The mission of Force 1 was to move through Arry and occupy Hill 400 in the Bois le Comte. Force 2 was to go down the main highway to Vittonville and then rendezvous with Force 1. The infantry attack on Hill 396 would have tank support.

The armor moved in fog at 0915, after a 30-minute preliminary artillery bombardment on known German positions. Force 1 managed to get through into Arry despite the zero visibility, which probably confused the enemy just as much. They soon reached their initial objective, and as the sun came out at midday, they consolidated for a further move to capture the villages of Mardigny and Lorry. Force 2 progress was slower on account of enemy opposition and the pervasive fog. It was not until late afternoon that Vittonville was secured. By the evening, Force 1 had managed to occupy Mardigny, but had to leave the attempt on Lorry for the following day. Only when that place was in their hands would they have a reasonable road out of the bridgehead.

The infantry jumped off at 0900. The two left companies of the reserve 3rd Battalion of the 10th Infantry were to move through the 1st Battalion lines, while the two right companies were to march through Arry and up a track leading to the summit of the hill that was their objective. Each pair of companies was accompanied by a force of medium tanks. On the right, the supporting armor was stalled at a roadblock on the way south from Arry, and after suffering casualties from shelling, the infantry passed through them. On the left, the infantry followed closely behind the tanks, although three of those vehicles bogged down on the steep slopes. By 1500, however, Hill 396 was firmly in American hands—a vital starting point for further expansion to the east. A counterattack on the morning of 17 September was repulsed after bitter hand-to-hand fighting.

With the completion of the above actions, the bridgehead was finally secure, anchored to the north and south at Corny and Vittonville respectively. The cost, however, had been high. The 10th Infantry Regiment had lost 25 officers and 700 men killed and wounded, roughly equivalent to the 11th Infantry losses at Dornot. As the reshuffle of XX Corps got under way, the rest of 7th Armored crossed the Moselle and the 2nd Infantry rejoined 5th Division. The time scale is also significant in view of the optimism with which the troops had set out on 7 September. It had taken ten days to secure one comparatively small bridgehead over the Moselle, which was situated in country that was extremely difficult for expansion by armor. Before the month was out, further bitter fighting was to take place there with negligible results.

ACTION TO THE WEST OF METZ

While on the right of XX Corps, CCB of 7th Armored Division and two infantry regiments from the 5th Division were picking their way down to the river to the south of the city, the major opposition should have been anticipated in the center. With the 90th Infantry Division echeloned to the northeast and heading for the Moselle at Thionville, CCA and the 2nd Infantry Regiment were all that was left to deal with the fortified salient. It was there that the main enemy forces were concentrated because, to defend the city, they had to occupy the high ground to the west.

When the main advance got under way on 7 September, CCA led the way in the center. They penetrated to the river bank, just north of the city and outside the fortified area, where they halted, under the assumption that they would undertake a crossing there. To the south of them, the 2nd Infantry Regiment, commanded by Colonel Roffe, moved due east toward Metz, linked to their neighbors by tenuous cavalry patrols and reconnaissance units. By the following day, they had become so detached from their parent division, that the command structure was changed by General Walker. He gave CCB to General Irwin, who thus commanded a composite armor and infantry force in the south. The 2nd Infantry and the other two combat commands (CCA and CCR) formed a central task force under the command of General Silvester of 7th Armored Division. The precise mission of 2nd Infantry was to occupy the enemy in the Metz perimeter to hinder them from reinforcing the crossing sites in the south.

As in the southern bridgeheads, armor was to be of little help on account of the difficult terrain. Only a few roads led down from the plateau through narrow ravines into the city; and the whole perimeter, apart from the main forts, was a network of skillfully placed field defenses—bunkers, barbed wire, trenches, and minefields. The perimeter was held by three German regiments that were probably equivalent in strength to an American infantry division. If one accepts the view that an attack against a fortified position requires a superiority of at least three to one, then it is obvious that XX Corps was faced with a difficult task. It had only one infantry regiment and some armor, instead of the required three good infantry divisions and massive artillery support.

In fact, the events of 1870 were due to be repeated, although on a much smaller scale. After their attempts to break out to the west had failed as a result of the battles between Vionville and Mars-la-Tour, the French retreated back toward Metz. They occupied a line from the river at Ars, through Gravelotte, and running north to Amanvillers and St. Privat (almost identical to the German line in September 1944 and with the same tactical and geographical conditions imposed upon the attacker). The battle known as Gravelotte-St. Privat was fought on 18 August 1870, and the opposing forces numbered some 330,000 men. The Germans were unable to break through the French lines and stalemate ensued until they besieged the French army in Metz, where it subsequently surrendered after a few halfhearted attempts to break out.

On 7 September, the 1st and 2nd Battalions of the 2nd Infantry Regiment stumbled blindly into the outer defenses held by the Officer Candidate Regiment along the line Gravelotte-Verneville-Aman-villers. To quote the official history of the campaign, "Limited intelligence information and inadequate ground and air reconnais-sance during the hurried drive to the Moselle forced the 2nd Infantry to attack blindly, groping in the midst of battle to feel out the contours of the German defense line."[15] The enemy was a first-class fighting unit, whose newly commissioned members were yearning to distin-guish themselves. They adhered rigidly to the official German tactical doctrine of immediate counterattacks to regain any ground lost—regardless of casualties.

The two infantry battalions were brought to a halt by the field works and stubborn resistance of the Germans. Thus pinned down, they were subjected to heavy artillery fire, although Krause states that the Metz garrison was chronically short of ammunition. The 2nd Battalion managed to drive the enemy outposts out of Verneville, but the 1st Battalion was driven back from Amanvillers. The following morning, the latter unit was savagely counterattacked by a fairly large German force which managed to capture or kill two officers and sixty-six men before being repelled. After reorganizing, and with all four companies in line, the 1st Battalion gallantly returned to the attack. Again they were stopped short of the village, caught in the open by a withering hail of small-arms fire and an artillery barrage. The 3rd Battalion was pulled out of reserve and thrown into the line to the east of Malmaison in an attempt to bolster the weak front. The *History of the 5th Infantry Division,* in a masterpiece of understate-ment, describes these initial assaults as "unexpected."[16]

On 9 September, a task force from CCA (Task Force McConnell) was attached to the infantry in an effort to break the deadlock. The mission of this unit was to turn the flank of the Officer Candidate

Regiment along the line from Amanvillers to Gravelotte, by hooking around and behind them from the north out of St. Privat. However, a glance at a contour map should have shown them that this maneuver would have been impossible, for the very simple reason that behind Amanvillers the road down to Metz runs through a ravine with almost vertical rocky sides. In order to carry out their orders they would have to cross this at right angles, and it would have been quite impassable for armor.

However, they did not get near enough to make the attempt. During the morning the American artillery pounded away at the known German positions, and at 1330 both armor and infantry moved off. Task Force McConnell only managed to progress a short distance east from St. Privat, when they were subjected to heavy fire from the high ground in front. German artillery eliminated seven tanks and two SP guns, forcing the column to beat a retreat back into St. Privat. From there the task force tried without much success to execute a direct flank attack in support of the infantry, still trying to batter their way into Amanvillers.

Neither did the rest of the regiment have any particular success that day. The 2nd Battalion made a gain of a "few hundred yards" to the east of Verneville, described in terms reminiscent of the First World War, while the 3rd Battalion tried to move east from Malmaison toward Moscou Farm. This latter feature was composed of a number of strong stone buildings and had been stoutly defended by the French in 1870. Improved since by the addition of bunkers and barbed wire, it managed to hold up the Americans in 1944. That night, Colonel Roffe reported to his superior, General Silvester, that his regiment had lost 14 officers and 332 men in three days of inconclusive fighting—the 1st Battalion alone had lost 228 casualties at Amanvillers. Colonel Roffe registered a strong protest about sending his men "uselessly" against "20-odd forts."[17] He sensibly pointed out that artillery had proved ineffective and that aircraft and heavy bombs were needed.

These references to the forts pose a problem to the historian. The 2nd Infantry was fighting the German outpost line that was about a mile in advance of the main ridge on which the forts were situated. If you walk over the area today, the peaceful farm fields are still dotted with ruined concrete bunkers and the indentations of bomb craters and trenches. All the American reports speak of the very heavy bombardments by German artillery, who were supposed to be short of ammunition. Cole, on the basis of the official documentation, refers to fire being received from Fort Kellermann and the Lorraine Group. He states that when seven battalions of American artillery fired at the Lorraine Group, their fire subsided briefly; but field pieces had little effect on fortress batteries, which were in steel emplacements, located on rear slopes, and requiring high-angle fire to reach them.[18] We know from Krause that, at the beginning of the battle in early September, the only fortress guns in working order were one battery at Driant and possibly three 150-mm howitzers at Jeanne d'Arc, which could "only go into action after combat engagements with the enemy had begun on 6 September."[19] Fort Kellermann never had any turret artillery fitted; it was built purely as an infantry strongpoint. The Lorraine Group originally had six 100-mm guns and six 150-mm howitzers, and two of the latter were in working order in November. It is, of course, possible that they had been made operational much earlier and did in fact fire at the 2nd Infantry Regiment during the second week in September. One can state, however, that only a small proportion of the shells fired at that unit could have come from fixed batteries in the forts. This in turn poses another question. If not from the forts, where did the gunfire come from? Krause states quite definitely that his antiaircraft guns were removed to the rear to guard the supply lines and that he had no armored self-propelled artillery in Metz. He lists his available ordnance as a Replacement Artillery Detachment armed with horse-drawn Russian 7.5-cm cannon, located around Gravelotte, and a battery of four 10.5-cm guns in the St. Privat area. That number of guns could not have brought down such an amount of fire as is described in American accounts of the battle, leaving one to assume either that these were exaggerated or that the Germans received heavy reinforcements which were not noted by their divisional commander.

Colonel Roffe's request for air strikes was difficult to meet, as the available aircraft were thinly spread along a wide front. Everyone was hollering for them, but on 10 September, three squadrons were released for attacks on the Amanvillers sector. The P-47's swooped in and dropped their 500-pound bombs with little effect. When the infantry resumed their attacks, they met with just the same bitter opposition as before. By switching the armor around to the south flank of the 1st Battalion, they managed to advance to within a hundred yards of the outer buildings of Amanvillers. In the center, the

2nd Battalion struggled forward a few more yards, and on the right, the 3rd Battalion clung to their positions around Malmaison and Gravelotte.

The latter unit was engaged with the enemy on historic ground. Directly to their front was the ravine in which ran a small stream known as the Mance. The scene of great slaughter in 1870 when the troops of the Prussian General Steinmetz attempted to cross it, it was to prove a deathtrap in 1944. The Germans were positioned on both banks and had sited machine guns to fire along the base of the ravine. The 3rd Battalion had tried to push patrols across without success, and so they then attempted to outflank the position by moving around it through the Bois de Génivaux. Whenever they managed to move forward over the unfamiliar terrain, groups of the enemy slipped back behind them and cut off their patrols. Equipped with inadequate maps, an American infantry battalion was stumbling around in country over which their enemy had spent many months of training and had become familiar with every bush and rock.

That evening, reinforcements arrived in the shape of CCR, which had at last been extricated from the traffic jam in the defiles south of the city. General Silvester decided to use this force to try another wheeling movement from the north to get in behind the enemy positions, while at the same time the unfortunate infantry made a frontal attack. In the early morning of 11 September, the armor moved off to the east toward the village of Pierrevillers, where they came up against concrete roadblocks covered by antitank guns, probably manned by elements from the NCO School Regiment. To avoid these, the armored column swerved to the south toward Semécourt along one of the main roads leading into Metz. This led around the north flank of the fortified zone, but to their right was the Fèves Ridge, on which the Canrobert forts were situated. These had no turret artillery, but were faced by a vertical concrete wall the entire length of the ridge. Accurate fire from well-concealed gun positions again halted the American armor. The commanding officer and two battalion commanders were wounded. A final effort was made by dismounted troops, who managed to gain a toehold on the Fèves Ridge, but by then the attack by CCR had shot its bolt, deflected by the fortifications.

In the meanwhile, the planned infantry attack was initially delayed by German counterattacks that disturbed the American timetable. In the center, the 2nd Battalion became involved in a seesaw battle, in the process of which it lost half its strength and some of its hard-won ground. The 1st Battalion, still clinging to the edge of Amanvillers, was dislodged by intense fire and forced to pull back some five hundred yards. The unit was so shattered that during the night it had to be relieved and placed in reserve. To replace it, the 3rd Battalion was brought north, while their positions on the right were taken over by the 87th Cavalry Reconnaissance Squadron.

However, the battle had to go on. The 3rd Battalion was given the task of regaining the ground lost the previous day, which they succeeded in accomplishing in two more days of bitter fighting. By then the infantry were drunk with fatigue and no longer capable of functioning as an efficient force. Even so it took a lot of persuasion on the part of General Irwin to get corps to abandon the attack, which was finally authorized on 14 September. In the process, General Irwin's division had virtually ceased to exist, having lost about half its strength. During September they received the highest total of replacements of any month of the war—5,180 officers and men.

THE ATTACKS IN THE NORTH

Having followed the fortunes of the right and center of XX Corps in their efforts to comply with Field Order No. 10 during the opening stages of the Battle of Metz, we come now to the left wing. This was formed by the 90th Division, whose primary mission was to capture Thionville and effect a crossing of the Moselle in that area. The initial objective set was the capture of the high ground to the west of that city.

We have seen that, on the right of the division, CCA had advanced as far as the river and was established on the west bank to the north of Metz, the enemy having withdrawn to the far side, from which they shelled the armor. The 90th Infantry Division was faced with a difficult task. They formed the left flank of the Third Army which was, in fact, hanging in the air, there being no solid contact with V Corps of 1st Army, who were operating in Luxembourg. Until such contact was established, General McClain's troops could not advance in a solid phalanx to the east, but had to echelon northeast with the three regiments spread out over a front of some 15 miles. In classic military terms, this invited defeat in detail. The enemy opposing them, however, was just as thinly spread, with only two regiments of the 559th Volksgrenadier Division between the 90th Division and the Moselle. Running in an arc north of Thionville and parallel to the Luxembourg frontier was the Maginot Line. In this particular sector the Germans had made no attempt to turn it around. Besides, they did not have the manpower available to garrison it. As far as the defenses of Thionville were concerned, although these were of the same type and vintage as the Metz forts, they were far less sophisticated. There were three of the *feste*-type works, one on the heights to the west of the city and two on the east bank of the Moselle. All were apparently in some sort of working order, but were not joined by field works and bunkers as in the Metz perimeter.

During 6 September the 90th Infantry Division assembled near Étain, and the following morning moved off on foot. On the right, the 357th Infantry Regiment became involved with a rear guard of the 559th VG Regiment, who were holed up in the small but important mining town of Briey. Attacking frontally, the 2nd Battalion was checked by determined opposition, but the other two battalions moved around to the rear and surrounded the town. It surrendered the following day and 442 prisoners were taken.

Unknown to General McClain, however, trouble was brewing, in the form of the 106 Panzerbrigade Feldherrenhalle, which was under the command of Colonel Baeke. This was one of a number of armored brigades which were formed at the end of August from remnants of divisions that had been shattered on the Russian front, and which were equipped with tanks fresh from the factories. Von Rundstedt had appealed for armored vehicles to be sent to existing divisions in order to be able to rebuild them, but Hitler insisted on "creating" new formations. Most of them were sent to the Moselle in the "stop Patton" bid.[20] Generally, such formations consisted of one armored infantry battalion (*panzergrenadier*) and a tank battalion equipped with 33 Panthers and 11 SP assault guns, plus a company of engineers and service troops. This unit had assembled to the south of Luxembourg. Also newly arrived in the area was the 19th Volksgrenadier Division. The term "Volksgrenadier" requires a few words of explanation. These divisions, like the independent tank brigades, were the product of the barrel-scraping carried out after the defeat in France. As a direct result of the abortive bomb plot in July 1944, Himmler was appointed as Commander of the Replacement Army (*OB des Ersatz-heeres*). As such he became responsible for raising new divisions, rather then reforming old ones, which were given the rather grandiloquent title of "People's Grenadiers." They had the normal three-regiment setup, but each regiment had only two battalions, giving a divisional strength of approximately 10,000 men. The aim was to raise forty of these units, manned by combing out rear area headquarters and replacement depots, a wholesale redrafting of air force and navy personnel, calling up of men employed in industry, and lowering the enlistment age to sixteen. Between August and October, Himmler produced an additional 500,000 men.

General von Knobelsdorf, the German First Army commander, managed to get permission to use the 106th Panzerbrigade for an attack on the American left flank, but this employment was limited to 48 hours.[21] As per Army Order No. 11, the brigade moved off from its start position near Audun-le-Romain during the evening of 6 September. The original attack was ordered for that night but was postponed because the supporting infantry (59th Infantry Regiment, part of the 19th VG Division) were not ready. During the early hours of the following morning, the brigade divided into two groups, with the infantry sitting on the vehicles. From there they reconnoitered to the south as far as St. Privat, blew up a bridge, and left the infantry to man positions. The armor retired back toward Aumetz.

In the meanwhile, the other two regiments of the 90th Infantry had advanced without meeting any real trouble, and by evening were established along the road from Briey to Longuyon. The Divisional CP was set up in the small town of Mairy.

During the late evening the 106 Panzerbrigade was again ordered to attack toward Briey in order to help the 19th Volksgrenadier Division take up their positions. They set off in the dark in three columns, and, quite fortuitously chose to drive through Mairy, where they encountered the 90th Division CP. At least half the German unit passed on through before the American staff realized what was happening. A series of haphazard actions then ensued as the HQ troops joined in with anything that came to hand. One source states that General McClain himself was awakened by gunfire at 20-yard range and that some of the enemy rifled the classified files before rejoining the rest of their unit.[22]

In the dark it was difficult to separate friend from foe. William McConahey, a doctor with the 357th Regiment some miles to the southeast at Briey, heard a lot of tanks moving about in the night and a lot of firing going on. The divisional artillery staff were completely surrounded for a while and had to fight their way out on foot. Captain Baird of the 358th Infantry managed to stop one of the German columns by disabling the lead tank with a well-aimed bazooka rocket. He then hit the second vehicle, and although wounded, led a successful counterattack, for which he was later awarded the Distinguished Service Cross.

As soon as dawn broke, the fate of the Germans was sealed. They were way out on a limb and more or less surrounded. Tanks and tank destroyers were brought up and the divisional spotter planes soon located their extended forces. At 0935 the commander of Column 1 requested permission to withdraw to the east and was sent Column 2 as a reinforcement. The German attack had lost all momentum and the bulk of their vehicles were destroyed during the day. The remainder broke off combat at 2000 and retired northward to lick their wounds. The 90th Division claimed thirty tanks destroyed or captured, plus sixty half-tracks and a hundred other vehicles. According to Army Group G,[23] the brigade was reduced to nine tanks and assault guns. In their own unit war diary, the German unit commented on their experience: "On account of the lack of our own aerial reconnaissance, the brigade had operated in an area in which the available enemy forces and their positions were totally unknown, and the brief road reconnaissance had too many gaps." There is no evidence in any of the German sources to show that there was any previous knowledge of the position of the 90th Division HQ.

While the rest of the division was busily mopping up the German tanks, the 357th Regiment took the surrender of Briey. There they interrogated a number of prisoners and captured certain documents, all of which indicated that another counterattack was imminent— although it failed to materialize. The 1st Battalion, which earlier in the day had been counterattacked by a small force, were later able to watch from cover while an enemy battalion (probably from the 559th VG Division) attacked an unoccupied hill. With the aid of artillery the Americans managed to cut down the majority of the enemy who had been so busily engaged in such a fruitless operation.

In expectation of the threatened counterattack from the north, the division consolidated its positions and remained static during 9 September, but resumed its advance the following day. The plan was to close up to the river by 11 September, by which time contact would have been established on the left with the American First Army, enabling the division to move to the east. They were moving into difficult country, hilly and cut up with defiles. The enemy disengaged slowly in front of the division, which fought gradually forward from hill to hill. The 359th Regiment was kept in reserve to force a crossing of the river once Thionville had been secured. By the evening the enemy hold on the heights above the town had been broken, and the 358th Infantry was poised to descend into the valley where Thionville was situated on either side of the Moselle. In the process, the regiment captured intact Fort Guentrange, the large work on the hills above the city. The Germans made no attempt to defend it, since General von Knobelsdorf had decided to withdraw all his scanty forces back across the river.

During 12 September, the 357th Infantry on the right moved down to the river bank at Uckange, where they took up defensive positions. The bulk of the 378th Infantry rode on tanks into Thionville, whose streets were littered with mines. Apart from minor disturbance from the enemy, the part of the city to the west of the river was cleared by the evening, except for a small perimeter at the head of the main bridge across the river to the suburb of Yutz. This was defended by a barricade of concrete machine-gun nests and iron rails. During the night, however, this rear guard withdrew and the bridge was completely demolished.

The far bank of the river in the city area was defended, and there seemed to be little point in attempting to storm across. General McClain already had cavalry patrols roving out to the north along the river, and accordingly he planned to make his crossing there and to take the German defenses in the rear. He had already dispatched part of his reserve regiment, the 359th Infantry, in that direction, when he received orders from XX Corps to seize a bridgehead in Thionville. However, hardly had these new plans been sorted out, when at about midnight on 13 September, the division was told to suspend its activities and be prepared to move south to contain the Metz perimeter.

SUMMARY

The general regrouping of forces that took place on 13 and 14 September effectively ended the first phase of the battle to capture Metz.

Of the original aims, little was left. On the plus side, XX Corps had a small bridgehead over the Moselle to the south of Metz; and in the north, half of Thionville had been seized. But at what cost! The 5th Infantry Division had had its fighting strength halved, and 7th Armored had been unable to achieve anything in such difficult terrain. General Walker found himself responsible for a 40-mile front from north of Thionville, to Vittonville, halfway between Metz and Pont-à-Mousson. His difficulty was that he was being subjected to pressure from above. Prestige was at stake; Patton had received his first bloody nose of the campaign.

Walker was not a fool. He fully realized the costs of the frontal attack against the fortifications and the fact that the area was unsuitable for armor. He had been given orders that had seemed to all concerned to be practicable when they were issued, and he had attempted to carry them out. It was obvious to him, however, that the original aim of a double envelopment of Metz had become impossible. Such a maneuver would admittedly put both the 5th and 90th Divisions across the river, but they would be miles apart and separated by the Metz fortifications. A determined enemy with interior lines of communication could, in theory, defeat them in detail. He decided therefore that, as he had the bridgehead at Arnaville, it should be expanded, in spite of the risk in weakening the left and center, in order to obtain the necessary manpower.

In the background, naturally, there is still the "great argument" and the subsequent controversy that this caused. The blame for the lack of success in capturing Metz and the Moselle crossings in early September is naturally laid at the door of the notorious five-day delay caused by the lack of fuel. This is fair enough as it certainly gave the Germans time to reorganize and establish a cohesive line of defense. There were, however, other factors which have to be borne in mind. The attack got under way as the autumn rains commenced, and Lorraine is a notoriously wet part of France. The concentration on fuel on the assumption of a mobile warfare situation led in turn to a shortage of artillery ammunition when the warfare became static. Bad weather also affected air support, although the main problem there was the lack of available aircraft to cover such a broad front.

The above factors, however, also applied to other sectors of the Allied front. Locally, the real reason for the defeat of XX Corps was poor planning based on false optimism, and lack of reconnaissance and detailed information about the terrain and the forts. The tragedy was that, at this stage, no radical rethinking of the problem was undertaken, with the result that similar tactics were continued in an attempt to retrieve something from the original plan.

The Continuation of the September Battle

STRATEGIC BACKGROUND

While the gallant men of XX Corps were fighting along the Moselle against an equally brave and determined enemy, the strategic background to the campaign had altered somewhat. As a result of the German decision to concentrate their reserves on the Moselle to halt Patton, the First Army on the left found the going somewhat easier. By 10 September its two leading corps were approaching the German frontier on a line between Aachen and Trier. In accordance with Eisenhower's general strategic directions the emphasis should have been to the left to support Montgomery's northern thrust, but as a result of Patton having been given fuel to advance to the Moselle, the right of the First Army had to be given extra supplies to keep up with him. This tended to dilute the First Army operations, but they did score one major triumph—they were the first to penetrate the legendary Siegfried Line and the first Allied force to enter Germany. The result was banner headlines in the press for a minor penetration that occurred on 11 September to the north of Luxembourg—the First Army had won the race.

The main change of emphasis during September, however, was the operation known as Market Garden or more commonly, the Arnhem campaign. This did not directly affect Patton, but it represented a further shift of attention from the embattled Third Army. Its indirect effects, however, were considerable. Market Garden itself is outside the scope of this book, but some mention must be made of it in connection with the supply situation and the general direction of strategy.

Montgomery conceived the plan in early September with a view to breaking the deadlock and to seizing a crossing over the Rhine by outflanking the Siegfried Line. The original intention was to start it on 17 September and to employ the bulk of the otherwise idle Allied Airborne Army. This would entail a shift of direction from the east toward the north, and the flank would have to be protected by the First Army. To comply with this, the First Army would have to sideslip to the left and its southern sector would have to be taken over by the Third Army; thus stretching the latter's weakly held front even further and precluding action on the Moselle. Eisenhower turned down this proposal at a conference held in Brussels on 10 September, forcing Montgomery to take other steps. If he could not have support from the First Army, he had to plug the gap between his forces and the Americans somehow. He therefore decided to pull VIII Corps forward from the Seine, a task for which there were insufficient stocks of fuel and transport. Montgomery therefore warned the Supreme Commander on the following day that he would have to postpone the Arnhem operation until 23 September. This brought an immediate reaction. General Bedell Smith flew the following day to see Montgomery and promised him delivery of 1,000 tons daily to Brussels. He also apparently promised that the offensive by Patton toward the Saar would be stopped and that the bulk of American resources would be switched to the First Army. It would seem that Montgomery had got what he wanted.[1]

But then another contradiction appears. Two days later, Montgomery proposed that a diversionary attack should be mounted along the Metz-Nancy front between 14 and 26 September. Although he rescinded this on 16 September because the Third Army operations were having the desired effect anyway, it seems an odd idea.[2] An additional backwash effect of Market Garden was the need for transport to provide the promised 1,000 daily tons. If we agree that extra infantry was required to crack the Metz fortifications, three such newly arrived divisions waiting for deployment in Normandy were stripped of their vehicles, which were then employed on the Red Ball Express routes. This was robbing Peter to pay Paul with a vengeance and did nothing to contribute to the overall strategic plan that was still lacking.

While General Eisenhower tried to impose some sort of control over the diverging aims of the two main national groups in the Allied forces, the American camp was thinking along lines different from those of Montgomery. As late as 11 September, Bradley was still issuing ambitious orders about advancing to the Rhine to "secure bridgeheads . . . from Mannheim to Cologne." If possible, Patton was to cross as far south as Karlsruhe. At the same time Bradley laid down that First and Third Armies would have equal supply. This can hardly be reconciled with Eisenhower's direction that priority had to be given to supporting the thrust toward the Ruhr. The following day, however, Bradley had to attempt to put on the brakes. He warned Patton that the Arnhem plan had been accepted by SHAEF and that "Third Army might have to hold the west bank of the Moselle defensively." Patton, who reported that he had four days of ammunition and enough fuel to go to the Rhine, naturally did his best to plead. He said, "Don't stop us now, Brad, but I'll make a deal with you. If I don't secure a couple of good bridgeheads east of the Moselle by the night of the 14th, I'll shut up and assume the mournful role of the defender."[3] His aim was to get himself so involved beyond the Moselle that Eisenhower would be forced to supply him. Bradley gave Patton the two days, and told him that if he failed, he would have to assume the defensive.

Patton of course got his bridgeheads by the deadline and assumed that that gave him the green light to continue his attacks. On 15 September, Eisenhower issued a new directive emphasizing his broad-front policy but again giving priority to the northern thrust and the clearance of Antwerp. He stated quite unequivocally that "all possible resources of the Central Group of Armies (Bradley) must be thrown in to support the drive of First U.S. Army to seize bridgeheads near Cologne and Bonn in preparation for assisting in the capture of the Ruhr."[4] These arrangements, however, were not to take effect until the Third Army was securely established along the Moselle. This sort of compromise may have been justified in strategic terms, as the presence of Patton would hold German forces on the Moselle. But, by giving permission for further operations of a limited nature to secure the Moselle position, it paved the way for Patton to attempt to "edge" eastwards.

However, after the bitter fighting in early September, it should have been obvious that to make a serious dent in the enemy along the Moselle, a massive injection of fresh manpower was needed. The granting of facilities for limited operations merely cost American lives and achieved little. Either Patton should have been massively reinforced with infantry and unlimited air support, or he should have been ordered to stay put. Again, political necessity was allowed to triumph over military common sense.

REALIGNMENT OF FORCES IN THE XX CORPS AREA

In the previous chapter we have seen just how thin was the line of American troops containing roughly an equal number of Germans. The only area that could be exploited was the bridgehead in the south, but to do that, fresh manpower was desperately needed. The 5th Infantry was exhausted and really needed a breather to absorb the flow of replacements.

On 14 September, General Walker issued Field Order No. 11, which initiated the regrouping of the whole corps for a new attack, to begin the following day. The idea was that the right wing would be reinforced and the whole of 7th Armored Division would cross into the bridgehead. From there they would move east and then north, circle around behind Metz and roll up the German line along the Moselle north of the city. This in turn would enable the 90th Division to cross unopposed in the Thionville area. In the reshuffle, the latter unit was relieved of responsibility for a 23-mile front to the north of Thionville, which was transferred to the reinforced 43rd Cavalry Reconnaissance Squadron. They were to be assisted by a deception team to simulate the presence of an armored division in the area.

CCA and the 2nd Infantry Regiment would then be pulled out of the line to the west of Metz and would rejoin their divisions in the bridgehead. Their responsibilities would be taken over by the 90th Division, who would sideslip to the right and resume the attack against the forts on 15 September. This movement was carried out during the night of 14/15 September. This left the 358th Infantry holding the line of the river from Thionville to Uckange, while the 90th Reconnaissance Troop patrolled the bank south to Talange. In the center, the 357th Infantry was positioned at right angles to the cavalry across the flood plain in front of Maizières-les-Metz and as far around the fortified perimeter as St. Privat. In front of the main forts was the 359th Infantry, which relieved the 2nd Infantry as far south as Gravelotte.

General Walker, under pressure from Patton, who in turn was being pressured by Bradley, had to be seen doing something. With the benefit of hindsight and mature reflection, it seems incredible that the same mistakes were about to be repeated—attacks with too few troops on too wide a front against a well-entrenched enemy. General Walker, however, had his orders and they were to capture Metz and advance to the Rhine. His bulldog tenacity would not permit him to let go, and as no reinforcements were forthcoming, he had to make do with what he had. The fighting that was about to begin was to be perhaps the bitterest of the whole campaign in Lorraine. All hopes of rapid movement became lost in a sea of mud, and combat degenerated into a war of attrition fought by the infantry in conditions reminiscent of the First World War.

The Germans, however, also had their problems. They too had a chronic manpower shortage that they could not easily alleviate. General von Knobelsdorf, the army commander directly responsible, believed that Metz could not hold out for long if seriously attacked. He felt that the Americans, with their air superiority, could simply pass to the north and south, and encircle the city. But Knobelsdorf needn't have feared; XX Corps didn't have the resources for the sort of maneuver that had been envisaged in their original aims. Knobelsdorf realized, however, that if such an operation were to be carried out, his First Army would have to withdraw to avoid being split in two, and would thus lose contact with the garrison of Metz. Such a gap would be difficult to plug in view of the manpower shortage, besides which, the school troops in Metz were too valuable to lose. He therefore reported to his superior, Blaskowitz, commander of Army Group G, that Metz should be abandoned and the German First Army should withdraw to a line more easily defended. Blaskowitz, however, believed that Metz should be held and that contact should be maintained with the field units on either side. As was usual at that stage of the war, the decision had to go right to the top—to Hitler himself. His doctrine on fortified places was that they should be garrisoned by second-rate troops and then be left to their own devices to hinder the enemy as long as possible.[5] On 15 September he ordered that the garrison should allow themselves to be surrounded; but the following day he simply changed his mind, possibly prompted by the cooler heads in his operations staff. He issued new orders that the German First Army should reinforce the shoulders of the Metz salient and hinder any attempt at encirclement.[6]

In Metz itself there was also a change of regime. Lieutenant General Krause was relieved on 18 September and transferred to the Führer Reserve—which in effect meant that he was put on the shelf. Knobelsdorf described Krause as not being "a strong personality,"[7] but it would seem that during his period in command of 462nd Division, he did a pretty good job. He himself stated that when transferred, his successor, Major General Luebbe, "received from me a stable defense front on the western bank of the Moselle."[8]

EXPANSION OF THE ARNAVILLE BRIDGEHEAD

With the successful capture of Hill 396 on 15 September and the breakout of the armor to the south, the bridgehead was regarded as secure. On that day, CCR had crossed the Moselle and CCA was on its way south. The plan for the employment of 7th Armored Division had been worked out largely by the Third Army staff, and called for an advance by two parallel combat commands (CCA and CCR) with CCB in reserve. They were to slip past the forts to the south of the city, cross the Seille River, and while CCR guarded the right flank, CCA would then cross the Nied and swing around behind Metz. This was a real Pattonesque plan in its very boldness, and once the armor had shaken free from the broken country along the river, they would be on better terrain: open uplands sparsely wooded and dotted with small villages. In theory, neither the Seille nor the Nied was a formidable military barrier. The road network, however, was poor; and if the bad weather continued, the tanks would be restricted to the few hard-surfaced highways which would simplify the defenders' task by canalizing the attack. The forts to the south and east of the city did not represent a serious threat, as they had been disarmed before the war—although the turrets and carriages were left in place, the barrels had been removed.

In fact, the southern and eastern fortified belt was destined to play little part in the battles for Metz. One of the forts was severely damaged during mid-September, although I have been unable to determine the exact date. The Fortified Group "Marne," the last of the major fort groups to be built, was used by the Germans to store torpedo warheads. A P-47 pilot returning empty-handed from a sweep noticed a line of German trucks on the road leading into the central barracks, and as he had a spare bomb, swooped down. The bomb hit one of the trucks, causing it to explode; and in a chain reaction, the others ignited like a powder train leading into the fort. What followed must have been one of the mightiest explosions heard during the Second World War. The huge concrete barracks simply disappeared from the face of the earth, leaving a crater large enough to swallow a cathedral. All that can be seen today is a few lumps of concrete littered around a peaceful pool of deep blue water much favored by the local anglers. What was left of the fort became the headquarters of the 17th SS Panzer Grenadier Division during the coming battles.

In spite of its boldness, the Third Army plan had a number of inherent defects. First, the plan did not allow for the weather, which was not going to improve at that time of the year and would thus curtail air support—which was scarce anyway. Thus, that most potent weapon of the Second World War, the fighter-bomber, which the Germans feared so much, would be denied to the armored columns. Second, the plan did not consider that the Seille and Nied, "just two more rivers," could hold up armor unless there were sufficient supporting infantry. The infantry, however, in the shape of the battered 5th Division, would be fully occupied containing the Metz garrison to the north and in getting over the Seille themselves. To the south, XII Corps was busy in the Nancy area, and although they had bridges over the Moselle, they were not in a position to move parallel to guard the exposed flank of 7th Armored. This meant that their columns would be advancing in a pencil-like thrust deep into enemy territory, without any form of solid reserve to back them up and with their flanks insecure. Experience had shown that the enemy was prepared to make a stand in the area, and when the armor had passed, could easily filter back and menace their communications. If the 7th Armored had in fact fulfilled their mission of penetrating to the Moselle north of Metz, their communications back to the Arnaville area would have been some 20 miles long.

Moving through CCB early on 16 September, CCR jumped off to continue the immediate expansion of the bridgehead and to start the race to the Seille crossings. They took Lorry, which had been left over from the previous day, but then ran into trouble along the road from there to Sillegny on the Seille. The enemy had entrenched themselves in woods on either side of the highway and were supported by artillery firing from Sillegny. The Americans managed to fight their way through into the open, but were then driven back into the shelter of the trees by intense and accurate shelling. On the left, CCA was in position by the early afternoon. They were to pass through the old infantry positions on the hills and seize Marieulles and Vezon. From the start their vehicles were more or less useless on account of fog and the slippery, steep ground. Some of the tanks had to be hauled by winches over the crest to reach their start positions. Therefore they had to resort to using their armored infantry battalion (the 48th), but when they started down toward Vezon, they were hit in the flank by fire from the Verdun forts on their left. Their commanding officer then redirected them toward Marieulles, which was plastered in a preliminary bombardment by field artillery. The enemy, however, crawled back out of the cellars when the guns lifted, and repulsed the armored infantry.

The 5th Infantry Division spent the day regrouping their units and in patrol activity. The 2nd Infantry moved in to relieve CCB on the right of the bridgehead area, while 10th Infantry re-formed all three battalions in the center. On the left, 1st and 3rd Battalions of the 11th Infantry took up positions facing north toward Metz. Their shattered 2nd Battalion was left on the west bank to hold the line around Fort Driant, still largely minus weapons and helmets that had been thrown into the river during the withdrawal from the Dornot bridgehead. On their left, the 5th Reconnaissance Troop kept contact with the 90th Infantry at Gravelotte.

Apparently Patton was highly dissatisfied with the day's activities and voiced his displeasure during a visit to corps HQ. Walker passed on his comments to General Irwin as follows: "General Patton is here and said if we don't get across the Seille he is going to leave us here and contain Metz while he goes across with the rest of the army to the Rhine."[9] This was probably one of Patton's well-known pep talks, designed to spur on his subordinates; but it does show, I believe, that he was still not aware of the problem posed by Metz and was still obsessed with the symbolic Rhine—if only he could get there, he would have won the war. The problem was that, as the Germans were not stupid, they soon realized that XX Corps was on the defensive to the north of Metz. Pressure in the south enabled them to strip the northern front and concentrate their resources to meet the 5th Infantry Division and 7th Armored Division attacks. The main unit in the area was the inevitable 17th SS Panzer Grenadier Division. Admittedly it was short of armor, but its artillery battalion was intact and was to play a crucial role during the next few days. We have seen how the division fought against the Dornot bridgehead, yet the XIII SS Corps chief of staff did not think much of its personnel. He stated that after the retreat from the Seine, where it lost most of its vehicles, it was filled up mainly with air force and ethnic German personnel.[10] In the case of the latter, they would have been from the eastern territories rapidly being overrun by the Russians—if Germany lost the war they would no longer have homes to which they could return.

The infantry got off to a bad start on 17 September. Just after dawn, and well sheltered by fog and driving rain, a party of Germans estimated at battalion strength crept up the defile leading west from Vezon. There they fell upon the boundary between 10th and 11th Infantry Regiments, where confused hand-to-hand fighting ensued for most of the morning. The Germans were armed with Panzerfausts and the Schmeisser machine pistols, known to the Americans as "burp guns." Much of the fighting took place around the command post of I Company, which was attached to the 1st Battalion, 11th Infantry. Both the company commander and the executive officer were wounded, but when the enemy was finally forced to retire, the survivors of I Company counted 94 dead Germans in front of their positions. As they had only arrived there during the night, it was to their credit that they gave no ground. One platoon of L Company had to surrender after they were overrun but most of them later escaped when their guards became involved in the running battle. The Germans finally withdrew when a few tanks arrived on the scene and sprayed the line of retreat with their machine guns.

On the right, CCA spent most of the day trying to capture Marieulles, where some 500 men from the 17th SS were holding out. The first attempt by the 48th Armored Infantry and the 23rd Infantry (from CCB) was driven off with heavy casualties, caused by a number of the dreaded 88-mm antiaircraft guns, which fired high explosive shells into the packed ranks of the attackers. The Germans were using them like shotguns. In the afternoon, two battalions of 155-mm artillery fired for precisely one minute into the small town. The short bombardment was a declaration of poverty in that it was all the ammunition ration would permit. It is this sort of situation that made a mockery of the grandiose intentions of swanning off to the Rhine. After this brief barrage, the unfortunate infantry returned to the assault, only to be driven off again by the high-velocity guns. A final attack, supported by light artillery and led by tanks, finally cleared Marieulles, although the enemy did not give up easily—the German rear guard fired their machine pistols from the hip at the tanks trundling down the main street of the village. They left behind, however, the 88's and 135 prisoners.

While this bitter fighting was in progress, CCR on the extreme right spent a frustrating day removing roadblocks in order to establish a start line for the advance to Sillegny. These blocks were covered by preranged artillery emplaced on the far side of the Seille, which caused a number of casualties among the close-packed armor. It was difficult to return the fire as the fog and rain made observation more or less impossible.

This type of weather was but a foretaste of things to come throughout the Metz campaign. The armored vehicles bogged down in the sticky mud and could seldom be used properly except as supporting artillery, while the infantry had to bear the brunt of the fighting. Gradually the realization began to dawn on officers and men that the glorious days of headlong pursuit were over and that they were in for a long, hard slog.

The objectives for the following day were a number of villages strung out along the road from Metz to Cheminot, which ran roughly parallel to the meandering Seille. On the left, Pournoy-la-Chétive was to be taken by the 2nd Battalion, 10th Infantry. The 1st Battalion, 2nd Infantry, was to capture Coin-sur-Seille, and CCR was to aim for Sillegny. CCB, pulled out of reserve to replace CCA, was to attack Lonqueville-les-Cheminot. Today these villages are unremarkable and have been rebuilt, although the odd bullet scar can be seen on the few older buildings left standing. In September 1944, the bulk of the 37th and 38th SS Panzer Grenadier Regiments chose to make a stand in them in front of the river, instead of retiring behind the Seille in accordance with normal military practice—never fight a battle with a river at your back.

The attack started all along the line early on 18 September. On the right, CCB found their way hampered by the mine-strewn village of Bouxières, and a lot of time was wasted in clearing a path for the tanks. Once through, their attached armored infantry set off for the river, only to come under fire from guns in concrete emplacements on Hill 223, which was not even marked on their maps. As a result, they had some difficulty in persuading their divisional HQ that the opposition was genuine. These bunkers were not new; they were part of a line of outer defenses built by the Germans in 1916 after it had seemed that the Battle of Verdun was unlikely to be conclusive. Had the armistice not intervened in 1918, it is highly probable that American troops would have had to storm that line. (While researching for this book I received a letter from a man who had fought in the U.S. 60th Division toward the end of 1918. He was involved in combat in the Pont-à-Mousson area and distinctly remembers seeing a signpost which read "Metz—33 kilometers.")

On the left, the infantry advanced against light opposition toward Pournoy and Coin. Their verve, however, seems to have been missing at this stage, which is hardly surprising. Between 10 and 16 September, 10th Infantry is said to have lost 24 officers and 674 men, and they had been fighting without a break for eleven days under appalling conditions. The wet weather was beginning to produce the first of a crop of nonbattle casualties on account of the Metz malady, trench foot. In the official history, H. M. Cole states that further progress would have brought them under fire from the forts around Verny and that aircraft were needed to silence the guns.[11] These forts were the Fortified Group "Aisne" which had been disarmed before the war. Any guns there would have been field pieces. On account of the weather, the few planes that got through only managed to drop some token napalm bombs.

Had the Aisne group been in full working order, the Americans would never have got near the Seille because the fort had been built to guard the crossings. Originally the fort was armed with four 150-mm howitzers and four 100-mm guns under turrets, plus two 150-mm long-range guns in open emplacements. In addition to the two armored batteries there were three fully self-contained infantry strongpoints. As subsequent events were to prove, this type of fort was impervious to anything that the Americans could throw at it. To get over the river they would either have had to bring in a squadron of Lancaster bombers loaded with superheavy "earthquake" bombs, or have resigned themselves to a lengthy siege.

In the center, CCR launched its first assault on Sillegny during the afternoon. Supported by tanks, the 38th Armored Infantry Battalion moved off; but as soon as they broke cover from the woods, they were met by a hail of artillery. The tanks managed to close in on the village but were forced to withdraw when their ammunition ran out. The enemy fire was so intense that the infantry refused to move any further and fell back into the woods. Colonel Heffner, the commander of CCR, reported back that he had thrown in nearly all of his troops and that he had only two platoons in reserve—even if they were used it seemed unlikely that Sillegny could be taken with the limited forces available. However, he was ordered to try again. Using the last two platoons, his men moved once more out of the woods into the curtain of fire from the panzer grenadiers. Unnerved by the steady enemy fire, the men broke, only to be rallied by their commanding officer. Reorganized, at dusk they were sent in again, making "a splendid comeback." They followed the tanks right to the edge of the town, where they managed to dig in. At daybreak they even managed to take a few of the outlying houses before being once more repelled by the enemy, who had apparently been reinforced during the night.

The day on which the 38th Armored Infantry would win glory was 19 September, but it ceased to be a fighting force in the process. Throughout the day a savage battle raged in and around Sillegny, reminiscent of some of the close-quarter fighting of the great trench battles during the First World War. The enemy too achieved his share of glory.

During the morning the commander of the 38th, Lieutenant Colonel Rosebro, was mortally wounded and the executive officer was killed. The next in seniority, Major Wells, took over, only to be killed in his turn. Headquarters then sent forward Lieutenant Colonel King, commander of another battalion, and at 1100 he withdrew the troops, leaving the already ruined village to be pounded by the supporting artillery. After reorganization, and reinforced by a fresh company, the infantry returned to the fray in the afternoon, only to find that, in the meanwhile, the enemy had evacuated Sillegny. However, there was no advantage to be gained for the men of the 38th, as they were subjected to murderous shellfire from the high ground to the east, which forced them to take cover in the cellars.

At this stage, the Germans decided to counterattack with infantry and tanks. However, as they moved up, their column was strafed by fighter-bombers, which were in the area on a mission against the Aisne forts. Although the majority of the enemy were dispersed, a few tanks got back into the village, followed by infantry. Two American tanks which were on the spot managed to knock out the leading German tank, but finding that their own infantry were in the cellars, moved back to avoid being cut off. At this stage, Colonel King was wounded, the third battalion commander in one day. By 1830 the enemy were once again in possession of the ruins, cutting off in the process an American captain and 23 men who were holed up in a large house. Contact with them was lost after some tanks made a fruitless attempt to relieve them.

The fourth battalion commander, Lieutenant Colonel Rea, finally received permission to disengage. The 38th Armored Infantry had lost three-quarters of its strength, and nearly all the officers had been killed or wounded. The survivors were pulled out the following morning and replaced by CCA.

On the left in the 5th Division zone, the day was relatively quiet, since the divisional commander had called off the planned assaults on Pournoy and Coin to await the outcome of the armored attack on Sillegny. An attempted German counterattack from Coin was foiled by divisional artillery. On the right, CCB managed to dislodge the stubborn enemy from the bunkers on Hill 223. By dusk, and fighting all the way, they managed to seize Longueville, a village directly on the Seille. However, they failed to take Cheminot on the opposite bank, and five tanks were lost to well-aimed antitank guns from the other side of the river. Cheminot was to remain a potential threat to the right flank of 7th Armored until its garrison withdrew voluntarily three days later.

By the afternoon of 20 September, CCA was established in position in front of Sillegny. It was then decided to try a pincer movement in coordination with CCB to get across the river, but both moves failed, although some elements did manage to penetrate to the edge of the water. On the far side the Germans had antitank and machine guns emplaced in solid concrete bunkers. By this stage, the 7th Armored

Division was more or less exhausted. As an illustration of the losses suffered, CCR had eight different commanders between 1 and 21 September. Their line of advance to the river was outflanked by the enemy in Cheminot and the Germans were still able to reinforce. There is some evidence that part of the 559th VG Division was in the area, having been brought down from the Thionville sector where the Americans were on the defensive. Daylight movement became impossible, but after dark on 21 September, CCB managed to ford two companies of infantry across the Seille. Plans were immediately made to construct a bridge, until it was discovered that there was insufficient material available on the spot. The reason for this calamity was that three trucks full of engineer stores had been destroyed by shellfire during the day. The infantry had to be pulled back, and further plans for an all-out assault had to be abandoned as the division was notified that it was to move north to assist the First Army.

On the left, the 5th Infantry fared no better. A combined assault with the 7th Armored had been planned for 20 September, but the delay caused by the reshuffling of the latter, left the infantry to go it alone. Hopes of large-scale air support were dashed by the overcast skies, and this was compounded by a chronic shortage of artillery ammunition. However, the attack had to be mounted, and General Irwin sent his deputy, Brigadier General Warnock, to coordinate operations on the spot—Warnock often functioned as Irwin's "fireman."

Fighting their way slowly forward through a hail of tank, artillery, and mortar fire, the 1st Battalion, 2nd Infantry, managed to occupy Coin by the evening, only a few hundred yards away from the mainstream of the river. On the left, however, the 2nd Battalion, 10th Infantry, soon found themselves in trouble. The battalion was up to strength, having been filled with fresh men to replace the Arnaville losses. Supported by engineers, tanks, and tank destroyers, they moved off from the woods toward Pournoy with about two thousand yards to advance across fairly level open ground. Low clouds prevented any air strikes and the artillery was still chronically short of ammunition.

As soon as they broke cover, the battalion was subjected to murderous fire from front and from the right flank. Caught in such a cross fire, they either had to advance or be cut down. The supporting armor opened up and the infantry replied with their heavy weapons. Through this storm the men advanced, steadily firing from the hip, but the mounting toll of casualties made it extremely difficult to sustain momentum. Two company commanders were killed and one wounded, but in spite of this, the infantry managed to get into the village. Operating with rifles, bayonets, and grenades, they flushed the Germans out of the ruins and by early evening had managed to occupy about a third of Pournoy. There they were promptly counter-attacked by tanks and were finally forced to withdraw about three hundred yards, where they dug in. One company, disorganized by loss of officers and shattered by the almost continuous shelling began to straggle back, but was steadied by the more experienced soldiers.

One of the heroes of Pournoy was Private Catri, who was a member of the G Company bazooka team. When the German tanks appeared, his teammate was wounded, but Catri grabbed the weapon and ran under fire to a shallow depression about fifty yards from the nearest tank. Operating the bazooka alone, he disabled the tank and shortly afterward forced another to withdraw.

The battalion commander, Colonel Carroll, and the few remaining officers managed to restore some sort of order to the tattered ranks, and the 10th Infantry returned once again to the attack. The attached armor moved around to the sides of the village while the infantry once again drove out the enemy. This time they managed to clear all the houses and dug in to the east.

The American occupation of Pournoy formed a dangerous salient in the German lines, and it was soon apparent that the enemy would not rest until they had eradicated it—ground must not be sacrificed, regardless of the cost of regaining it. It was, however, the key to the whole 5th Division position. The line held by the 2nd and 10th Infantry ran south to north parallel to the Seille and through Coin and Pournoy. From there the line bent back at right angles all the way to the Moselle. Thus Pournoy was like a finger pointing at the 17th SS Panzer Grenadier Division. During the evening the divisional commander did the rounds of the regiment, where he was told that a further advance would be impossible unless more artillery ammunition could be procured. When this information was passed back to corps, the 5th Division were told to stay put and hold on. Throughout the night, shells continued to rain on Pournoy, both from heavy guns sited to the rear and from 88's and smaller guns just over the river and on both flanks. This shelling had the effect of disorganizing communications; and during the early hours of 21 September, a force of enemy, estimated at two companies, got behind F Company, who were holding the outpost line to the east of the town. There was a delay until retaliatory artillery could be called in, during which the Germans got into the village streets and cut off F Company, afterward striking at E Company. By dawn the battalion managed to reestablish their line close to the town; but by then, half the effectives had become casualties: of the 800 men who started off for Pournoy, only some 450 were left.

The key to the German attacks that took place throughout 21 September was another village to the north, Coin-lès-Curvry (not to be confused with Coin-sur-Seille to the south, which was occupied by the 2nd Infantry). From there the enemy moved in with armor and motorized infantry supported by apparently unlimited artillery. One man said later, "We were shelled just once at Pournoy; that was all the time." Although reinforced by a fresh rifle company during the morning, the men of the 2nd Battalion could not leave their foxholes in daylight to get food or water. They were only saved from being overwhelmed by the performance of divisional and corps artillery who, hoarding their precious ammunition supplies, blasted Coin-lès-Cuvry off the map. Throughout the night and the following day, the pressure was kept up; although on 22 September the counterattacks slackened off—the Germans too had suffered heavy casualties from their suicide tactics. By 23 September, the 2nd Battalion, 10th Infantry, was at the end of its tether and the commanding officer requested that they be relieved. During that night they withdrew their shattered companies, which were replaced by the 1st Battalion.

The irony is that as a result of decisions imposed upon corps by wider demands of strategy and allocation of manpower, Pournoy was shortly to be abandoned, and the whole 5th Division was withdrawn to a holding line to the west. Thus, the attacks on the Seille line and the resulting casualties had been in vain—the only positive factor was that a great many of the enemy had been killed and wounded. Battles of attrition, however, do not lead to immediate decisions, and their effects are only felt in the long term—which is small consolation to those who are killed and wounded in the process.

CONTINUATION OF THE ATTACKS AGAINST THE METZ PERIMETER

In spite of the terrible losses suffered by the 2nd Infantry Regiment, the efforts to penetrate the fortified western salient were continued. The general regrouping that took place on 14 September brought two of the 90th Division regiments south to occupy the positions previously held by 2nd Infantry and CCA of the 7th Armored Division. On the right, the 359th Infantry were positioned on either side of the Gravelotte-Metz road, facing the notorious Mance ravine. On their left, the 357th Infantry took over the old positions in front of Amanvillers.

The division commander, General McClain, thus found himself holding a front of some 20 miles, as his other regiment, the 358th, was strung out along the river almost as far as Thionville, padded out with cavalry elements. He had no depth and no reserves to call upon. He was extremely lucky that the enemy troops on the far bank of the Moselle showed no particular inclination to attack, but as we have seen in the preceding section, there is evidence that the Germans stripped this front to reinforce their troops counterattacking in the southern bridgehead. Had the Germans north of Metz indulged in active patrolling across the river, the 90th Division could well have found itself in trouble.

General McClain's two southern regiments were hard up against the main belt of the Metz fortifications, about which little had been discovered during the first week of fighting, in spite of constant patrolling and air reconnaissance. Each small gain of territory uncovered a further line of bunkers and other obstacles. Artillery spotting proved most difficult as the German guns were placed on the reverse slopes of the wooded ridges and could be easily moved along good lateral roads.

The 357th Infantry was facing the 1010th Security Regiment, the combat efficiency of which "left much to be desired" according to their division commander, General Krause. The 359th Infantry had to deal with the Officer Candidate Regiment, who in addition to their zone of fortifications were fronted by the Mance ravine. General von der Goltz, one of the Germans involved in the 1870 battle, later wrote of this feature, "A stronger position in the open field can hardly be imagined." Thus, on paper, two American regiments were facing two

German ones. The 90th Infantry Division were comparatively fresh, not having suffered heavy casualties during their advance from Verdun. There, however, the similarity ended. The Americans were plagued by a chronic lack of ammunition and the appalling weather which they had to withstand in open foxholes. Their opponents were generally warm and snug in their permanent emplacements, and in addition, had expert knowledge of the terrain they were defending. The job of the 90th Infantry was to occupy the Germans to such an extent that they would be unable to send reinforcements to the south of the city.

The first attack was launched on 15 September, with each regiment deploying one battalion. On the left, the 1st Battalion, 357th Infantry, was ordered to effect a penetration along the St. Privat-Metz road where it passed to the south of the Canrobert works. They were supported by a platoon of engineers equipped with flamethrowers, the first recorded use of this weapon during the battles against the Metz defenses. The official historian states that the flamethrower was little employed in the operations of the Third Army: "Little training was given in its use and most of the troops regarded this weapon with a jaundiced eye."[12] Portable flamethrowers were effective against pillboxes, providing that the operator could get near enough to aim the oil into the firing slits. The type of flamethrower tank known as a "Crocodile" and used by the British forces might well have proved effective at Metz, as it had a greater range.

At this stage some confusion has crept into the official record, probably due to difficulties with nomenclature. Cole refers to the narrow gap between the Canrobert and the Kellermann works, while some American reports refer to the latter as "Fort Amanvillers." The two were completely separate entities, Kellermann lying some 500 yards southeast of the defensive work known officially as the Ouvrage des Carrières d'Amanvillers (Amanvillers Quarry Works).

The infantry, advancing through dense scrub, crossed the light railway that ran up and along the Fèves Ridge, and drove in the German outposts. By evening, they were hard up against the Amanvillers quarries in which they managed to gain a foothold. Their sister battalion, the 2nd, sent out a patrol to try to get around the Canrobert line from the north, but the idea was abandoned when it was discovered that they would have to move across open ground under the fire of the Fort de Fèves.

On the right, and covering ground already tried by the 2nd Infantry, the 2nd Battalion of the 359th Infantry moved off from Malmaison to try to attack the Jeanne d'Arc fortified group. This was the largest of the Metz forts in the area, and some of its turret artillery was in operation at the time. The place was also probably in reasonable repair as it had been used as the headquarters of General Condé's Second Army during the Battle of France in 1940. The aim was to avoid the Mance ravine deathtrap by moving around to the north of it. Initially the infantry made some progress, but in the early afternoon, they were held up by a large pillbox in the woods to the east of Malmaison. The 2nd Battalion discovered that bazooka rockets bounced off the pillbox, and the tanks and engineers with flame-throwers who were called in had an equal lack of success. Although the bunker was kept under fire, it was not captured, and by evening the attack had petered out.

Thus the first day ended with little achieved, which was not surprising in view of the failure of previous attempts in that sector. Representative of the feelings of many who fought there, here is a quote from the memoirs of William McConahey, battalion surgeon with the 2nd Battalion, 357th Infantry: "We were pulled out from our position south of Thionville and thrown into futile and suicidal attacks on the great forts of Metz. Bitterly we cursed the Germans and our luck as we shivered in the fall rains, and slipped and slid in the ankle-deep mud. The poor infantrymen lying out there, soaking wet, covered with mud, and under murderous fire from the forts, were really taking it again. Slowly it began to dawn on us that our sweep across France had not beaten the Krauts, and that maybe we'd have a winter war on our hands. . . . The second battalion was ordered to try a predawn attack. All we had to do was to cross a mile-wide, muddy, soaked field swept by machine gun and artillery fire, traverse a deep moat filled with barbed wire, scale the walls on the other side and then assault a series of huge concrete fortresses built into a hill. It would have been suicide."[13]

That evening, General McClain surveyed the situation and sensibly concluded that formal assaults on the fortified perimeter were pointless unless additional troops could be brought in. He therefore instituted a policy of nibbling at the German positions with a series of limited-objective attacks, and ordered intensive patrol activity to keep the enemy occupied. This was designed to fulfill the original mission of hindering the Germans from pulling troops out of the salient for use elsewhere, and at the same time minimizing casualties.

However, the following day, the attacks were continued on much the same basis. In heavy fog, the 1st Battalion, 357th Infantry, had another go at the St. Privat-Metz road. The fog gave them welcome cover from the attentions of the enemy gunners, but caused them to lose their way and run up against the concrete wall in front of the Canrobert position. The battalion commander then decided to sideslip south and try to move through the gap at the end of the wall. The regimental commander sent in the 3rd Battalion to form a blocking force on the right while this attempt was made, so as to provide extra fire power. However, as the two companies detailed to spearhead the assault were forming up, they were hit by a detachment from the Officer Candidate Regiment. As the regiment was not in their sector, one can only assume that the detachment was part of a mobile striking force made available for just such an eventuality—a threatened American breakthrough. As was usual with such tough troops, the action was fast and furious, ending with hand-to-hand fighting before the Germans finally withdrew. Their casualties are not recorded, but the 357th lost seventy two men—losses they could ill afford.

To the south, the 359th Infantry had another crack at getting to grips with the enemy in the Mance ravine. This time they skirted to the north through the woods and then tried to move south along the bed of the ravine. Once there they came under intense fire from enemy machine guns and mortars. Crawling from cover to cover, they managed to penetrate some 200 yards until they reached the main Gravelotte-Metz road, which plunges down into the valley and rises up the steep bank on the other side. Once there they could go no further and added a liberal quantity of dead and wounded to the toll already exacted by the ravine—15 officers and 117 men, roughly the equivalent strength of a good rifle company.

Pecking continued without success on 17 September, when corps finally agreed that such limited attacks were far too costly for the advantage gained. After that, the 90th Division remained in a holding capacity, only hindering the German garrison from breaking out. This gave the men a valuable breathing space until the end of the month, when a few more attempts were to be made.

While all this infantry action was in progress, the artillery had not been idle, in spite of limited ammunition. Serious attempts were made to bombard the forts into submission. With the benefit of hindsight, we now know that this was a total waste of precious ammunition; but at the time, and with air missions strictly curtailed, it seemed to be the only way to support the infantry. The 90th Division Artillery was using at least one battery of captured 10.5-cm artillery, and at least some of their tanks were firing captured 75-mm ammunition. American reports indicate that when they opened fire on a fort, the guns there ceased to operate—only to reply when the fire was lifted. There is a fairly simple reason for this. It involved the type of construction employed by the Germans for their fixed batteries, installed prior to the First World War. Contemporary French turrets were of the disappearing type, which had to be raised by counterweight into the firing position—a total lift of some 4 feet. The German turrets were of the fixed rotating type, whereby the dome sat on an apron of hardened steel embedded in the concrete roof of the battery. The muzzle of the gun was mounted in a ball joint in the curved wall of the dome. To fire, the dome (or cupola) was raised only a few inches to allow it to be traversed mechanically. Under bombardment, the noise inside such a turret was simply deafening and the crew had to be withdrawn into the shelter below. As soon as the enemy artillery ceased action, the crew could return to the gun chamber, raise the turret, and reply.

The Americans used 155-mm and even 240-mm artillery against the forts, concentrating their fire against Jeanne d'Arc and Driant, without being able to put a single gun out of action. The Germans, however, also had their problems with the turret guns. We have seen that they had no proper sighting equipment, and their ammunition was also often faulty on account of old age. The Americans on the receiving end noted a large number of duds, one instance of which was cited in a letter from Charles Bryan, who commanded L Company of the 358th Infantry. He wrote to me as follows of their period in the line at Gravelotte, facing Fort Jeanne d'Arc: "The fort shelled us at first whenever a target presented itself. The shells were large caliber 8″ or 10″ (the most they could have been were 6″ or 150mm) but two thirds were duds. . . . One dud ricochetted off the paved street and lodged above the door frame of a house that was occupied by an M.G. squad. I told the men not to use the door until the engineers could remove the shell. The next day on inspection I noticed that the shell was gone, and I knew that the engineers had not come up as yet. I was notified that one of the men got tired of crawling through the window, so he yanked it out and carried it across the road to a ditch."

A further amusing piece of information from this sector of the attack is also worth mentioning. One of the few remaining documents concerning the 462 Division is a brief report of its activities compiled some time in October. This includes a translation into German of an article from the 19 September edition of the *Stars and Stripes*. The article stated that the Officer Candidate Regiment had been pushed back five miles, together with a lot of other nonsense. This was obviously circulated to the regiment, together with a few pungent comments written by their commanding officer, Colonel von Siegroth. This is but one illustration of the folly of relying upon contemporary newspaper reports as historical evidence.[14]

On the same date as the above piece of fiction, the Third Army noted that "the 90th Division less detachments was to contain Metz, while the 5th Infantry Division and the 7th Armored Division proceeded on assigned missions."[15] At the same time, XX Corps received information that a threat still existed to the extended northern flank of the 90th Division strung out along the Moselle, and Corps was instructed it reinforce the sector with tanks and tank destroyers.

STALEMATE

The cessation of serious attacks against the salient by the 90th Division and the calling off of the assaults on the Seille line in the south mark the effective end of the first stage of the Battle of Metz. As late as 17 September, the Third Army was still talking about the Rhine and issuing orders specifying exactly where crossings were to be made.[16] By then, however, it was plainly obvious that the Third Army had been defeated in a major defensive battle and their victorious advance had been halted. In this they were not alone, as the Arnhem operation had ended indecisively when the last troops were withdrawn from the bridgehead over the Lower Rhine on 25 September, and the First Army was still trying to batter its way through the Westwall in the Aachen area. By mid-September, the supposedly beaten enemy had performed miracles of regeneration and had achieved the aim of creating a solid defensive crust along and in advance of their frontier defenses.

Here again, the proponents of both points of view in the "great argument" have had their say. Those supporting the narrow thrust in the north against the Ruhr have said that the Eisenhower's broad-front strategy permitted small groups of low-grade German troops to hold up the Allied advance, whereas a single thrust could have easily disorganized their thin crust. Both Patton himself and his supporters have argued that if he had been given the resources, he could have bulldozed his way to the Rhine with comparative ease. Eisenhower, however, was still plagued by logistic problems which would only have been aggravated if one of his two army groups had charged off into the wilderness. It was clear to the SHAEF planners that only a major offensive on as broad a front as possible would put the Allies across the Rhine, and this could only be sustained once the port of Antwerp was in full operation.

The strategy that was to shape operations during the latter part of 1944 was laid down at a conference held at Eisenhower's new head-quarters at Versailles on 22 September—in the presence of all the Allied top brass, with the notable exception of Montgomery. The Supreme Commander was quite definite in his statement that the possession of an additional deep-water port on the northern flank was a vital prerequisite for the final drive into Germany. Therefore, the opening of the line of the river Scheldt would be the immediate priority, followed by the attack to envelop the Ruhr in the north by 21st Army Group supported by the First U.S. Army. We have seen that the Third Army drive to the Saar was always regarded by SHAEF (if not by Patton) as a subsidiary operation, but as a result of Eisenhower's decision its importance would be still further reduced. Bradley was instructed that the Third Army was to take "no more aggressive action than is permitted by the maintenance situation after the full requirements of the main effort had been met."[17]

These decisions were passed on to General Patton in a letter from Bradley; it confirmed the gist of the conversation that they had had at Bradley's headquarters at Verdun on 23 September. Patton was told that he would have to relinquish the 7th Armored Division, which was to go north to help the First Army, and that his right-hand corps (XV) would be transferred to General Dever's 6th Army Group (the forces which had landed in the south of France). There was a sound logistical reason for this in that the corps could be more easily supplied through Marseilles, but it seemed to Patton that his beloved army was break-ing up around him. At the time there was even mention of removing responsibility for the Metz front from the Third Army and handing it over to the newly arrived Ninth Army of General Simpson, which was inserted between First and Third Armies.[18]

The wider strategic implications of the Allied campaign provided no comfort to Patton, who saw his hopes dashed. Having been stymied at Metz, he had decided to pin his hopes on an attack by General Eddy's XII Corps. This was planned to start on 18 September and would lead to the desired penetration of the Westwall—thus outflanking the Metz garrison. Some armor was to be rushed in through this gap in an attempt to grab a bridge across the Rhine at Worms. A second division would hold the gap open while the third division mopped up any enemy forces remaining between the Moselle and the Saar. This was an extremely bold concept to be executed with such meager resources and without reserves. Metz would still have remained the fly in the ointment and was far too tough to be simply left in the rear of such a slender armored advance—the garrison had already demonstrated their determination to resist.

However, just as Eddy was about to jump off, the enemy launched a major counterattack in the Lunéville area which was sufficiently serious to hold up the planned advance until the stop order was received by the Third Army anyway. This effort was the culmination of Hitler's bid to stop Patton and was carried out by the Fifth Panzer Army commanded by General Manteuffel. In the end, the Germans suffered a major defeat, losing the bulk of their armor and inflicting few casualties on the Americans. The point was, however, that their surprise attack caught XII Corps off balance and imposed a delay, which in view of the reallocated priorities could not be made good. Patton was therefore forced to assume the defensive along the entire front and like Dickens' Mr. Micawber, wait for "something to turn up."

His reaction was predictable. In private and in front of war correspondents, he was caustic, blaming his troubles on the Mafia at SHAEF and on the machinations of Field Marshal Montgomery. However, as a loyal subordinate, he complied promptly with the spirit of his orders and wrote an eminently sensible letter of instruction to his senior commanders on 25 September.[19] Pointing out quite correctly that the supply situation had been the cause of the decision to assume the defensive, he made it plain that this had to be concealed from the enemy—who might otherwise take the opportunity to move troops to other fronts. Therefore, no wiring, mining or, digging in was allowed. Instead, the front was to be held by outposts backed by strong mobile reserves who should be prepared to carry out local counterattacks. The aim behind this was to secure a suitable line of departure for the "future offensive" and ended characteristically with the Patton touch—"We only await the signal to resume our career of conquest."

In the context of securing this line of departure, Patton then put a number of operations of a strictly local nature to Bradley for authorization. The latter wrote to Eisenhower on 25 September justifying further action on the Moselle in terms of authorization given to Patton to "make some minor adjustments in his present lines." These were set out as a list of priorities, the second of which was an operation to drive a wedge into the fortified perimeter of Metz. In this respect, XX Corps had realized that the key to the whole position was Fort Driant, the large work at the southern end of the salient, and it was accordingly decided to reduce this strongpoint. Even if they were on the defensive, there was no reason for the fighting to stop.

During the course of the above Allied deliberations, the situation "on the other side of the hill" opposite the Third Army had altered. General Blaskowitz, commanding Army Group G, was sacked as a result of the failure of the counterattack at Lunéville and two new brooms arrived on the scene. General Hermann Balck took over command of the army group, assisted as chief of staff by Colonel (later Major General) von Mellenthin. On their way to take up their new positions, the two men were received by Hitler on 18 September. During that meeting the Fuehrer prophesized that the Allied advance would come to a halt on a line from the Scheldt to Metz, and that he would use the opportunity thus created to launch a counteroffensive in November (the Ardennes operation). Balck was ordered to hold the Alsace-Lorraine area at all costs and to avoid getting into a situation whereby forces earmarked for the offensive would have to be diverted to Army Group G. In the book he wrote after the war, Mellenthin stated, "We now know that Third Army received categorical orders to stand on the defensive. The rights and wrongs of this strategy do not concern me, but it certainly simplified the problems of our Army Group G. We were given a few weeks grace to rebuild our battered forces and get ready to meet the next onslaught."[20]

From this it is quite clear that the Allied halt enabled Hitler to start concentrating reserves for the Ardennes operation—which had been in his mind as early as the beginning of September. Naturally, had Patton been given the means to reach the Rhine, he would have outflanked the German area of concentration, assuming that his advance would have got that far. However, the problem of Metz in his rear would still have been unsolved.

$$\equiv 6 \equiv$$

The Attack on Fort Driant

The Fort Driant action, of a purely local nature, can easily be examined in isolation because it took place while the rest of the XX Corps was strictly on the defensive. All those concerned could give the operation their undivided attention. However, the idea of attacking and neutralizing Fort Driant was not new; the plan should be seen in the context of operations during September.

Fort Driant was the key to the whole fortified position to the west of the Moselle and, by crossing its fire with the two forts of the Verdun Group, it linked up with the eastern defenses. Its construction was started in 1899 as part of the Germans' initial program to modernize the Metz fortress. (Other works of the same period were Lorraine, Jeanne d'Arc, and the Verdun Group.) It was built on a plateau to the southwest of the city and divided from the rest of the fortifications by the Mance ravine. Its mission was to hinder an enemy advance toward Metz from the south along the Moselle valley and to cross its fire with the guns of Fort Jeanne d'Arc. On a full war footing, its garrison would have been roughly 2,000 men, including infantry, artillery, and engineers.

As in all the pre-1914 German forts in the area, Driant consisted of a number of elements inserted into the terrain. It was originally

known as *Feste Kronprinz,* but when taken over by the French in
1918, it was renamed *Groupe fortifié Driant,* after Colonel Driant, a
hero of the 1916 Battle of Verdun. The fort is roughly triangular in
shape, more or less level on the surface, and covers an area of 355
acres. It measures roughly a kilometer in length and the width varies
between 500 and 800 meters.[1]

The entire area was enclosed by a multistrand barbed-wire entanglement, and the central barracks was situated on the western side,
additionally protected by a wide ditch. The central strongpoint
housed the power plant, communication equipment, hospital, and the
bulk of the garrison. Running across the top of the fort was a line of
four batteries—two each of three 100-mm guns and two each of three
150-mm howitzers. In addition, there were five concrete barracks and
a large number of infantry shelters and armored-plated infantry posts,
pillboxes, and concreted trenches—all connected together by underground passages. The garrison could easily move from one part to
another, under cover and without being observed. On the southeast
corner and outside the main perimeter was a further battery (Battery
Moselle) armed with two 100-mm turret guns designed to give flanking cover along the wooded slopes. The only way up to the fort was via
a twisting road that led up from the Mance ravine near Ars-sur-
Moselle. During the attack this remained firmly in German hands.

When such forts were originally built, it was assumed that they
would be formally attacked by a large field army equipped with
superheavy siege artillery—the forts were designed before the Wright
brothers got themselves into the history books. Under the rules of
warfare at the time, if bombardment failed, the attackers would dig
themselves forward laboriously via saps, or might resort to mining. In
their abortive attempt to regain Alsace-Lorraine in 1914, the French
had no intention of getting involved in a siege of Metz and aimed their
attack to the south. One of the many ironies of the Metz story is that
Fort Driant only fired once in anger during the First War, and that
was against American troops in the Pont-à-Mousson area in 1918.

During the early stages of the operations in 1944 at Metz, Fort
Driant had helped to frustrate bridge-building efforts at Dornot and
Arnaville and had caused a large number of casualties to the infantry
trying to cross the Mance ravine to the east of Gravelotte. It was
therefore felt that if any penetration of the fortified salient was to
succeed, Driant had first to be eliminated. During the first part of

September, priority of air support had been given to the reduction of Brest, far away in Brittany, which finally surrendered on 19 September. All those concerned from the Third Army downward were convinced that air bombardment was the only way to silence the forts, which had so far resisted artillery and infantry attack. With this in mind, General Walker issued a tentative plan code-named "Operation Thunderbolt" on 17 September. This called for a coordinated air and ground attack to commence on 21 September and formed the background to the 5th Infantry Division and 7th Armored Division attacks on the Seille line. One of the primary objectives listed in the original plan was the reduction of Fort Driant. This was to be accomplished by heavy bomber saturation, initial infantry advance covered by artillery and medium bombers, and a final infantry assault.[2]

As is so often the case with such plans, the final edition was whittled down drastically. G-3 Air of 12th Army Group inserted the proviso that support would be by medium bombers only and that the missions would not be flown until the weather permitted and when the aircraft were not required by higher headquarters. In the event, most of the available aircraft were diverted to assist the First Army in its attempts to break through the Westwall in the Aachen area, and the Third Army came off second best. With the benefit of hindsight and the subsequent damage reports (see appendix), we can see that Thunderbolt would have been a waste of bombs anyway.

It appears that Colonel Yuill, commanding the 11th Infantry Regiment, was convinced that he could take the fort by storm and sold the idea to 5th Division. As the latter had suffered most from the artillery of the fort, it is not surprising that they were keen on the scheme. They estimated that the fort was garrisoned by three companies of the Officer Candidate Regiment. This would seem to be reasonable enough, although it has proved impossible to determine just how many Germans were in the fort at any one time. This estimate also helps to explain why it was decided to use just one infantry battalion to capture the fort, a decision that is hard to understand today. It has always been one of the basic tenets of war taught at military academies all over the world that, in attacking a fortified position, superiority of three to one is required. Although the bulk of the 5th Division was deployed to the east of the Moselle in the bridgehead, it will be remembered that the 2nd Battalion of the 11th

Infantry had been left to contain Fort Driant and the west bank of the river. It was this unit that had been virtually wiped out at Dornot and had since been absorbing a large number of raw replacements.

Having been forced to shorten their line by the withdrawal of the 7th Armored Division, 5th Infantry had been able to accumulate a supply of artillery ammunition for the Driant operation. Even so, they were still holding far more territory than they could cope with. Their good fortune was that the enemy had also been severely mauled and was not in a position to mount a serious counterattack. If they had stayed in their forward positions close to the Seille, they would not have been able to mount the attack on the fort at the same time.

On their left, the 90th Infantry was also in the process of realignment. Having ceased their operations against the western fortifications on 17 September, the two regiments involved were in desperate need to rest. However, on 27 September, the 358th Infantry Regiment, which had been left to contain the Thionville sector, was brought south and replaced by Task Force Polk, the reinforced 3rd Cavalry Group. The 358th was inserted into the line at Gravelotte, where its 3rd Battalion had been committed the previous day in another effort to cross the Mance ravine. As his contribution to Operation Thunderbolt, General McClain intended that his forces should move east from Gravelotte toward the Jeanne d'Arc fort, and a prerequisite for this was the capture of the road through the ravine.

As in all previous attempts, this was doomed to be a costly failure. On 27 September the whole regiment was committed, but by the evening the troops were exhausted. Once again the 90th Division went on the defensive, holding the line with outposts and rotating the battalions to the rear for rest and training. The division commander, however, still retained ambitions toward the elusive forts in spite of the casualties suffered by his men. He still dreamed of an attack on Jeanne d'Arc with two regiments, although at this stage he inserted the proviso that "above all, the operation is based on the prior capture of Fort Driant and our subsequent occupation and utilization of it as a flank anchor, OP and base of fire."[3]

The 2nd Battalion of the 11th Infantry Regiment was alerted on an almost daily basis to carry out the attack any time after 19 September. Weather and the chronic shortage of aircraft combined to delay the operation, however, which by then was all that was left of Operation Thunderbolt. The idea of massed air attacks was finally abandoned on 25 September, when Bradley gave orders cancelling them because there was insufficient ammunition available to support all-out operations against the Metz forts. Thereafter, support was on a day-to-day basis.[4]

At this stage we must digress briefly to discuss the problem of obtaining plans of the forts, plans which had been unavailable at the outset of the campaign. By the latter part of September, the map situation had improved somewhat as the road maps had been replaced by 1:50,000 sheets. The latter were not detailed enough for battalion and company operations, but the intelligence people had located some 1:20,000 contour maps in Paris. Also from Paris came Commandant (now General) Nicolas, a French army engineer who before the war had been responsible for detail construction work on the Maginot Line. He was attached as fortification consultant to the Third Army, from where he was sent to XX Corps. Also available was a certain Monsieur Tonnelier, who had been the head of the utilities section in the Metz engineer headquarters and who had an intimate knowledge of the fortifications. The breakthrough came, however, when Nancy was liberated on 15 September. Living there was a French officer, Colonel Collier, who before the war had been the head of the engineers at Metz, and just before the Germans arrived in 1940, he had taken the set of plans of the forts and had hidden them at Lyons in the south of the country. These were retrieved and rushed back to XX Corps HQ, where a planning unit was set up.

In an effort to save time the first drawings were reproduced directly from the French originals, but these proved to be too complicated for use by the troops. Commandant Nicolas then produced a series of excellent plans of the forts, gridded for artillery fire control, color shaded and lettered in English. These were supplemented by detail cross sections and extremely useful, exploded three-dimensional drawings of individual bunkers. When Metz was finished, the team went on to do the same work for the Maginot Line and also made a number of models of the Metz forts for study by the various units. They were assisted by air surveys, and the reproduction was carried out by an engineer topographic battalion and a group of expert model makers.[5]

Between 26 and 30 September, XIX Tactical Air Force fighter-bombers flew a series of missions against the Metz forts as a whole, using napalm and 1,000-pound bombs dropped from P-47 Thunderbolt aircraft. An eyewitness described one such mission as follows:

"From observation posts near enemy-held Fort Driant, some officers and men were watching American Thunderbolts attack Fort Verdun 3,000 yards away on the other side of the Moselle River. A pilot peeled off high above, diving straight down for one of the turrets of the fort as a thunderous roar of enemy ack-ack rolled across the valley. The pilot bore down so low that it looked as though he would crash. The plane made a quick upturn, and the bombs could be plainly seen as they dropped. In a second or two a huge flame shot up, 'that's napalm and plenty hot for any Germans there.'

"The ack-ack roar continued and the spectators held their breath hoping the pilot would get through. He turned and then headed down for the ack-ack with his machine guns blazing. What a show of audacity and bravery! The pilot pulled up and out on his way to safety, and a silent cheer went up from those on the observation post."[6]

27 September dawned with clear skies, and in order to gain the maximum advantage from air support, the division commander ordered the attack to start at 1415. Colonel Yuill, in addition to his 2nd Battalion, had the following elements in support: a company of tanks, a company of chemical mortars, and a medical company. The 19th Field Artillery Battalion was detailed for fire cover and divisional artillery was on call if required. In spite of having obtained plans of the forts, the detailed drawings were not ready by then for distribution, and the 11th Infantry assault companies had been briefed only on the basis of somewhat vague sketch maps of the surface of the target. While the troops were assembling in the woods to the southwest, fighter-bombers bombed and strafed the whole area of the fort. This probably contributed to raising the morale of the German garrison by demonstrating that their concrete protection was adequate.

Just prior to H-hour, American artillery fired a concentration from eight batteries, including 8-inch and 240-mm howitzers, without causing the enemy guns in the fort to do more than pause briefly when their turrets were lowered. The regimental commander had decided to commit only two companies (E and G), which during the preliminary bombardment worked along the open ground on the western flank of the fort. During this time the enemy remained fairly quiet, but at H-hour when the troops made their approach the Germans opened up with rifles, machine guns, and mortars. The chemical company laid down a smoke screen to cover the advancing infantry, who soon found themselves up against the barbed-wire obstacle covering the ditch to the northeast of the central barracks. This whole area could be swept with fire from a number of well-concealed pillboxes, and although the men could see a causeway leading over the ditch, they got no nearer than some three hundred yards. In the meanwhile, a number of tank destroyers had moved up and took on the pillboxes at short range, without achieving more than chipping the concrete.

The two companies hung on in swiftly improvised foxholes until the early evening, by which time it was clear that they would make no further progress. At 1830, the division commander gave permission for them to withdraw. In spite of the amount of opposition, casualties had not been heavy—only 18 men from the two infantry companies were incapacitated. It would seem that the greatest problem was posed by the depth of the wire obstacles, which made it impossible to get close enough to the pillboxes to use pole charges poked in through the embrasures. One squad from E Company did manage to cut through part of the wire but then found themselves in open ground without any form of cover.

The following day the rain started again, and further attempts were called off until a more comprehensive plan could be made. A detailed drawing of the fort did arrive by then, but as the men had had to abandon their demolition equipment when they withdrew, new supplies had to be made up.

By then, all concerned were facing a difficult problem. Although supplies were still short, the gravest lack was of experienced personnel, especially in the 5th Division. Generals Patton, Walker, and Irwin met on 28 September to discuss the progress of the campaign as a whole. It would appear that, for once, General Patton was not the firebrand on this occasion, as he instructed General Irwin to use the lull to recuperate his regiments. Walker, however, was all for action and made the suggestion that the failure of the first attack on Fort Driant was caused by lack of aggressive personal leadership at regimental and battalion level.

This was manifestly unjust, and Irwin pointed out the lack of available information—air photos had not shown the massed barbed wire and the network of pillboxes around the perimeter. This is just another example of the attitude of senior American commanders to the problem posed by permanent fortifications, a subject of which they had had no experience in previous wars.

Therefore the attack had to go on, being finally approved by Patton on 29 September. This was based on an operational directive issued the previous day which allocated priority to Metz in respect of limited and local operations.[7] Irwin himself was not keen on the idea as he realized better than anyone else, just how his division had suffered during the early stages of the Metz campaign. He was holding a front of some 12 miles split in two by the Moselle valley, and during September, the 5th Infantry Division had suffered 3,056 casualties—killed, wounded, and missing. These figures of roughly one quarter of the fighting strength do not include losses occasioned by sickness and combat fatigue, which were running at a high level by the end of the month. At that time, the division was in the process of absorbing nearly 4,000 replacements who had to be eased into the existing regimental framework.[8] The sensible thing to do would have been to contain Fort Driant until such a time as supplies and personnel permitted the operation to be carried out with some chance of success.

It is Walker's attitude that is difficult to understand. Admittedly, his vanity had probably been wounded by his lack of success at Metz compared to the advances made by other Allied units. He looked like a bulldog and had the tenacity popularly ascribed to that animal. However, with his personal experience of combat during the First World War, he should have realized that infantry were powerless against uncut wire flanked by machine guns. It would seem that at this stage of the campaign, he still had not realized that the nature of the war had changed and that the Allies had temporarily lost the initiative in the West.

On 28 September a detailed plan of the fort had finally been obtained, and the next stage of the attack was scheduled for 3 October. Planning was carried out at regimental HQ on the basis of a two-pronged assault by tank-infantry teams. Again, the sorely tried 2nd Battalion was to be involved, reinforced by B Company of the 1st Battalion. This time, B Company was to aim for the southwestern corner of the fort, while E Company would return to the northwest. G Company would remain in reserve, ready to exploit whichever approach seemed to be the more favorable. The whole of corps artillery was allocated to support the operation, and support of a more immediate nature was provided by a composite tank company manned by picked men. This comprised eleven medium tanks, five light tanks, four self-propelled 105-mm howitzers, and two tank-dozers. The latter were normal tanks fitted with bulldozer shovels for filling in ditches.

The attached engineers had prepared a formidable arsenal of explosive devices to deal with the obstacles. In addition to the usual bangalore torpedos, satchel and pole charges, and flamethrowers, a number of "snakes" had been constructed. These were long pipes filled with explosive which were to be pushed by the tanks into the barbed-wire entanglements and then exploded. The chemical mortars were on hand to provide smoke screens and a preliminary softening up was to be carried out by the fighter-bombers. On paper, the plan was well thought out and it was clear that the 5th Division meant business. The day before the attack, Technical Sergeant Reeder from B Company carried out a daring reconnaissance of the planned line of advance. In spite of enemy fire, he wormed his way through the wire at the southwestern corner of the fort, and once inside he made his way around his unit's initial objective, the battery marked E on the plan. Returning safely, he again set out over the same route with one of the tank company's officers.

Owing to the inevitable bad weather the promised air support failed to arrive, although during the afternoon the fighter-bombers did manage to drop some napalm. Unwilling to wait, General Irwin gave the order for the attack to commence on schedule at 1200. During the preliminary assembly, however, disaster was already hovering in the wings. One of the tanks lost its "snake" and both tank-dozers were in trouble—one with a broken fuel line and the other with a slipping clutch. By the time the troops reached the wire covered by a smoke screen, all the "snakes" had become detached and were abandoned.

B Company managed to penetrate the wire in the southwestern corner as the supporting armor blasted a way through for them. Leaving the pillboxes to be mopped up later, the men rushed through aggressively, using the cover provided by the many shell craters and the bushes which grew on top of the fort. They headed for the two concrete barracks (3 and 4), being met with determined opposition from enemy small arms. Technical Sergeant Reeder was wounded early in the attack, but the troops had been well-briefed on the terrain. The supporting tanks used their guns and machine guns to occupy the defenders while the engineers made futile attempts to blast their way into the barracks. By 1400, however, B Company was established on and around its initial objectives.

E Company in the northwest corner was not so lucky. They managed to break through the wire, but as on the previous occasion, they were then met by an intense hail of fire. As the tank-dozers, whose job had been to fill in the ditch, were inoperative, the supporting tanks could not get inside the fort and had to content themselves with firing at the outlying pillboxes. The slopes were too steep to permit them to advance ahead of the infantry, who had no choice but to dig in just outside the wire. There they remained, most of the time under heavy fire, for four days until they were relieved—only 85 officers and men marched back out of a complement of 140.

Therefore, the rest of the story of the Fort Driant operation is concerned with the activities in the southwestern corner.[9] The commander of B Company, Captain Anderson, arrived inside the fort hard on the heels of his leading squads, accompanied by a small staff of radio operators and runners. One of the radiomen, looking for a place to set up his equipment, investigated a bunker, which proved to be still occupied by the enemy. He alerted Captain Anderson, who jumped into the trench in front and heaved a grenade into the bunker. Not satisfied that it had gone off properly, he chucked in another, only to discover that the occupants had escaped from the rear entrance down into the tunnels. The fact that nearly all the various bunkers and observation posts were connected to the underground communications system was to bedevil American attempts to clear the surface of the fort throughout the operation.

Captain Anderson then returned to the breach in the wire to hurry on the next platoons, but his suspicion was aroused by another bunker. Collecting grenades from his runners and covered by a rifleman, he approached this large concrete structure and threw a phosphorous grenade at the entrance. The doors to such bunkers in the Metz forts had a blast wall in front of them with a way around at each end, but a favorable wind blew the smoke inside. As nobody shot at him, Anderson went nearer and heaved in two more grenades for good measure. Out stumbled six Germans waving a white piece of cloth, three of whom were badly wounded. One of the two officers was found to be from the Officer Candidate Regiment, the 3rd Battalion of which formed the bulk of the garrison, under the command of Captain Weiler.

The bulk of B Company by that time were occupied in trying to force an entrance into barracks 3 and 4. These were two-story concrete blocks whose walls were more than four feet thick. Their roofs were flush with the ground, but their rear walls were exposed in a trench and the doorways were barred by an iron palisade. Although tanks and one of the self-propelled guns had been brought to within 30 yards range, they could only chip the reinforced concrete, and it was at this stage that the momentum of the attack was temporarily lost. The neighboring forts and other German artillery had opened up on the top of Fort Driant, which coupled with machine gun and mortar fire, began to take a steady toll of the attackers.

The man who regained the initiative was Private Holmlund who managed to clamber on top of Barrack 3 where he found a number of ventilator shafts. Although under fire, he simply kicked off the covers and stuffed bangalore torpedos down the openings. The explosions went off in the basement and the occupants came tumbling out. Holmlund later reported, "I could hear 'em swearing and trampling over one another trying to get out."

It soon became clear that most of the enemy had escaped along the tunnel to Barrack 4, because when the Americans had cleared the first building and tried to get into the passage they were driven off by a burst from a machine gun. Holmlund was awarded the Distinguished Service Cross for his part in this action but was later killed on the fort when checking the positions held by his squad. The men on the surface at Barrack 4 were unable to perform the same feat as there was an accurate cross fire laid on the roof, but one of the self-propelled artillery tubes managed to blast in one of the doors. By then the American squad was down to only four men, but they rushed inside and cleared the bunker room by room.

Another platoon passed through the men fighting around the barracks and moved toward the southernmost battery (E). They had four flamethrowers with them, but only one could be persuaded to work properly. The 2nd Platoon established themselves around Battery D; and the commander, Lieutenant van Horn, in an example of foolhardy bravery, rushed the entrance to the main barracks (A), supported by only one rifleman. Both men were killed on the spot.

Although his men were on their objectives, Captain Anderson was in difficulty during the late afternoon. His men were scattered all over the surface at the southern corner of the fort, and it was clear that with the available weapons the men were not going to make much of an impression. He had to organize the position for defense and simply try to hang on against enemy counterattacks and an ever increasing volume of fire. He set up his command post in Barrack 3, around which he placed the tanks, guarded by infantry who simply dug in where they could.

At 1700, the reserve G Company, commanded by Captain Gerrie (who distinguished himself at Dornot), began to arrive on top of the fort, although far too late to be able to achieve anything, as darkness was already falling. Had they brought up promptly behind B Company, they might have gained their objectives, which were the two northern batteries B and C. As it was, they could not see where they were going and the inexperienced men went to ground on the right flank of B Company.

It is probable that, during the night, the German garrison was reinforced, which was quite easy as they held the road up from Ars-sur-Moselle and the lower end of the Mance ravine. Erupting from the maze of tunnel exits onto the surface, they pressed home a number of vigorous counterattacks. Toward dawn it seemed that G Company would be routed; but just in time, reinforcements arrived in the shape of K Company, 2nd Infantry Regiment.

Thus by the morning of the second day, the Americans had a toehold on the southern edge of the fort occupied tenuously by three infantry companies, two of which had suffered heavy casualties. Below them sat an enemy virtually undamaged and secure in the knowledge of adequate overhead protection. Neither of the two barrack blocks that had been captured was in any way vital to the overall defense of the fort, and 110 casualties had already been suffered (roughly 50 percent of the first two companies deployed!). Colonel Yuill was ordered by the divisional commander to hang on and extend his area of occupation, and in the background, General Patton is reported to have said, "if it took every man in the XX Corps, [he] could not allow an attack by this army to fail."[10] Thus, the die was cast.

During the day, further futile efforts were made to break into the batteries and the main barracks, while the Germans brought up every gun available to fire onto the surface of Fort Driant. Movement on the surface in daylight became impossible, and the only method of bringing in supplies was by the tanks that had been allocated to the artillery observers. The men simply went to ground wherever they could in the maze of trenches and concrete shelters, and any attempts to break into the tunnels were beaten off by the garrison. As soon as darkness fell, the Germans again burst out onto the surface from all directions, causing confusion and more heavy losses among the dwindling band of Americans. The enemy had all the advantages— surprise and knowledge of the ground, safe cover from their own and American artillery, and secure communications with the rear.

During 5 October, the enemy artillery kept up their pounding of the surface of the fort, while the GI's, who had intended to be the besiegers, became in turn the besieged. Although the actual guns of the fort could not be depressed sufficiently to fire against attackers on the surface, the two guns of Battery Moselle were used most effectively to create tree bursts over the approaches to the southwestern corner. During the late afternoon, the following report was received at headquarters from the officer commanding G Company. The poor grammar can be accounted for by the fact that the officer concerned had had no sleep for at least 48 hours and little food.

"The situation is critical a couple more barrages and another counterattack and we are sunk. We have no men, our equipment is shot and we just can't go. The troops in G are done, they are just there whats left of them. Enemy has infiltrated and pinned what is here down. We cannot advance nor can K Co., B Co. is in same shape I'm in. We cannot delay any longer on replacement. We may be able to hold till dark but if anything happens this afternoon I can make no predictions. The enemy artillery is butchering these troops until we have nothing left to hold with. We cannot get out to get our wounded and there is a hell of a lot of dead and missing. There is only one answer the way things stand. First either to withdraw and saturate it with heavy bombers or reinforce with a hell of a strong force. This strong force might hold here but eventually they'll get it by artillery too. They have all these places zeroed in by artillery. The forts have 5-6 feet walls inside and 15-roofs of reinforced concrete. All our charges have been useless against this stuff. The few leaders are trying to keep what is left intact and that's all they can do. The troops are just not sufficiently trained and what is more they have no training in even basic infantry. Everything is committed and we cannot follow attack plan. This is just a suggestion but if we want this damned fort lets get the stuff required to take it and then go. Right now you havn't got it. (*signed*) Gerrie, Capt. Inf."[11]

This was a sober statement of fact written by a gallant soldier, not a panic-stricken cry for help. At about the time this message was received, it was obvious to the division commander that the attack was stalemated and that a painful decision would have to be made. B and G Companies had been reduced to around a hundred men between them, and after a meeting of the company commanders present at the fort, a number of officers reported back to the battalion command post. On the basis of information received, General Irwin decided that the only course was to denude the line even further and to bring in fresh troops. He therefore organized a task force to be commanded by the assistant division commander, Brigadier General Alan Warnock, who was to take charge of the continuation of the Driant operation.

During the night of 5/6 October, the battered remnants of the 2nd Battalion, 11th Infantry were relieved by the incoming 1st Battalion, 10th Infantry. The men were pulled back to the shelter of Barracks 3, and from there stumbled through the dark to safety, carrying their wounded on stretchers. The following morning, more troops from the 3rd Battalion, 2nd Infantry, arrived, and together with the entire 7th Combat Engineer Battalion, they made up the strength of Task Force Warnock. It was decided that the attack would restart on 7 October, but as daylight surface movement had proved to be more or less impossible, the emphasis would be placed on an attempt to penetrate underground into the tunnel system.

During the whole operation, a vast concentration of American artillery had been amassed to counter the enemy batteries and to support the infantry. In spite of ammunition shortages, virtually the whole of corps artillery became involved, including 8-in. and 240-mm howitzers. They certainly managed to cause casualties when the Germans emerged during the night, but little damage was done to the fort itself in spite of somewhat optimistic American reports. The corps artillery historian wrote, "Our 240-mm and 8-in. howitzers had been unable to knock out or neutralize the steel-turreted guns of Forts Driant and Verdun. A few direct hits had been obtained but they merely 'slipped off' without causing damage."[12] This was fair comment as a recent inspection of Fort Driant made by the author produced no evidence of any of the guns having been dismounted. All that can be seen are grooves and abrasions on the surface of the turret plating. However, the above source goes on to state that 155-mm self-propelled (SP) guns sited in open emplacements fairly close to the target "entered into a gruelling dangerous six-week duel to emerge victorious in the end. . . . As the enemy guns elevated into firing position, that was the start of a furious direct-fire duel. By faster and more accurate fire our gun crews made it so hot for the enemy that they invariably broke off firing and retracted to non-firing positions. In this manner our gun sections achieved almost complete neutralization of the enemy guns. . . . The failure of an enemy gun to reappear indicated damage inflicted. Subsequent inspection after the final surrender of the forts revealed several of the guns damaged." All that is certain is that field artillery of the calibers available in 1944 was not adequate for dealing with forts designed to withstand the siege guns of a bygone era.

The plan for 7 October called for a simultaneous attack both above and below ground. Careful scrutiny of the newly-arrived, detailed plans showed that the tunnel ran from 3 and 4 Barracks to Battery P and from there via Battery D into the main central barracks. It was decided to attempt to penetrate along this tunnel while the troops on the surface extended their slender hold and kept the enemy occupied. The previous day, the fresh troops engaged in some preliminary skirmishing, during the course of which a troublesome pillbox to the south of battery E was captured. An infantry squad was installed inside and a sound-power telephone link with battalion headquarters was rigged up. During the night, frequent calls to this post were made, to be answered with assurances that everything was OK. At headquarters, the plans for the attack on the following day were discussed in the vicinity of this phone, but unknown to those present, the bunker had been recaptured by the Germans. An English-speaking officer had been placed there with orders to answer the telephone, which he apparently did to the satisfaction of all concerned! At any rate, the attack failed to achieve surprise.[13]

Preceeded by an artillery barrage, the 1st Battalion, 10th Infantry, jumped off at 1000 hours on 7 October and succeeded in recovering much of the ground in the south of the fort during the day, ground which had been abandoned when the 11th Infantry withdrew. That, however, was all, and during the afternoon they were severely counterattacked from both flanks. Two valuable platoons were wiped out and the commander of B Company and two forward artillery observers were taken prisoner. Stiffened by 3rd Battalion, 2nd Infantry, troops, the 1st Battalion managed to hold their positions, but between then and the abandonment of the operation, no further useful gains were made on the surface.

All hopes were thus pinned on the subterranean campaign; although Commandant Nicolas, as the expert on the spot, advised against it. C Company, 10th Infantry and engineers entered the tunnel at Barracks 4 but found their way barred by an iron door. Working in the cramped space of the passage (three-feet wide and seven-feet high) the engineers blew a hole in the two-inch thick door, only to find that the other side had been blocked by a tangle of scrap metal, including old gun barrels and other debris. This extended 20 feet back along the tunnel and was stacked right up to the ceiling, having obviously been placed there by the Germans when the Americans captured the surface areas of the two barrack blocks.

The only way to shift that lot was to cut it piece by piece, and a lull ensued until welding equipment could be brought up during the night. Working in the dark, the men managed to clear the debris by mid-morning of 8 October but were then faced by another iron door which was presumed to be the last hurdle before reaching Battery E. These limited gains, however, had not been made without great difficulty. The main problem was the fumes caused by the explosion of the charges and from the welding gas. After each charge the men had to be evacuated and the issue of respirators proved to be ineffective. In addition, it was thought that enemy were about to take a stand, as sounds of digging were plainly heard in the tunnel indicating the possibility of a countercharge.

To counter this, a 60-pound beehive charge was rushed into the tunnel and placed against the door. When it was exploded, the carbide fumes released were so intense that the area had to be evacuated for two hours. In fact, the fumes crept back into the upper parts of the barracks where many of the troops were sheltering and the wounded were being tended. The half-gassed men rushed to gulp fresh air through the rifle slits in the outside walls, and the bolder spirits chose to risk the artillery outside rather than the fumes within. All sorts of expedients were tried to create some form of ventilation, but visibility below ground remained limited to a few feet in any direction.

Finally an engineer officer managed to crawl back into the tunnel, to discover that only a small hole had been blown in the door. But before more explosives could be produced, the Germans opened fire with a machine gun and grenades along the tunnel. Sergeant Klakamp, an engineer, jumped forward and frantically began to build a parapet of sandbags, helped by the few men who could be deployed in the limited space. The enemy countered this by exploding a charge, but when the fumes cleared again, the Americans managed to mount a machine gun on top of their barricade, exchanging occasional fire with the enemy during the night.

On the surface, an attack on the two southern batteries (E and D) planned for the night of 8/9 October was abandoned owing to the general confusion. General Warnock had brought in fresh troops in the shape of the 3rd Battalion, 2nd Infantry, and had stationed them in Barracks S, but it had proved impossible to establish cohesive company and platoon positions in the limited space available. The daylight attacks had proved too costly, but night operations tended to degenerate into individual combat against the Germans, who swarmed up from the tunnels and bunkers. Between 3 and 8 October, 21 officers and 485 men were either killed, wounded, or missing. In view of the relatively small numbers of troops involved and the total lack of success, this was a high price to pay indeed.

During the morning of 9 October, General Patton sent General Gay to represent him at a meeting with Generals Walker, Irwin, and Warnock, where the whole question of continuing the operation was discussed.[14] General Warnock pointed out that further surface attacks would be far too costly, and stated that in his opinion the fort should be surrounded and the enemy destroyed underground. As this would have required an extra four infantry battalions, it was clear that the idea was a nonstarter, and General Gay reluctantly gave the order for the operation to be abandoned. In doing so he obviously had Patton's agreement, who showed great common sense in this case, although this was the first publicized defeat suffered by his Third Army. Previous reverses in the Metz area had been cloaked by placatory "bromides" but the actual withdrawal from a publicized objective could not be easily hidden.

In the meanwhile, the subterranean skirmishing continued, the 2nd Infantry having relieved the 10th Infantry in the unenviable task. They set about improving the baffle wall, and in spite of the dust and the choking fumes, made it six-feet thick and reaching almost up to the roof. On top they mounted both a machine gun and a bazooka crew to control the line of the tunnel, in spite of the fact that the Germans could be heard busily working in the vicinity. Then it happened. At about 1650, a tremendous explosion ripped through the tunnel, killing four men and wounding eight others. Fumes filled the whole of the confined space, seriously gassing a further 23 men. What caused the explosion seems to be unclear—either it was accident or design on the part of the Germans. What is incredible is that it did not bring down the roof of the tunnel, as the men on the spot estimated its force as three times that of the standard 60-pound beehive charge.

Again, as soon as the fumes cleared, the intrepid men actually went down inside and rebuilt the wall, stationing an NCO and two men on top to keep the enemy from occupying the tunnel. This was a suicide job as relay after relay was picked off by sniper fire or grenades bounced off the floor.

This stalemate was to continue for an additional three days as the state of the troops steadily worsened. Water was getting short and ammunition began to run out. Fighting in fact ceased as the men clung to their positions with ratlike tenacity. The dead and wounded piled up, and those who survived in the open stood in their foxholes in their own filth, unable to move for even the most basic human needs. Those under cover fared little better as they lay choking in the dust and fumes.

The actual evacuation was carried out after dark during the night of 12/13 October with hardly a shot being fired by the enemy. The tired and dazed men staggered away down the hill and through the woods. In addition to many dead and some prisoners, they left behind them six tanks, which were later destroyed by American artillery. As the infantry evacuated the shelters, the rear guard parties of engineers moved in with orders to blow up everything that could possibly be used by the garrison at some later stage. They placed their charges in the bunkers, shelters, and tunnel entrances, with fuses timed to explode at various delayed intervals, and as a further refinement, bangalore torpedos were left in the utility conduits with six hour delay fuses. In all, a total of 6,000 pounds of explosive were left behind as a memento of their brief stay.

The last troops left the surface of the fort at 2330 hours under the blanket of a massive artillery barrage, and an hour later, the first explosions from inside the fort were heard. All that remained was to try to surround the place as far as was possible and to wait for a more favorable opportunity.

Thus, somewhat ingloriously, ended one of the toughest and most difficult small operations of the war. Although such comparisons may be invidious, it is tempting once again to look back at the First World War, as the Driant operation reminds one of the small actions fought by groups of survivors among the German redoubts around Thiepval on the first day of the Somme battles in 1917. Even if they had been available, it would have been pointless to pour in more troops as there was no room to maneuver on top of the fort. The only method of dealing with the place quickly and cleanly would have been the special RAF bombs, but they too were not available. Although the initial idea of capturing the fort would have improved the position for a general attack when supplies became available again, it would not have led to a general rolling up of the German front. For this there were simply not enough allied troops available, and those that were would have been faced with a succession of Fort Driants, being forced to fight from fort to fort.

In the attack, 5th Infantry Division lost 64 killed, 547 wounded, and 187 missing—roughly half the attacking force, and many more were temporarily disabled by gassing or simple exhaustion. German casualties are impossible to calculate, but were almost certainly not nearly as high. Their high command made a field day of the victory, and the Wehrmacht Report of 19 October included the following statement: "In the course of the successful action at Fort Driant, Captain Weiler, commander of the 3rd Battalion, Regiment Stressel [misprint for Stössel, CO of the Officer Candidate Regiment] and Lieutenants Woesner and Hohmann displayed exemplary courage. With their assault groups they surrounded and destroyed superior enemy forces in the casemates and tunnels of the fortress."[15]

The only positive result of the affairs from the American point of view was that the commanders concerned finally recognized the futility of attacks on the forts with the facilities at their disposal. A crash training program was instituted while the fort garrisons were contained by outpost lines until the time would be ripe for a grand encircling movement. The story of the operation was then conveniently forgotten, being far too unimportant to be worthy of a place in the generals' memoirs. From his lofty perch as army group commander, General Bradley was able to inject a note of impatience into the otherwise tragic event. "During October he [Patton] undertook an unauthorized pecking campaign against the enemy fortress position at Metz. When I found him probing those battlements, I appealed impatiently to him. 'For God's sake, George, lay off,' I said, 'I promise you'll get your chance. When we get going again you can far more easily pinch out Metz and take it from behind. Why bloody your nose in this pecking campaign?' George nodded but the diversion went on. 'We're using Metz,' he said, 'to blood the new divisions.' Though I was nettled over George's persistence in these forays at Metz, I declined to make an issue of it."[16]

This was nonsense as there were no "new" divisions in the area; the only troops "blooded" were the poorly trained replacements who were thrust unprepared into the heat of battle. Fort Driant deserves to be remembered as a monument to the courage of two great combat units, the Officer Candidate Regiment and the U.S. 5th Infantry Division, and especially to the 2nd Battalion, 11th Infantry, who had already given of their best at Dornot.

A 1940 German air photo of Metz, showing some of the forts and the line of hills to the west. (*A. Kemp Collection*)

150 mm howitzer turrets of "B" battery at Fort Driant. (*O. Andersen*)

Surface exit of a troop shelter. It was from positions such as these that the American troops on top of Fort Driant were constantly attacked. *(O. Andersen)*

A "snail" type observation post. *(O. Andersen)*

Artillery armored observation post near Thionville.
(*O. Andersen*)

A typical infantry firestep in a "Feste" type fort.   (*O. Andersen*)

Tanks abandoned on top of Fort Driant after the attack was
called off. (*A. Kemp Collection*)

An M-10 tank at the Koenigsmacher Fort near Thionville.
(*National Archives*)

Troops of Third U.S. Army advance under fire into the outskirts of Metz.
(National Archives)

Street fighting in Metz.   (*National Archives*)

Barracks entrance at Fort St. Quentin, one of the last to surrender.
(A. Kemp Collection)

Soldiers of Third U.S. Army carry the American flag over the grass-covered roof of Fort Jean d'Arc, the last Metz fortress to surrender.

(National Archives)

Fifth Infantry Division troops clear S.S. barracks in Metz.

(National Archives)

Fifth Division troops pinned down in Metz. *(National Archives)*

Mopping up in Metz. (*National Archives*)

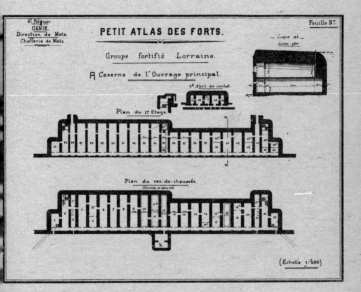

Plan of main barracks in the Lorraine fortified group.

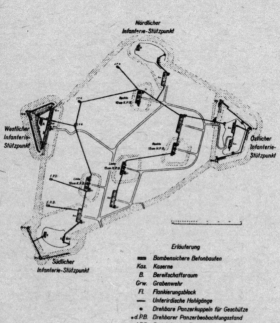

Nördlicher Infanterie-Stützpunkt

Westlicher Infanterie-Stützpunkt

Östlicher Infanterie-Stützpunkt

Südlicher Infanterie-Stützpunkt

Rechte 10cm K.P.B.

Rechte 15cm K.P.B.

Linke 15cm K.P.B.

Linke 10cm K.P.B.

Erläuterung

▬	Bombensichere Betonbauten
Kas.	Kaserne
B.	Bereitschaftsraum
Grw.	Grabenwehr
Fl.	Flankierungsblock
───	Unterirdische Hohlgänge
●	Drehbare Panzerkuppeln für Geschütze
● d.P.B.	Drehbarer Panzerbeobachtungsstand
● f.P.B.	Feststehender Panzerbeobachtungsstand
	Infanterie Wachtürme
░░░	Drahthindernis
---	Für 5 cm Kan. oder MG. vorgesehen gewesene
───	Für 7,7 cm Kan. Scharten (Schußrichtung)

Bild 28

Feste Kaiſerin bei Metz (Bauzeit 1899 bis 1905)

Plan of Fort Jean d'Arc, Metz

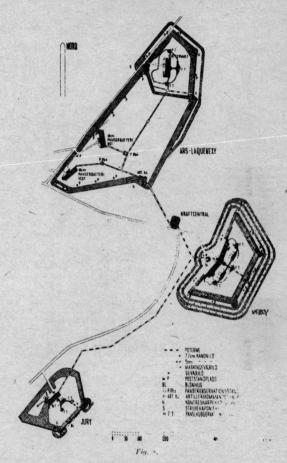

Fig. 8.

Plan of the Marne fortified group

AFFUT CUIRASSE POUR CANON DE 10 c/m (Type allemand)

_____ Echelle approxim.te 1/20e _____

_____ Légende _____

A	Calotte en acier extra dur au nickel (0,16 + 0,04)
B	Avant-cuirasse en fonte dure
C	Culasse
D	Bâti
E	Pointage en direction
F	Flasque
1	Volée renforcée
2	Collier d'embrasure
3	Doublage en tôle (eau)
4	Articulation de la crémaillère
5	Jaquette
6	Rainure guide
7	Point d'attache de la chaîne du contrepoids
8	Frein
9	Manivelle pour le soulèvement de la coupole
10	Plateforme
11	Plancher
12	Contrepoids
13	Levier
14	Couronne dentée
15	Monte-charge
16	Chaîne de Gall

Cross section of a 100 mm gun and turret mechanism of a Metz fort

THIRD ARMY DISPOSITIONS
Evening, 5 September 1944

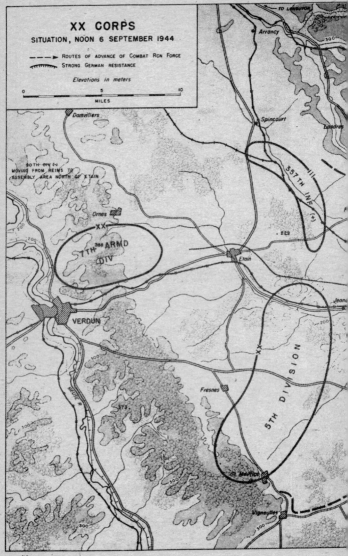

XX CORPS

SITUATION, NOON 6 SEPTEMBER 1944

- - - ► ROUTES OF ADVANCE OF COMBAT RCN FORCE
mmmm STRONG GERMAN RESISTANCE

Elevations in meters

0   5   10
MILES

TO LONGUYON

Arrancy

Spincourt

Landres

Damvillers

357TH INF (+)

90TH DIV (-)
MOVING FROM REINS TO
ASSEMBLY AREA NORTH OF ETAIN

Ornes

228

XX

7TH 388 ARMD

DIV

Etain

Jeanne

VERDUN

XX

200

300

5TH DIVISION

Fresnes

373

St. Maurice

300

300

Vigneulles

300

F Barnell

Rombas

Elms 48

Audun-
le-Roman

3 Rcn

THIONVILLE

341

Nilvange

B 43 Rcn

Trieux

Hautecharge

569 V G

Mairy

Uckange

Mondelange

Briey

258

Talange

Houconcourt

Maizières-
lès-Metz

Abbeville

200

Ste. Marie
aux-Chênes

Argancy

C 43 Rcn

St. Privat-
la Montagne

Amanvillers

Conflans

Jarny

Verneville

No. 462

Gravelotte

Mars-la-Tour

Rezonville

Bois
des Ognons

METZ

Vionville

Ars-sur-
Moselle

3 Rcn

17 35

Buxières

Chambley

Gorze

Dornot

Novéant

Corny

Arnaville

3 Rcn

Lorry

Pagny-
sur-Moselle

3

Thiaucourt

Le Pont-à-Mousson

XX
XII

Vigny

MOSELLE R.

SEILLE R.

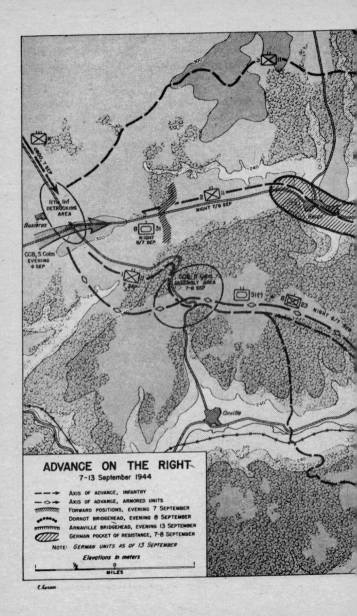

ADVANCE ON THE RIGHT
7-13 September 1944

- - -> AXIS OF ADVANCE, INFANTRY
- - o> AXIS OF ADVANCE, ARMORED UNITS
FORWARD POSITIONS, EVENING 7 SEPTEMBER
DORNOT BRIDGEHEAD, EVENING 8 SEPTEMBER
ARNAVILLE BRIDGEHEAD, EVENING 13 SEPTEMBER
GERMAN POCKET OF RESISTANCE, 7-8 SEPTEMBER

NOTE: GERMAN UNITS AS OF 13 SEPTEMBER

Elevations in meters

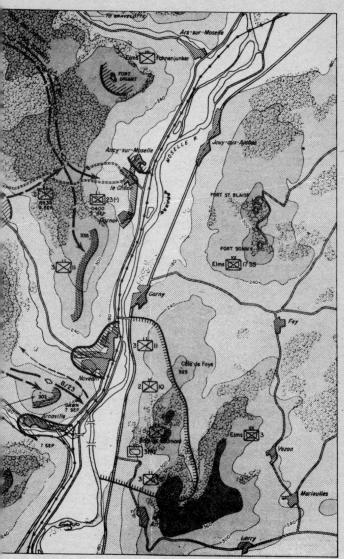

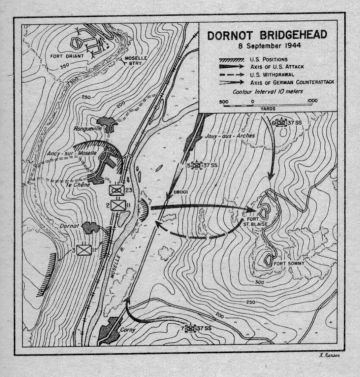

DORNOT BRIDGEHEAD
8 September 1944

/////////	U.S. Positions
	Axis of U.S. Attack
	U.S. Withdrawal
	Axis of German Counterattack

Contour Interval 10 meters

500   0   1000
YARDS

FORT DRIANT

MOSELLE BTRY

350

300

250

200

Rangueville

Ancy - sur - Moselle

le Chêne

Dornot

Jouy - aux - Arches

6 ⊠ 37 SS

5 ⊠ 37 SS

0800

23

2   II

3   II

FORT
ST. BLAISE

FORT SOMMY

300

250

200

Corny

7 ⊠ 37 SS

R. Hansen

ADVANCE ON THE LEFT
7-13 SEPTEMBER 1944

Unit positions, night 7/8 September

Axis of US counterattack, 8 September

Forward positions, evening 10 September

Forward positions, evening 13 September

Elevations in meters

Printed by Defense Mapping Agency Topographic Center

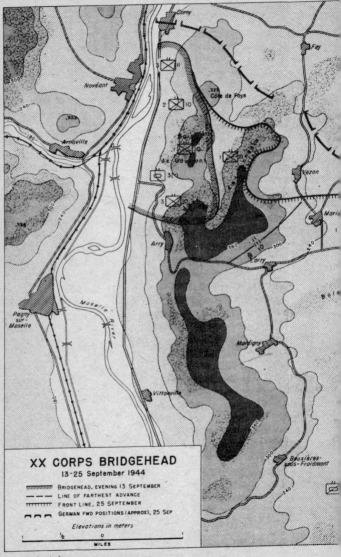

XX CORPS BRIDGEHEAD
13-25 September 1944

⊓⊓⊓⊓⊓	BRIDGEHEAD, EVENING 13 SEPTEMBER
– – –	LINE OF FARTHEST ADVANCE
⊓⊓⊓⊓⊓	FRONT LINE, 25 SEPTEMBER
▭ ▭ ▭	GERMAN FWD POSITIONS (APPROX), 25 SEP

Elevations in meters

½   0   1
MILES

R. Johnstone

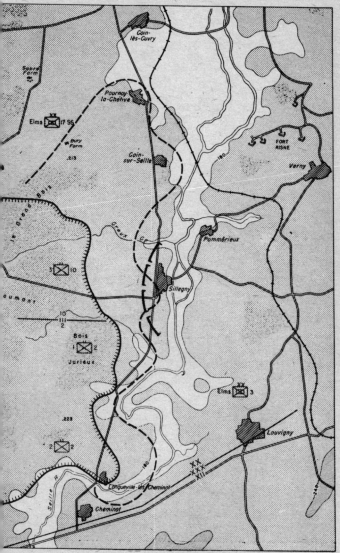

Coin-
lès-Cuvry

Sapré
Farm

Pournoy-
la-Chétive

Elms XX 17 SS

Bury
Farm

.213

FORT
AISNE

Coin-
sur-Seille

Verny

190

Le Grand Bois

Pommérieux

Greux

3 XX 10

Sillegny

10
2

Bois

2 XX 2

Jurieux

Elms XX 3

.223

Louvigny

2 XX 2

XX
XXX
XII

Seille R.

Longueville-lès-Cheminot

Cheminot

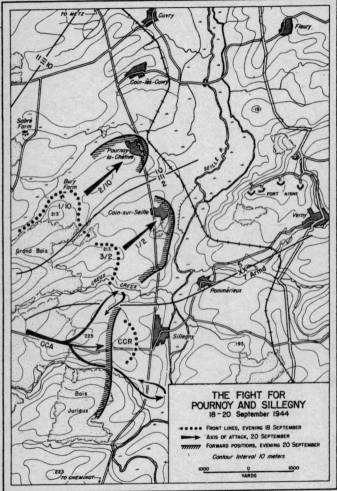

THE FIGHT FOR
POURNOY AND SILLEGNY
18 - 20 September 1944

••••• FRONT LINES, EVENING 18 SEPTEMBER
▬▬► AXIS OF ATTACK, 20 SEPTEMBER
/////// FORWARD POSITIONS, EVENING 20 SEPTEMBER

Contour Interval 10 meters

1000   0   1000
            YARDS

R. Hanson

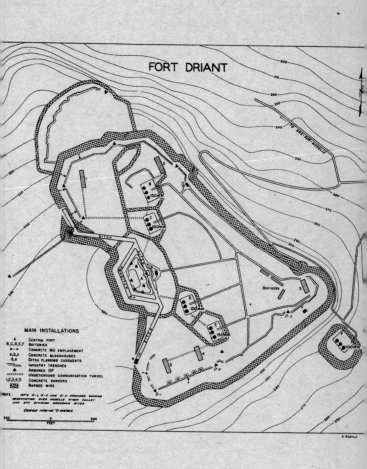

FORT DRIANT

MAIN INSTALLATIONS

A	CENTRAL FORT
B,C,D,E,F	BATTERIES
↦	CONCRETE MG EMPLACEMENT
a,b,c	CONCRETE BLOCKHOUSES
d,e	DITCH FLANKING CASEMENTS
⊥⊥⊥⊥	INFANTRY TRENCHES
▲	ARMORED OP
═══════	UNDERGROUND COMMUNICATION TUNNEL
1,2,3,4,5	CONCRETE BUNKERS
▨▨	BARBED WIRE

NOTE: OP's O-1 AND O-2 PROVIDE SUPERB
OBSERVATION OVER MOSELLE RIVER VALLEY
AND 5TH DIVISION CROSSING SITES

Contour interval 10 meters

500   0   500
FEET

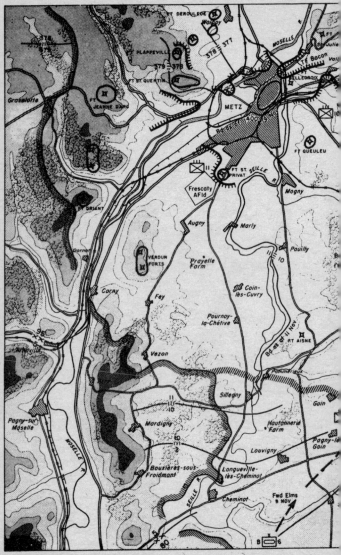

FT DÉROULÈDE

Woippy

FT ST. Julie

MOSELLE R.

378 — 377

FT Bacon

PLAPPEVILLE

BELLECROIX

379 — 378

FT ST. QUENTIN

METZ

Gravelotte

FT JEANNE D'ARC

Bd. 95. of 1300 IS 16

FT QUEULEU

FT DRIANT

FT ST. SEILLE
PRIVAT

Frescaty
AFld

Magny

Augny

Marly

Dornot

VERDUN
FORTS

Prayelle
Farm

Pouilly

10

Coony

Fey

Coin-
lès-Cuvry

Pournoy-
la-Chétive

Vezon

Bd. 95 of 11 Nov

FT AISNE

Pommérieux

Arnaville

Sillegny

Goin

Pagny-sur-
Moselle

MOSELLE R.

11
10

Mardigny

Hautonnerie
Farm

Pagny-lè-
Goin

10
11

Louvigny

Bousières-sous-
Froidmont

SEILLE R.

Longueville-
lès-Cheminot

Cheminot

Fwd Elms
8 NOV

80

B   6

R. Limbach

BATTLE FOR METZ

ENVELOPMENT FROM THE SOUTH

8-19 November 1944

///////// FRONT LINE, MORNING 8 NOVEMBER
C⊃ 5TH DIVISION OBJECTIVE
///////// POSITIONS REACHED 12 NOVEMBER
➤➤ AXIS OF ADVANCE, CCB, 6TH ARMD DIVISION
➤ AXIS OF GERMAN COUNTERATTACK, 13 NOVEMBER
▬▬▬ FORWARD POSITIONS, NOON 19 NOVEMBER
⬭ GERMAN POCKET, NOON 19 NOVEMBER

ELEVATIONS IN METERS

0   200   250   300   350 and above

0   1   2   3
MILES

Printed by Defense Mapping Agency Topographic Center

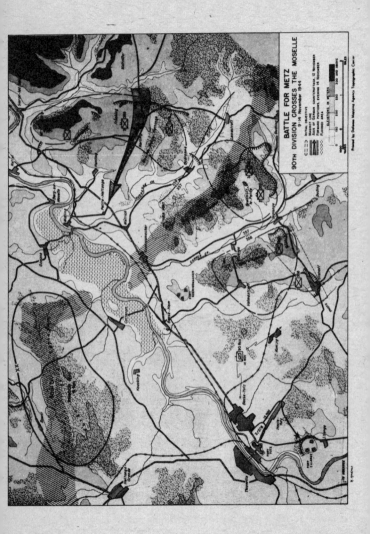

BATTLE FOR METZ
90TH DIVISION CROSSES THE MOSELLE
9–14 November 1944

INITIAL OBJECTIVE
ARREST LINE
AREA OF GERMAN COUNTERATTACK, 12 November
FORWARD POSITIONS, EVENING 14 November
FLOODED AREA

ELEVATIONS IN METERS
0   50   100   150   200   200 AND ABOVE

Prepared by Defense Mapping Agency Topographic Center

$$\equiv 7 \equiv$$

The October Lull

Apart from the activities of one regiment of the 90th Infantry Division, which was occupied in trying to capture Maizières-les-Metz, fighting along the XX Corps' front virtually ceased after the abandonment of the Driant operation. The Third Army was still a victim of the general logistical shortage, and with the limited manpower available, there was nothing for it to do but contain the enemy positions and wait for better times. Combat became reduced to patrol skirmishing and long-range artillery duels—as and when the ammunition shortage permitted. Along the 40-mile front of XX Corps, two U.S. infantry divisions strengthened with cavalry and other miscellaneous units faced four understrength German divisions, which had the advantage of well-fortified positions, and in the north, the line of the Moselle.

During part of the lull, the American manpower crisis in the sector was relieved a little, but not enough to warrant offensive action. From 21 September to 11 October, the 83rd Infantry Division was loaned to XX Corps to guard the northern flank. This unit temporarily replaced the cavalry screen to the north of Thionville and occupied positions from there northward into Luxembourg. Its activities are of no concern to the history of the Metz operation, but the presence of the division did mean that the weak spot on the left wing of the corps could be strengthened. After 11 October, when the 83rd was transferred to the control of Ninth Army, it was replaced by Task Force Polk, which returned to guard the line of the Moselle. This was the reinforced 43rd Cavalry Reconnaissance Squadron, filled out with some artillery, a poorly equipped FFI (*Force Française de l'Intérieure*) battalion, a combat engineer battalion, and a "simulated" armored unit.

In such a position of stalemate, one automatically tends to think in terms of the situation on the Western Front during the First World War. There, however, the trench lines were continuous and constructed (at least by the Germans) in depth. During the autumn of 1944 in Lorraine, the Americans held their line extremely thinly, relying on chains of outposts with the few available reserves held in the rear. To keep the outpost line manned, they were forced at times to rely on engineer units insufficiently trained in infantry tactics and on platoons of service troops. It was in fact lucky for XX Corps that their opponents also had problems of their own and were not seeking much in the way of active confrontation.

General Walker was able to put the lull to good use by instituting a much needed period for rest and training. The tired units were pulled out of the line in rotation and sent to rest camps in the rear. For the first time since the breakout from Normandy, the mens' personal comfort supplies arrived together with such items as sports equipment. There was mail from home and the chance to write letters in reply, hot baths, clean dry clothing, and adequate hot meals. Shows and films were laid on to boost morale. More importantly, a serious training program was organized in the area of the Maginot Line forts to the west of Thionville. There, the men were taught how to attack fortified positions, benefiting from the lessons learned during the earlier part of the campaign. A whole variety of new methods were tried out, based on a firm determination not to become involved in another Driant fiasco.

As far as the wider strategic background was concerned, the emphasis was still in the north. During October, Montgomery's 21st Army Group was busy attempting to clear the Scheldt estuary leading up to Antwerp, where the First Canadian Army was involved in bitter fighting against an equally determined enemy. The first minesweepers did not reach the port until 3 November, and it was not until the end of that month that Antwerp was fully operational. First U.S. Army continued their battles around Aachen until 21 October when they finally captured it—the first major German city to fall to the Allies. This freed the U.S. First Army to take part in a new general offensive, but by the end of the month, no serious dent had been made in the western defenses of Germany.

From the middle of the month, planning was in progress at various levels for a resumption of the Allied advance. This will be dealt with later in detail insofar as it concerns the final attack on Metz, but the overall SHAEF plan still placed the emphasis on the northern thrust toward the Ruhr. However, the broad-front strategy would still apply in that the Third Army would ultimately be released to go for the Rhine when the supply situation permitted. Patton had to use the enforced lull to conserve stocks and build up a reserve capable of putting him over that distant goal.

The commanding general prowled around his sector during this time "like a caged tiger" in the process living up to his nickname of "Ol' Blood and Guts." Draconian penalties were meted out to units that did not live up to his high standards of appearance, and according to the cartoons of the period, drivers in transit would rather make a detour of several hundred miles than risk driving through the Third Army rear areas. There is, however, no real evidence that his love of spit-and-polish caused a morale crisis in the Third Army. It may at times have been resented, but the men were proud to belong to Patton's outfit. Their real enemy was the weather. It rained in torrents, making it extremely difficult to comply with the dress regulations. Polished boots were an impossibility in the clogging mud of Lorraine that autumn.

It was not until the third week of the month that the first reinforcements arrived in the form of the 95th (Victory) Infantry Division. This unit was fresh from the United States and was commanded by Maj. Gen. Harry Twaddle. Between 18 and 21 October it relieved the battered 5th Infantry in the southern bridgehead, where it received a valuable and comparatively gentle introduction to combat conditions. The 95th did not apparently suffer from the usual teething problems suffered by other "green" units, and when the time came for action, it operated well at all levels. In point of fact, the 5th Division had been in constant contact with the enemy for 44 days on the date that they were relieved.[1]

The other stalwart unit of XX Corps, apart from engaging in the attack on Maizières-les-Metz (to be described separately), was still containing the western fortified salient while other parts were strung out along the banks of the Moselle toward Thionville.

THE GERMAN SITUATION DURING OCTOBER

We have already seen that there was a change of command at Army Group G toward the end of September, when General Balck took over. Although Cole states that the first intimation Balck had of the planned Ardennes offensive was on 1 November,[2] this is belied by the former's chief of staff, von Mellenthin. At a meeting with Hitler on 20 September, the two German officers were taken into the Fuehrer's confidence and told about the offensive in outline.[3] Balck's mission was to hold Alsace-Lorraine at all costs and to avoid forces earmarked for the offensive having to be sidetracked to Army Group G.

The German commanders were under no illusions about their ultimate fate, fully realizing that the quiet period was but the lull before the storm. Their basic problem was to foretell when and where the attack would come, and the solution was not difficult as there were few possibilities. Mellenthin correctly divined the future course of the battle, as a good staff officer should: "We anticipated that the next American attack would come through the historic 'Lorraine Gateway' between Metz and the Vosges. This was the aim of the notorious 1914 Plan 17, and Castelnau was defeated by Rupprecht between Chateau Salins and Morhange.... During late October it became very clear to me that another big offensive was impending on our front.... We estimated that one of the American thrusts would come through Thionville and we anticipated another big push in the Château Salins area, aimed directly at Saarbrücken; the effect of these two drives would be to 'bite out' the fortress of Metz."[4]

The lull in active combat was also utilized by the Germans for a wholesale regrouping of their forces. Of immediate importance to the future conduct of the Metz battle, Division No. 462 was forced by OKH (Army High Command) to part with the Officer Candidate and NCO School troops. They were transferred out of the fortress, as on no account could they be allowed to be left behind in a futile siege operation. Many of them were needed as cadres for the new Volks-grenadier divisions that were in process of formation. This in effect meant that two of the three regiments directly defending Metz were more or less dissolved. The crack troops were replaced by a number of low-grade units that had originally been intended for use in the Westwall. According to Mellenthin, "The defensive strength of the Metz garrison was reduced, not numerically but in fighting efficiency."[5]

In recognition of their fighting abilities, the members of the Officer Candidate Regiment were granted the right to wear an armband inscribed *Metz 1944*.[6] Their commander, Colonel von Siegroth, was promoted to major general and became a minor hero. The resistance put up by the regiment was used by the propaganda people as a justification of Hitler's doctrine of holding positions and immediately recapturing ground lost by counterattacking. Their fame, however, was well deserved, whatever one may think about the ideals for which they were fighting. In addition, it must again be emphasized that they were not SS troops, in spite of American opinions current at the time.

When the crack troops were withdrawn, the Metz garrison was reorganized as the 462nd Volksgrenadier Division with three regiments, each of two battalions. Under the command of Major General Luebbe, the division remained an organized force and the Ia (chief of staff) was Major Zimmermann after 5 October. The exact order of battle is somewhat confused, but was probably somewhat as follows:

1. 1215 VG Regiment, Made up from the remainder of the Officer Candidate Regiment; new commanding officer, Colonel von Stoessel.
2. 1216 VG Regiment, Made up from remainder of the NCO School Regiment; commanding officer, Colonel Stolz.
3. 1217 VG Regiment, Parts of the 1010th Security Regiment plus the replacement battalions; commanding officer, Lieutenant Colonel Richter.
4. Artillery Regiment 1462, 3 light and 1 heavy batteries; Colonel Palm.
5. Anti-tank battalion 1462, 3 companies; commanding officer, Captain Lautenschlager.
6. Fusilier Company (or battalion?); Probable commanding officer, Major Voss.
7. Pioneer Battalion 1462; commanding officer, Captain Hasselmann.

8. Communication company 1462; commanding officer, Captain Friemel.
9. Divisional Combat School, Field Replacement Battalion 1462; commanding officer, Captain Gratwohl.

The authority for the above order of battle[7] states that the latter formation included an independent unit known as *Festungsgruppe Driant* (Fortress Group), which I have been unable to confirm elsewhere. The only documentary evidence for the activities of the division from this period to survive is a section of "Daily Orders." These in themselves are uninteresting but do illustrate that, in any army at any time, there is someone in the orderly room busy with a typewriter.[8] The following are a sample:

No. 14. 18.9.44   The fuel position requires that as far as possible all motorized vehicles be replaced by horse-drawn transport.

No. 24. 28.9.44   This includes orders concerning the issue of soap, dusters and brooms. It also forbids "requisitioning" from civilians. In this context it must be remembered that Lorraine was not occupied territory but an integral part of the German *Reich* where the citizens were protected by German law.

No. 37, 11.10.44   Orders concerning delivery of *Heeresdruckschriften.* (Army printed forms.) The whole series of these orders is full of examples of all sorts of forms that were required.

No. 60. 5.11.44   An order forbidding manufacture of "souvenirs" from *Wehrmacht* metal.

Another odd item from this period was the presence of a large German railway gun in the area. It seems that this weapon was used along the main north-south railway lines running parallel to the front because it fired both at XX Corps and XII Corps. On 5 October, the XX Corps Artillery command post, located in the buildings of a school at Jarny, was shaken by a number of explosions from heavy enemy artillery. Immediately a number of men were sent out to search for shell fragments, during which the assistant S-2 was shot in the leg by an overenthusiastic sentry and had to be evacuated to England. Calculations established the fact that the shells fired were from a 280-mm gun, but finding it was not so easy, as the gun was parked in a convenient tunnel during the day. It fired again on 7 October and immediately American heavy guns opened up on the suspected position, possibly inflicting some damage, as it disappeared for nearly two weeks. On 19 October, firing from a position to the southeast of Metz, it fired 20 rounds at Jarny, and the following day, information was received that a large railway gun was in the repair shops at Metz. Helped by air observation, the 733rd Field Artillery Battalion poured 120 rounds from their "Long Toms" onto the target, starting large fires and demolishing the sheds. Subsequent information from intelligence stated that a large-caliber weapon had been destroyed and a number of the crew killed.[9]

Besides those in Metz, there were other changes along the rest of the German line facing XX Corps. To the south, the opposition in the bridgehead was still the 17th SS Panzergrenadier Division. Mellethin says that on account of the loss of experienced officers and NCO's and the arrival of inexperienced replacements, its combat efficiency was impaired. However, according to Colonel Koch, the Third Army intelligence chief, this division was one of the Third Army's "favorites."[10] "Whenever it appeared, things were bound to happen. When it broke contact, things were bound to happen elsewhere." He tells the story of a patrol from the 17th SS that crossed the Moselle at Corny during the night of 31 October and was captured the following morning at Bayonville. When searched, it was found that one of the prisoners was carrying a map showing the precise location of the division command post near Peltre (southwest of Metz). As a result, this was heavily bombed on 8 November and apparently heavily damaged.

To the north of Metz, along the line of the Moselle as far as the Thionville area, were two divisions. On the left was the 19th Volksgrenadier Division, the two regiments of which had suffered losses of between 15 to 20 percent. It had ten heavy antitank guns, one medium and two light artillery battalions, but no self-propelled assault guns. On the right was the 416th Infantry Division. This had arrived from Denmark at the beginning of October to replace the 559th Volksgrenadier Division. Having been occupied in a static security role, the 416th had no combat experience and was composed mainly of elderly men. The German command slightingly nicknamed it the *Schlagsahne* (whipped cream) division on account of the calorie-filled individuals who served in it. Mellenthin regarded it as fit only for defensive combat.

The German numerical superiority, however, was a delusion as none of their units had more than a small proportion of armor and general motor transport was almost nonexistent. Allied air power meant that it was extremely difficult for the Germans to move supplies and reinforcements, and convoys and trains had to run at night. Patton may well have grumbled about priority of supply to the north, but Balck was in the same boat. His needs were always subservient to those of the units fighting around Aachen and in Holland, as well as those units being assembled for the Ardennes operation.

The latter also meant that Balck had to reckon with losing most of his armor, which was his only chance of being able to hold a mobile reserve capable of reacting to the American attack that was bound to come. For example, 3rd and 15th Panzergrenadier Divisions were withdrawn into reserve behind the Rhine; and although in theory under the command of von Rundstedt as Commander-in-Chief, West, in practice only Hitler could authorize their employment. Balck had been glibly ordered to form a reserve of four infantry and three armored divisions, but OKW had failed to provide the means. In effect, when the American offensive was launched in early November, only the 11th Panzer Division was available behind the German First Army front.

Although Mellenthin had predicted where the attack would come, the Germans were still not sure, but they did discount a frontal assault on Metz. They realized that their only chance lay in fighting a defensive battle as a delaying action and to use some form of elastic defense—in direct defiance of the Hitler doctrine of holding on to territory. The coming battlefield favored defense and had been somewhat improved by man. Apart from the Metz fortifications, there was the Maginot Line, which blocked the way to the Saar. Although this had been built by the French to stop an attack from the northeast and had been used by the Germans as a convenient source of scrap metal, some of the guns could be made to fire and the maze of ditches and pillboxes could be used for defense.

The Weststellung, the construction of which had been ordered as far back as 24 August,[11] was envisaged as a series of fieldworks in advance of the Westwall (with which it should not be confused). This work was to be carried out by the civilian population, and Himmler was in charge of the project in his capacity of chief of the replacement army. Local control was in the hands of the party officials, which in the case of the Moselle district, was the Gauleiter, Josef Buerckel. It was all very well for Hitler to issue such orders, but there were neither the skilled personnel nor the material available to carry them out. Interference by the Nazi Party led to clashes with the military authorities about where the line was to run; and in Lorraine, there was the additional problem of divided loyalties within the local population, who should have been wielding the spades. However, some antitank ditches were dug and a large number of mines were laid.

In view of the lack of antitank guns, mines were to form the main defense against American armored vehicles in the German First Army sector. Literally thousands were laid, but the mines could not compensate for the German lack of air support. Throughout October, the Germans apparently imposed strict ammunition rationing in order to be able to build up stocks, but this was not apparent to those American troops involved in Patton's "limited attacks" at Driant and Maizières-les-Metz.

THE OPERATION AT MAIZIERES-LES-METZ

A glance at the map of Metz and the fortified positions to the west of the city will show that there was a gap between the northern edge of the Fèves Ridge and the river. This flood plain is traversed from north to south by the main Metz-Thionville road and railway, and offered the only way into the city avoiding the fortifications. It was along this axis that the French forces made their last attempt to break out from Metz in 1870.

During September 1944, part of the 7th Armored Division had cleared this road as far south as the industrial mining town of Maizières-les-Metz, which at the time had a population of some 3,000 (it was known to the Americans as "Mazie"). Its possession would improve the start line for any advance into Metz itself.

Between 10 and 14 September, the 7th Armored had made a number of attempts to move into the town but had been forced to retire into the shelter of the Bois de l'Abbé—defeated by intense fire coming from the opposite bank of the Moselle and from the tops of the two huge slag heaps that dominated the area. When the armor departed to the south for employment in the Arnaville bridgehead, the sector was taken over by the 90th Infantry Division, whose 357th Regiment held a line about five miles long running roughly from

Talange on the river, to St. Privat to the southwest. As the rest of the division was occupied in the futile attacks against the fortifications, this section of the front was relatively quiet, although the opponents were a part of the NCO School Regiment.

The idea of capturing Maizières first appeared on 24 September, when the initial enthusiasm for frontal attacks had begun to wane. General McClain put the proposal to corps to use the operation both as a training exercise and to gain a valuable jump-off position. This was in line with General Walker's wise concept of "active defense," although some of the operations planned on account of this were hardly prudent. Walker reasoned that if an army were forced on the defensive through lack of resources to press home the attack, the enemy must be kept busy in order not to lose the initiative. As opposed to the Driant operation, the attack on Maizières was well thought out and not too costly in terms of casualties. The general advantage lay with the Germans; because of the general lull, they could reinforce the sector via their internal lines of communication, whereas the American line was overstretched, to say the least.

On 3 October, the same day as the main phase of the Driant operation got under way, two companies of the 357th Infantry Regiment moved out from the shelter of the Bois de l'Abbé and occupied the slag heap to the north of the town. This gave excellent observation over the whole area, and logically, it should have made Maizières untenable by the enemy. One account says that the attack was led at the charge by a sergeant blazing away with two pistols in true Wild West style. Just as he reached the top, he fell dead from a bullet in the head—one of three casualties suffered in the surprise assault. "So it was with good infantrymen—if they were good soldiers, they usually were killed."[12]

Although violently shelled and counterattacked, the two companies remained masters of the slag heap. However, instead of the Germans withdrawing from the town below, as they should have done according to theory, they simply dug in. The houses of Maizières were solid and many of them were built from stone. In addition, the mines, industrial plants, and railways formed a perfect defensive terrain. The only way for the Americans to reduce the place was to bomb it flat and then fight from ruin to ruin.

The next stage of the attack was planned for 7 October and laid down in Field Order No. 16, issued by the regimental commander,

Colonel Barth.[13] This called for the 2nd Battalion to send two companies into the town from the direction of the slag heap, supported by tanks, tank destroyers, and all the available artillery. The previous afternoon a fighter-bomber sortie caused heavy damage, and just after dawn, the assault went in. The enemy launched a diversionary counterattack against the slag heap. There the enemy were cut down by automatic weapons as they tried to scramble up the bare slopes, and the two American assault companies could thus move toward their objectives with little hindrance. By dusk they had managed to occupy most of the northern part of Maizières and had a foothold in the factory area. There, however, they were held up by determined infantry and large numbers of S-mines. The latter was a small but vicious antipersonnel device which, when triggered, flew into the air and detonated at waist height. All that could be seen of S-mines above ground were three small wires.

That night the Germans brought in reinforcements, including part of the 19th VG Division, which had not previously been part of the Metz garrison under the 462 VG Division. They also began to mass artillery, in spite of ammunition rationing; and in all, three battalions of guns were positioned to the northeast of Metz on the far bank of the river.[14] Within Maizières, almost every house was transformed into a miniature fort, held by a small group of determined Germans, strengthened with wire, mines, and sandbags. The central strongpoint was the Hôtel de Ville or city hall.

Emboldened by their initial success, the 2nd Battalion continued their attacks during the following days. They moved slowly forward using demolition charges and flamethrowers while their support artillery hammered the roads leading into Metz in an effort to discourage reinforcement. At the southern end of the town was another slag heap which was blanketed with smoke shells in an effort to hamper enemy observation. Some tanks were brought up after the mines had been cleared, but they proved a liability in such close range fighting. This was simply a job for the infantryman, who often ended up struggling eyeball to eyeball with his opposite number.

By 11 October, little further progress had been made by the one battalion committed, and Colonel Barth recommended the use of two. The inability to use sufficient troops to outflank the position meant that fighting had to take place along the main north-south street and among the maze of walled gardens and yards surrounding the houses. However, as was usual during the Metz operation, there simply was no spare battalion available, and the only solution was to replace the tired 2nd with the 3rd Battalion. But plans for a coordinated attack were stymied when on 13 October, a Third Army order instituted a freeze on all ammunition of more than 3-inch caliber, and a 95 percent reduction in expenditure was achieved.[15] This is but another graphic illustration of the straits to which Patton had been reduced by the supply situation and is in direct contrast to the popular image of the unlimited material resources of the U.S. Army at the time. One palliative was the extensive use made of captured guns and ammunition.

Without artillery support, it was obviously impossible to reduce Maizières by all-out assault. It was therefore decided to do the job piecemeal using the ruins as a practical (if dangerous) training ground for street fighting. Carefully-planned attacks with strictly limited objectives were made at company, platoon, and even squad level. Experiments were made and lessons learned. As an addition to the physical combat, a psychological warfare unit was attached, which used a loudspeaker to exhort the Germans to surrender. William Weaver, who was present at the time, wrote that this outfit might well "have been saved the rigors of battle for all the good it did. Those minions of the Great God Hitler, with whom we were confronted, were not gullible enough to fall for such persuasion and only laughed at it."[16]

The Germans seem to have been content to go along with this limited form of warfare, not taking the initiative themselves. It was during this period that General McClain left the 90th Division to take command of a corps, and he was replaced by Brig. Gen. James van Fleet. The latter had led the first regiment to land on D-day.

His appointment to command the "Tough Hombres" coincided with the completion of plans for the final assault on Metz, and as a result, ammunition supplies were freed for the Maizières operation. The situation had become intolerable with both Americans and Germans sharing the same town, and General van Fleet ordered the 357th Infantry to clear the place by 2 November. Colonel Barth, realizing correctly that the Hôtel de Ville was the key to the enemy defenses, decided that this had to be tackled first. On 20 October, a 155mm SP gun was brought up to within 150 yards of the building and fired 10 rounds into it. However, it took six more days before the infantry got near the place.

By 26 October, an infantry company managed to reach the lower floor but was driven out again by piles of burning mattresses and by flamethrowers. The following day, four ten-man assault teams were formed. Three of them were brought to a halt by mines and wire, but the fourth group managed to crawl in through a hole blasted by the SP gun. Once inside they fought hand to hand until all but one were killed or wounded. The survivors who could still move managed to escape while the one unwounded man held off the Germans.

On 29 October, five infantry companies with massive fire support were employed in what was to prove the final assault on Maizières. The divisional artillery fired counterbattery shots to keep the German gunners busy, while three infantry companies attacked abreast toward the town center from the south. Two more moved in from the north. As they advanced, the artillery fired a creeping barrage, smashing the houses and detonating mines. The enemy began to fall back in some confusion and to surrender in small groups. By the evening the bulk of the town was in American hands, except for the city hall and a few houses to the south and east.

The following day these remaining pockets were cleared, and when the infantry finally entered the city hall, they found only corpses. Both the commanding officer of the 3rd Battalion, Lieutenant Colonel Mason and the regimental commander, Colonel Barth, were awarded the Distinguished Silver Cross for their part in the operation, the latter having been wounded while leading a platoon attack.

Although the fighting had been bitter, the American casualties had been surprisingly light—55 officers and men during the final attack. German losses cannot be accurately given, but it is certain that the best part of a battalion was wiped out. This was purely as a result of the hold-fast tactic in untenable positions—a delay was imposed but troop losses were out of all proportion to the value of the object defended. However, with the reduction of Maizières-les-Metz, the 90th Division had removed an important roadblock on the way to the heart of Metz and had opened the way for a movement to outflank the fortified salient to the west.

$\equiv 8 \equiv$

Preparations for the Final Battle

THE AMERICAN PLANNING

Although throughout most of October there had been little fighting in
Lorraine, that did not mean that the commanders and their staffs at
various levels had been idle. All were aware that the situation could
not go on forever and that the final assault toward the Rhine was but
a matter of time. Paper planning, however, is a frustrating exercise for
a general, especially one with a temperament like Patton's.

In mid-October, General Eisenhower was faced with an agonizing
choice. He could dig in for the winter with the troops he had, build up
supplies through Antwerp, and strike the knockout blow in spring.
The alternative was to resume the offensive immediately with the
resources that were available. The former plan had the disadvantage
that the enemy would also have time to build up stocks of men and
materials. On top of this, those responsible for the war in the air feared
that production of jet fighters and possession of the proximity fuse
would enable the Germans to break the stranglehold of Allied air
superiority and thus gain a respite from the attentions of the stretegic
bombers.

On 18 October, Eisenhower met Bradley and Montgomery at

Brussels for a top-level conference on future strategy. There, the "great argument" once again reared its ugly head, having been slumbering during the past weeks of comparative inaction. With the prospect of once again getting on the move, both army group commanders staked their claims for the relative slices of the supply cake. Montgomery naturally pleaded priority for his northern thrust to cut off the Ruhr, on the grounds that there were insufficient resources available to support an attack along the whole line. Bradley demanded a double advance to envelop the Ruhr, with Patton coming in from the south via the Saar Basin. The result had to be a compromise between varying national aspirations. Eisenhower agreed, as he had before, that the northern thrust was more important. To appease Bradley, Patton was given the green light for the Saar campaign, "when logistics permit."[1] Bradley, however, writing after the war, stated that the "target date for the First and Ninth Armies" offensive (north of the Ardennes) was fixed for 4 November. The Third Army was to go "by the tenth."[2] The operations of the latter, according to Eisenhower would be "subsidiary to" and "so timed as best to assist the main effort in the north."[3]

Although the Supreme Commander's instructions placed the role assigned to the Third Army in perspective, it would seem that Bradley interpreted this policy declaration somewhat liberally. On 21 October he sent instructions to his army commanders ordering all three armies to be prepared to advance to the Rhine. As far as the Third Army was concerned, the mission was to cross the Rhine in the Mainz-Worms area, but if a crossing could not be immediately forced, the army was to turn northward toward Frankfurt and Koblenz to clear the west bank of the river. The target date for this operation was set for 10 November. However, at a meeting on the same day, it was agreed between Patton and Bradley that "the date of the attack, fixed by weather conditions rather than by the calendar, being after 5 November."[4]

This agreement, however, was preceded by some optimistic pleading on Patton's part. By 17 October his staff had produced a plan for an offensive which would start with a movement by XII Corps to seize a bridgehead across the Seille. Once this was secure, two armored divisions would pour through, one to secure the high ground to the west of Metz while the other would head straight for the Rhine. XX Corps would cross to the north of Thionville, join up with XII Corps behind Metz, and its 10th Armored Division would join in the race for the Rhine. This is odd, for the 10th Armored did not arrive on the XX Corps front until early November!

In a letter, Patton outlined the plan and went as far as to promise Bradley that he could make it to the Westwall in three days, and at the 22 October meeting, he waxed eloquent. He begged to be able to resume the advance at once, and if the Army Group's ammunition reserves were pooled, he could start *within forty-eight hours,* with excellent prospects of success. Bradley, however, was cautious and said that he preferred to wait until the entire Allied front could get under way.[5]

This was a piece of blatant optimism on Patton's part, as he was holding a front of 85 miles with only nine divisions. His XII Corps was fairly concentrated to the east of the Moselle, but to attack within 48 hours as promised, he would have had to completely reshuffle XX Corps, concentrate it in the Thionville area without an armored division, and then assault across the river. Many of the troops were spread out in rest camps and training centers and the inexperienced 95th Division was just settling down in the bridgehead south of Metz. The result would have been chaos, if we can believe the account of the meeting with Bradley.

As a complete contrast to their commander's optimism, the Third Army After Action Report stated, on 30 October, "The supply situation is still incapable of sustaining an offensive if launched immediately." This was the sober judgment of staff officers, but things were obviously on the mend. On 5 November, the date tentatively set by Bradley, the same source reported, "In preparation for renewal of offensive, supplies of gasoline and rations were in a sound condition." Much of this was due to the opening of new railheads directly behind the front line, but items such as tires and diesel fuel were still in short supply. As we have seen, ammunition had become a particular problem in the static war conditions that had prevailed, with XX Corps relying largely on captured guns; but on 6 November, "artillery ammunition again became available for expenditure in substantial quantities."

It is a paradox that Third Army planning at this time was based on the employment of III Corps, which, in effect, never took part in the Metz operation. This unit had arrived as a staff formation from the U.S. and had been assigned to Patton on 10 October—since then it had sat in Normandy for lack of divisions to make it operational. Plans A and B are given in detail in the After Action Report for 18 October 1944, but are summarized below only as an indication of how planning for a major attack can alter right up to the moment of assault. Plan A was the above-mentioned scheme for the two main corps to advance on either side of Metz with the new III Corps operating on the left wing. Plan B called for III Corps to make the Thionville crossing while the other two corps moved together south of Metz. The one common factor of all the schemes put about at the time was an obvious determination not to assault Metz frontally, but rather to surround the city.

It soon became apparent, however, that there would not be enough troops available to employ III Corps and that Patton would have to make do with what he had. At a meeting with his air and ground commanders on 1 November, he laid down the essence of what was to be the final scheme for the main offensive on the Third Army front, except insofar as timing was concerned. It was assumed that the First Army would attack in the north on D-day, and on D+1, XII Corps would move across the Seille. At the same time, the 95th Division would carry out a diversion, followed on D+2 by the 90th Division who would cross the Moselle north of Thionville. As soon as the XII Corps had cleared the front, the 5th Division would attack from the XX Corps southern bridgehead. Even then, III Corps appeared in the outline as it would ultimately be given some troops "to mop up the Metz pocket."

However, there were problems in the north which led to the postponement of the First Army attack, and on 2 November, Bradley asked Patton if he was prepared to go it alone. The answer was predictable and it was agreed to go as soon as good flying weather enabled the fighter-bombers to get to work—if not, the attack would be started on 8 November regardless of the weather. As a result, Bradley issued an operational directive on 3 November, ordering the Third Army to envelop Metz from north and south and to destroy enemy troops withdrawing from the area, *after which* they were to advance to the Rhine. This is the first written confirmation that I can find of Metz being treated as a specific objective by 12th Army Group. All previous directives had spoken in broad terms of the Saar and the Rhine.

The same day, Patton issued his directives for the coming operation. The XX Corps was to contain the fortifications to the west of Metz and to cross the Moselle at Koenigsmacker with a minimum of one infantry and one armored division. Once safely across, the corps was to seize road and rail facilities in the vicinity of Boulay, and in conjunction with XII Corps to the south, to destroy enemy forces retiring from Metz. Only then was there talk of the Rhine.[6]

One problem facing the whole of the Third Army at the time was one which could not be solved by the best of planning staffs. The Lorraine area was in the throes of the worst autumn weather for years, characterized by cold temperatures and torrential rain. At the beginning of October, total strength was down to 220,000; 18,000 of whom were out of action with influenza, trench foot, and other weather-conditioned ailments. Vital supply space had to be taken up with shipments of extra blankets, socks, tents, and waterproof clothing. Ultimately the weather was to prove the undoing of much of the optimistic planning, not only on account of bogged-down vehicles, but because it also negated so many of the vital air support missions—the one great advantage that the Americans possessed over the Germans.

From army level, we now step down to corps. Although General Walker's staff had also been busy committing plans to paper, their final scheme was based on Patton's letter of instruction of 3 November. The corps had the veteran 5th and 90th divisions, the 95th, and newly arrived from America, the fresh 10th Armored Division, commanded by Major General Morris. On the left wing there was still the 83rd Division, but this played no role in the battle for Metz. Walker only had "operational control" over this unit and it was limited to providing fire cover for the Koenigsmacker crossing. With the above order of battle, the corps had 30 infantry battalions, some 500 tanks, and more than 700 guns. In addition, large stocks of engineer bridging equipment and special supplies for dealing with fortifications had been built up. All this was in contrast to the haphazard efforts to get over the Moselle in September. Patton always scoffed at Montgomery as only being capable of set-piece attacks, but here he was having to force a major river crossing by plan rather than improvization.

On 3 November, XX Corps issued Field Order No. 12 to the division commanders.[7] Although an earlier plan had spoken of the "reduction" of the Metz forts, this order specified the corps mission:

encircle and destroy the enemy in the Metz garrison and capture a bridgehead over the Saar. The primary aim was the "destruction or capture of the Metz garrison without the investiture or siege of the Metz forts." The lesson of the fiasco at Driant seemed to have been well and truly learned.

In detail, the plan called for the 90th Division and the 5th Division to encircle Metz from the north and south, while the western salient would be contained by the 95th Division. Once the city was surrounded, the latter would move in to mop up any remaining enemy resistance. The 10th Armored would cross the Moselle through the 90th Division bridgehead and strike out for the Saar. As a small refinement, the 95th Division was given an additional mission. At 1500 on D-day they were to make a demonstration by crossing the Moselle at Uckange and hold out there for a minimum of 15 hours. Thus the attack was to be two-phased: first, Metz was to be surrounded, and second, the corps would cross the Saar.

However, before this could be put into operation, the troops had to be shuffled around extensively. Between 31 October and the evening of 2 November, the 5th Division moved from their rest areas to reoccupy their old positions in the southern bridgehead, relieving in the process the 95th Division. The latter, moving out regiment by regiment, sideslipped to the north to take up positions around the western fortified salient. There they freed elements of the 90th Division and the infantry of the 10th Armored. The latter unit had been concentrated around Mars-là-Tour, although some of their troops had been placed in the line to cover the reshuffle.

The assembly of the 90th Division was cloaked by a complicated deception scheme. Initially they were moved north into the training area around the Maginot forts near Aumetz—ostensibly for a course in demolishing fortifications. Their vacated gun positions were filled with rubber dummies, with a few real guns interspersed for firing an odd round or two. The deception was known as Operation Casanova, and employed all the tricks in the book. In addition to the dummy guns, sound-deception units were on hand to simulate the movement of vehicles and other equipment. The line of the Moselle in the area of the crossing site was held by the 3rd Cavalry, and 90th Division officers going forward on operational reconnaissance had to paint 3rd Cavalry markings on their jeeps. The 1st Battalion of the 377th Infantry Regiment who were to stage the demonstration at Uckange, were given the markings of the 359th Infantry, a 90th Division outfit. It was not until 7 November that the bulk of the 90th moved into their assembly area situated in the depths of the forest of Cattenom, directly opposite the crossing site—traveling without lights and with their vehicle markings obliterated and their shoulder patches removed.

We know the dates on which these troop movements took place and also the fact that the Metz operation was not given the go-ahead until 2 November. However, in the German Army Group G telephone log there is a record of a conversation between General von Knobels-dorf, CG of First Army, and General Balck, on 24 October. In this, Knobelsdorf says that he has received reports that the 90th Division had moved and "the army assumes" that the 5th Division had relieved the 95th, who in turn had moved to the west of Thionville.[8] This is very strange as there is no evidence from American sources of any deception having been organized before the first few days in November. However, as the subsequent attack by the 90th Division did achieve surprise, one can only assume that the deception operation was effective.

The movements detailed above placed XX Corps on the positions from which it would mount its attack. There was, however, one small nuisance that first had to be eliminated. The Germans had been left with a small bridgehead on the west bank of the Moselle to the north of Thionville. They still occupied the small town of Berg which directly overlooked the planned 90th Division crossing site, a state of affairs that could not be tolerated. Accordingly, during the night of 3 November, the 3rd Cavalry Group was sent to eliminate this outpost. The following morning, operating on foot, the cavalry managed to establish themselves on the hill overlooking the town, but were dislodged by a counterattack during the afternoon. They returned the following morning with massive artillery support, retook the hill and cleared the town—this time for good. This small attack was just one of the many operations that contributed to the success of the Moselle crossing, and during the attack, two Distinguished Silver Crosses were won.

The overall scheme having been fixed, it was up to the divisions to make their individual plans and pass these on to the regiments, battalions, companies, and platoons which were to execute them. It would seem that there was a fair amount of optimism in XX Corps at the time, the men being relieved by the prospect of action once again and having been enlivened by the many pep talks that Patton had been delivering up and down the line.

THE GERMAN SITUATION AT THE TIME OF THE ATTACK

Owing to the lack of surviving documents from lower-level formations, and the fact that many German accounts were written after the war with the benefit of hindsight, it is difficult to accurately assess their situation. However, there is enough information to give a reasonable picture of the opposition facing XX Corps at the beginning of November 1944. This is essential if we are to understand what went wrong in September and why the attack succeeded two months later.

The right wing of the First Army was held by the three divisions of LXXXII Corps, covering a front from Metz along the Moselle to where that river is joined by the Saar. As before, the 462nd VG Division was in Metz; and from there to Koenigsmacker, a front of some 20 miles was occupied by the 19th VG Division. This was commanded by Colonel Karl Britzelmayer, and had a total strength of some 9,000 men. On their right, there was still the 416th (whipped cream) Division under the command of Lt. Gen. Kurt Pflieger. This unit was organized in the normal three regiments, but like a Volksgrenadier division, each had only two battalions. Its strength was estimated at 8,500. The corps had no tanks, although some antitank and SP guns had arrived toward the end of October. Artillery was also limited and included a number of Russian booty weapons.

South of Metz was the XIII SS Corps, although this was SS in name only—most of its units were from the ordinary army. Facing the 5th Division in the southern bridgehead were their old adversaries, the 17th SS PG Division. The chief of staff of the XIII SS Corps was Colonel Kurt von Einem. In a report prepared after the war,[9] he wrote as follows concerning the expected attack: "After combat ceased on 19 October 1944, the corps was of the opinion that the Americans along the whole front had achieved the desired start line for a major offensive. After two weeks had passed from this date, it had to be reckoned with that the enemy preparations had been completed and that the offensive could begin any day. . . . The corps was fully aware that it could not deal with an enemy attack carried out along a broad front. Apart from the well known enemy superiority in materiel, the corps was minus any form of reserve and reinforcements were not to be expected."

At the highest levels there was some confusion about the status of Metz and exactly where the attack would be launched. OKW, OB West, and Army Group G were all involved. The basic question to be settled was whether the Metz garrison should be left to fend for itself or whether it should still be included in the army front. The latter posed a problem if, as expected, the Americans broke through to the north and south. In this case, the wings of the German First Army would be bent back, leaving Metz as a dangerous salient. It would be good tactical sense if the army could withdraw to a more easily defended line, leaving the city to tie down as many American troops as possible. Von Rundstedt did not have much faith in the value of Metz as a fortress, and twice during October he proposed that it be abandoned. OKW, however, as the mouthpiece of Hitler, insisted that it be retained within the general defensive line.

It is quite clear that Army Group G was expecting an attack in the Metz area, and for this reason, the First Army was strengthened at the expense of the 19th Army, its neighbor on the left. From this same source it is also plain that the Germans had a pretty good idea of the American order of battle and were aware of some sort of concentration to the west of Thionville—which naturally led them to conclude that the main assault would be over the Moselle in the north. However, as mentioned in the previous section, there was confusion, no doubt fired by American deception efforts. In his book, von Mellenthin admits that they were convinced that the 14th Armored Division was at Thionville, whereas at that date it had not even landed in Europe. He also states that "during late October it became very clear to me that another big offensive was impending on our front . . . (there were) indications of a strong concentration in the Thionville sector north of Metz."[11]

Knowing that there was no concentration in the area until early November, one can only assume that the writer was confusing his dates or was looking where there was nothing to see. At any rate, as a result of these opinions, Army Group G reinforced the boundary between the 19th and 416th divisions with five field artillery battalions—precisely the position where the American attack was aimed. In addition, more than 20,000 mines were laid on both sides of Thionville.

However, there were contrary statements. On 29 October, in the course of a telephone conversation with Balck, General von Knobelsdorf said that he did not believe that an offensive was imminent as the enemy had stretched their resources far too widely.[12] Four days earlier, speaking to von Mellenthin, von Knobelsdorf said exactly the opposite, believing that the enemy would thin out his line in front of Metz and would try to take the city either with a pincer movement or by attacking from the north.[13]

Whatever the truth of the matter, the German sources admitted that the 90th Division attack achieved tactical surprise, although Army Group G was warned to expect an attack on 9 November. This particular date had a magical significance in Nazi mythology, being known as the *Tag der Bewegung* (the day of the movement). This was the anniversary of the 1923 beer hall putsch, and von Rundstedt sent a message to Balck: "The C-in-C regards a general attack as possible." The irony is that the Americans were apparently blissfully unaware of the significance of the date of their attack—which was determined by weather rather than sentiment.

For Metz itself, in spite of the lack of documentary evidence, we have the valuable postwar report prepared by Lt. Gen. Heinrich Kittel. He took over as fortress commander on 14 November, but had been in the city advising on defense measures since 8 November.[14] We have seen in the previous chapter that the garrison was organized as a Volksgrenadier division after the school troops left in early October, but one of its regiments was transferred to the neighboring 19th VG Division on 1 November (the 1216th VG). This left a gap, and to fill it, the old 1010th Security Regiment was extracted from the 1217th VG and reorganized under the command of Colonel Anton. It was composed of one heavy fortress machine-gun battalion and one fortress infantry battalion (the term "fortress" indicates that it was without vehicles), and Kittel states that its health was poor and the equipment was inadequate.

Thus his command was made up of the three understrength regiments (each worth roughly a battalion), the division troops listed in the previous chapter, and a hodge-podge of miscellaneous units, which were still coming in as late as 17 November. This was in keeping with Hitler's policy of garrisoning fortresses with *halb-soldaten*, and the additions included a number of fortress machine-gun and infantry battalions, a company of sailors, an understrength battalion of the *Reichsarbeitsdienst* (Labor Service), and a *Volkssturm* (Home

Guard) battalion. Of the latter, Kittel said, "Fighting qualities were equivalent to zero and reliability doubtful, as there were FFI men in the ranks." The only available reserve was the 38th SS Panzergrenadier Regiment, which was attached from the 17th SS PG Division and saw service in the city.

Kittel gives the total ration strength for the garrison as about 12,000, but states that the fighting strength of his division amounted to only 5,500 men, few of whom were proper combat troops.

Kittel was a defensive warfare expert who had distinguished himself on the Russian front. He did his best to build up the Metz defenses, until on 12 November, the fortress commander, General Luebbe, suffered a stroke. Thus Kittel was summoned to corps HQ and ordered to take over the unenviable task of stemming the American attack, which by then was well under way. He assumed command officially on 14 November in the command post in the Mudra Barracks which was in the center of the city on the Ile Chambière. The reason for this was that the communication center for the entire fortress was situated under the barracks in the casemates of the older defensive works, and was connected to the outlying forts by buried telephone lines.

The division artillery was split into two sections, due to the chronic lack of mobility, and its commander, Colonel Vogel, was in charge in the north, based on Fort Plappeville. The southern section was commanded by Colonel Palm, CO of the 1462nd Artillery Regiment. The available guns were a mixed bag. By early November, 30 of the turret guns in the forts were in working order, although still without optical sighting equipment or adequate range tables. The forts were still maintained to a certain extent by specialist engineers, who would not allow anyone (even the fortress commander) to enter the works without permission from the General of Engineers at OKH in Berlin!

The field artillery consisted of two battalions of light 105-mm howitzers, one heavy antiaircraft battery and two fixed heavy antiaircraft batteries. This was supplemented by a trainload of assorted guns, mainly Italian booty weapons, which was brought in on 15 November. Ammunition was generally scarce, but the main problem was lack of mobility. Motor-tractors were virtually nonexistent and there was a grave shortage of horses. It seems that the local population, not wishing to back the losing side, were extremely reluctant to sell draft horses to the Germans.

It is clear that during the October lull, the necessary steps had not been taken to ensure an adequate supply for the city. Kittel states that on 12 November (four days after the start of the American attack) there was food available for only two days. That day a train arrived, but instead of the requested rations for one month, only enough for two to three weeks was received. The last train came in on 17 November, after which the city was entirely cut off.

One problem common to both sides, which has been touched on before, was the presence of a large civilian population in Metz. As far as the Americans were concerned, on moral and political grounds, they were precluded from large-scale air and artillery bombardments in support of infantry attacks. They could, however, reckon with a flow of intelligence from French sympathizers and active support from underground FFI units. The Germans too could count on support from some sections of the populace, but had to be constantly on guard against potential fifth columnists. By the time the city was captured, most of the German civilians in the area had been moved away to the east, without much persuasion being required.

We have already seen that during most of October, the Americans were actually outnumbered if you count the divisions available on both sides. By the beginning of November, however, they had been reinforced by two fully-equipped fresh divisions. The Germans had been unable to use the lull to build up their forces and, in fact, their defensive capability had gravely deteriorated—both in terms of quantity and quality of manpower. Four fully-organized American divisions faced four weak German divisions along a linear front of some 40 miles, but as soon as the pincers closed around Metz, General Kittel found himself defending a perimeter of 45 miles with only one understrength division—the German First Army having been forced back and having lost contact with the city.

☰ 9 ☰

The Initial Stage of the November Battle

The XX Corps Field Order No. 12, issued on 3 November, specified that the date of D-day for this operation would be announced. This momentous decision had to be made by General Patton, who spent much of his time anxiously scanning weather reports. On 7 November, the intermittent rain changed to a torrential downpour which lasted for more than 24 hours. General Eddy, whose XII Corps was to lead off, came in to plead for a postponement, but Patton was adamant. He said that the attack would go on, with or without air support, the following day. Thus the die was cast for the assault that would carry his army over the Moselle and on toward the Saar—until the Ardennes offensive intervened to upset everyone's calculations. What follows is basically an account of the activities of XX Corps during the next three weeks as they struggled not only with the enemy but also with the elements and Napoleon's fifth element—mud!

For the sake of clarity, I have broken down the initial stages of the battle, where the units were still spread geographically, into separate accounts of the activities of the various divisions. Books about battles are often difficult to understand on account of the necessity for quoting strings of divisional, regimental, and battalion identifications. Once the various different formations moved into Metz, it has been possible to compress the narrative into a narrower compass.

THE UCKANGE BRIDGEHEAD[1]

As a small contribution to the overall plan, a sideshow was planned, to be carried out by the 95th Division on their northern flank to persuade the enemy that the crossing would take place to the south of Thionville. In addition, the division was to eliminate the small German pocket remaining to the south of Maizières-les-Metz after the 90th Division attacks in October. The regiment assigned to these missions was the 377th Infantry, while the other two divisional units, the 358th and 359th, contained the western fortified salient around Metz. The division field order specified that the attack would be carried out on 8 November—D-day for the XII Corps advance and one day before the rest of XX Corps would get under way. Thus first blood in the final battle for Metz was to be scored by the "new boys" of the 95th.

The 1st Battalion was chosen to make the river crossing, and after the move from the southern bridgehead, they were transferred to the riverbank in the Uckange area. All 95th Division markings were removed, fake message traffic was maintained and they disguised themselves as the 359th Infantry Regiment, by then on the way north toward Aumetz. Their mission was to cross the Moselle, move across the flood plain on the far side and occupy the small town of Immeldange astride the main north-south road between Metz and Thionville. There they were to dig in and wait to be relieved by troops moving down from the main crossing site.

The appalling weather conditions precluded the planned preliminary air attack on the enemy on the far bank, but an artillery concentration was fired. At dusk, a company of the 320th Combat Engineer Battalion slipped across the river, detonated mines, and blew a gap through the barbed wire. At 2100, C Company of the 377th paddled across in 17 assault boats, a distance of some 200 yards. Once over they met with no immediate opposition as the Germans were entrenched further back along the line of the main road, and the 73rd Regiment of the 19th VG Division required some time to react. This is surprising because the activities of the engineers must have made a tremendous racket.

The small group of infantry advanced some 400 yards across the featureless floodplain and then dug in to await daylight. It was then that enemy artillery homed in on them, as they were well within range of the concentration of guns that had been amassed to counter the earlier attacks on Maizières-les-Metz. However, most of the shells fell behind C Company on the crossing site where the engineers were frantically trying to construct a footbridge. On account of the shelling, this had to be abandoned, and A Company was ferried over in the early hours of 9 November. By then, however, the weather had begun to exert its baneful influence. During the previous night the river had started to flood, fed by the torrential rain, and by the morning had burst its banks. The turbulent waters had spread out over the flood plain, doubling the normal width of the river and vastly increasing the speed of the current. The approach road to the crossing site disappeared under the water and all efforts to get a telephone line across were frustrated by the current. Thus the only means of communication were via a frail radio link.

At the same time as the 1st Battalion crossed the river at Uckange, the other two battalions of the 377th launched night attacks on German positions around Maizières. There they ran up against dense minefields that had been laid by the 1215th VG Regiment. Three companies were dispatched at 2100 to drive the enemy from the slag heap to the south of the town, the woods north of Semécourt and around Brieux Château. Advance parties stumbled over trip wires that detonated whole sections of the minefield, causing heavy casualties. The explosions alerted the Germans who pounded the area with artillery, catching the attackers in the open. However, by the morning of 9 November, they held the woods at Semécourt in spite of having been repulsed elsewhere. During the afternoon they regrouped, and with the help of some tanks, they drove the enemy off the slag heap and from around the Château by nightfall. This was mostly grim hand-to-hand fighting as the 1215th was probably the best of the remaining German regiments. The CO of the 2nd Battalion of the 377th, Colonel Walton, led an assault squad personally. When several of the men were killed by a machine gun, he rushed forward. Although wounded several times, he managed to kill the crew and destroy their weapon. For his gallantry he was awarded the DSC—just one of several decorations earned in this series of actions. The enemy were left in possession of a small enclave around the village of Hauconcourt, but by the following day, the rising flood water had isolated the area and no attempt was made to clear it.

By daybreak on 9 November, the 1st Battalion had two rifle companies and a heavy weapons platoon across the swirling river. They then began to move off further inland, bypassed the village of Bertrange, and established themselves on a low hill to the east, out of reach of the spreading water. Although not directly menaced by enemy infantry, shelling and mortar fire were heavy and the men dug in to keep warm. At 0905, the battalion reported back to Regimental HQ: "Two companies are across river. River is very high and we're not sending others over."

The flood waters frustrated all attempts to supply the two companies, who were by then virtually cut off. The speed of the current and accurate enemy shelling made daylight movement across the Moselle more or less impossible—even when outboard motors were attached to the assault boats. It was therefore decided to try air supply by artillery spotter aircraft. Ten L-4's flew throughout the afternoon, each with a "dropper" who had volunteered to squat behind the pilot. Flying at only 25 feet, they managed to deliver 1,080 K-rations, 46,000 rounds of small-arms ammunition, 4,000 rounds of .50-caliber ammunition, medical supplies, cigarettes, water purification tablets, plasma, and even a sack of toilet paper. The drops were certainly accurate; and a platoon leader said, "We got all the rations we needed from the planes." Major Neumann, who flew several missions, reported that he "could see some of our men standing in water in their foxholes. They waved and shouted when we dropped some rations right down next to the foxhole." This was the first of several occasions during the Battle of Metz when such light aircraft were used for resupply missions to isolated troops.

An indication that gentlemanly conduct could still prevail was provided when a boatload of medical personnel, displaying the Red Cross, tried to get over the river. Dragged away by the current, they were met on the far bank by two German soldiers, who emerged from a dugout. In good English the medics were told that they were in the wrong place and were directed further downstream. Somewhat puzzled and suspicious, they managed to return to their starting point where they were redirected by the battalion commander. Setting off for another attempt, they crossed the river and paddled on across the flood plain until they arrived at the outskirts of Bertrange. There, a German officer appeared and told them, "No English troops here. We are taking care of one wounded American. Your troops? Up there." He then redirected them to where the Americans were dug in.

On 10 November, in spite of the danger from icing on the wings, further supply missions were flown. There was worry about dropping mortar rounds as it was feared that they would go off on impact. As an experiment, an aircraft flew over German-held Bertrange and dropped several rounds on the human guinea pigs below. Not observing any explosions, the pilots assumed that it was safe to drop the rounds on their own men.

During the night of 11/12 November, the flood waters began to recede, and the following night it proved possible to ferry across the remainder of the battalion. This was undertaken without loss, as the engineers carried out a feint crossing by running their outboard motors, to distract the German artillery observers.

The operation in the Uckange bridgehead failed to tie down any significant numbers of German reserves. The main attack which started on the following day was immediately recognized to be the more important thrust. Thus the point of the deception was lost. The 19th VG Division did not have any reserves to commit anyway and would soon have realized that only small numbers of Americans were involved. By then the Germans had identified the 10th Armored Division north of Thionville and had observed the buildup of bridging equipment in the area.[2] Even if the flood had not hindered the construction of the bridge, an unsupported battalion could not have achieved more than local harassment. As later transpired, a strong armored task force was required to penetrate into Metz from the north, and only succeeded after several days of bitter fighting.

THE 90TH DIVISION CROSSING NORTH OF THIONVILLE

It fell to the lot of the "Tough Hombres" to achieve what they had been unable to do in September: to force a crossing of the Moselle and establish a viable bridgehead. Although this was "just one more river" on the way to the Rhine as far as the higher echelons of command were concerned, for many 90th men, it would be the last river on the way to "Jordan." The division did not only have to conquer the Germans, but also had to cope with nature in the form of floods, bitter cold, and the ever prevailing mud.

Previous reconnaissance had selected a series of crossing sites in front of the villages of Cattenom and Gavisse. These were about a mile back from the river flood plain and on the opposite bank were the villages of Koenigsmacker and Malling, respectively. Just to the north, high ground ran right down to the river, thus channeling any German approach into the valley and providing a secure anchor for the left wing of the division. Opposite the crossing area there was again about one mile of flat ground until the main road between Thionville and Sierck was reached. Beyond this the terrain rose steeply onto wooded heights. Southwest of Koenigsmacker was a fort of the pre-1914 Metz type, and southwest of Malling was one of the larger forts of the Maginot Line, the *Ouvrage de Metrich*. Cole refers to the latter as a collection of bunkers and field works, but it was in fact, a highly sophisticated fort which had originally been equipped with a number of 75-mm and 135-mm guns in turrets. It was lucky for the assault force that this fort was not in operation at the time, as the Germans only made use of some of the surface shelters. A pair of 75's in a Maginot turret could fire 24 rounds per minute at a range of 12,000 yards. The French reckoned such a turret to be worth a battery of field guns.[3]

Fort Koenigsmacker had been built as part of the Metz-Thionville position prior to the First World War. Between the wars it had been maintained by the French as a backup position behind the Maginot Line. Smaller than many of the Metz forts, it had only one battery of turreted artillery equipped with four 100-mm guns, which were probably in working order. However, it seems that the garrison were unable to make use of them, and although American sources refer to fire coming from the fort, this came from weapons sited on the ridge behind. The position, however, dominated the crossing site, and for this reason the fort had to be neutralized. In spite of general reluctance to assault such works as a result of the Driant experience, the 90th Division would have to tackle the place directly, putting into practice the results of intensive training.

Two days prior to the start of the offensive, the 90th Division was moved under cover into the Forest of Cattenom, directly to the rear of the crossing area. As this was subject to enemy observation from the far bank, all movement was by night, and to hinder the local spies, all unit markings were obscured. The bulk of the troops had to move some 15 miles from the rest areas around Aumetz over roads made treacherous with a liberal coating of mud. The 3rd Cavalry Group patrolled actively to cover this movement and to keep German patrols at bay.

Shortly before the attack was due, the officers of the division were regaled with one of Patton's famous pep talks, which went roughly as follows: "I've been going up and down the line today giving hell to everybody, but I don't need to chew out you bastards. I just stopped by to say hello, because I thought you'd be insulted if I didn't. There's nothing I can tell you sons of bitches. You bastards sure know how to fight."[4] Oddly enough, these sentiments were echoed in a captured German document, which stated, "The enemy (the 90th) no longer considers combat a sport but fights fanatically to hold territorial gains. The morale of his troops is good and he attacks vigorously, even in the face of losses."[5] This reputation among the Germans must have been gained during the futile fighting to gain a foothold in the western fortifications during September.

During the night of 7/8 November, the last of the infantry was secreted in the forest and bridge-building equipment was dragged forward. The plan called for the crossing to be made before dawn on 9 November. On the right, the 358th Infantry was to cross at the Cattenom site, with the 1st Battalion detailed to attack Fort Koenigsmacker. The other two battalions were to move past the fort on the north and establish themselves on the ridge leading southeast. The 359th Infantry was allotted to the Malling site and was to occupy the high ground in front. The 357th, in reserve, was to cross behind either of the assault regiments, secure the town of Koenigsmacker, and then move along the main southeast ridge on which the works of the Maginot Line were situated. The emphasis on these ridge lines was important, because the only road leading out from the bridgehead at Koenigsmacker, ran between them. By following that direction, the 90th would ultimately meet up with the 5th Division men coming up from the south, thus closing the neck of the bag around the city of Metz. Once the bridgehead was established, the 10th Armored Division would cross and move off toward the Saar.

An eyewitness described the weather as "terrible—cold, muddy, and pouring rains. The mud was worst of all, I knew how the infantry must be feeling, The miserable weather and the nasty job ahead would not make their lot any easier."[6]

Just before midnight, the assault battalions of the 358th and 359th began the 400-yard trek to carry their boats to the edge of the water following tapes that had been laid by the engineers. By then the flood plain had degenerated into a bog into which the heavily-laden men sank up to their knees, which imposed a severe physical strain even before they got into action. The fields they were crossing were already partly under water from the rising flood, and the men tripped over barbed-wire cattle fences that were already partly submerged. After negotiating these hazards, the lead battalions clambered into their boats from waist-high water and pushed out into the raging stream. Luckily they managed to cross unscathed and most of them reached the far bank. Oddly enough, the high water had been to their advantage—although nobody would have admitted it at the time. Firstly, the flood had forced the German advanced posts out of their foxholes near the riverbank from where they had retreated to higher ground. Secondly, the water covered the extensive minefield that had been laid on the level ground, and the assault boats simply floated over them. Certainly, by attacking without a preliminary bombard-ment, they achieved a tactical surprise. By 0500 they were established on the far side of the Moselle where they were shortly joined by two more battalions, which did suffer from the attentions of the awakened enemy gunners.

At the other site, the crossing also proceeded according to plan and all three battalions of the 359th Infantry got across safely. They occupied Malling, established themselves astride the main north-south road at Petite-Hettange and then moved off to the east toward Kerling. This was a vital cross-roads village astride the ridge that was their initial objective. There they met the first serious opposition from the enemy, but the 3rd Battalion charged four antitank guns and captured the position.

At Cattenom, the 3rd Battalion of the 358th Infantry crossed, in spite of the fact that the commanding officer was wounded in the hand as he helped to carry a boat. Eight men were needed for each boat and one of his group slipped in the mud, discharging his rifle and manag-ing to hit the colonel. Charles Bryan commanded L Company, and described his unit's part in the operation: "Our assembly point was a cement factory. The Germans had a listening post on the riverbank which was occupied at night. A squad was assigned the job of elimi-nating this. We didn't want any prisoners until after daylight. Their mission was accomplished with a minimum of noise. A two-man German patrol came by the factory while we were there. The security ambushed them, but one was wounded so we put him in a room in the factory. The Battalion HQ and Aid Station was moving in there before daylight. About 0400, K and L Companies had assembled all their men and formed a line of departure on a railroad track running parallel to the river. When it was light enough to see, we advanced up a low hill over open ground. Some Germans were dug in on this hill but we were on top of them before they woke up. Most surrendered but some tried to fight. Since we were integrated, we couldn't fire and had to resort to hand-to-hand combat. One of my best sergeants who had just returned from hospital (wounded in Normandy) could not extract his bayonet from a German's chest. He had to fire his gun and blow the man to pieces. He was able to free the bayonet, but he was smeared with blood and flesh. If he could have changed his clothing and bathed, he would have been alright. As time wore on and the temperature rose, the smell got on his nerves. He was evacuated that night for battle fatigue."[7]

From there the 3rd Battalion of the 358th moved past Fort Koenigsmacker toward Inglange, and as planned, the 1st Battalion occupied the small village of Basse Ham below the fort. From there they began to climb up through the woods toward the perimeter. The fort was roughly pentagonal in shape, measuring some 800 by 700 yards. It was surrounded by the usual multistrand barbed-wire entanglement and a ditch revetted on the outside by a stone wall. Oddly enough, unlike the Metz forts, there was no iron palisade. Inside there were three concrete barracks and the single turreted battery "which had never been fired."[8] These were supplemented by a number of concrete infantry shelters, armored observation posts and trenches. The fort was garrisoned by some 300 men of the 74th Infantry Regiment of the 19th VG Division (an understrength battalion).

This time the attackers were prepared, being equipped with adequate plans of the fort and its underground installations. At 0715 that attack started, and the two companies (A and B) moved through gaps in the barbed wire which had been blown by bangalore torpedos. Initial surprise was achieved in that the attackers managed to get through the wire, across the ditch, and into the trenches inside the fort before the garrison reacted. Once there, however, they came under fire from mortars zeroed in on the trenches, and from sentries in the armored observation posts.

Had the defenders been properly trained in the use of such fortifications, the Americans would never have got that far. Each arm of the ditch could be flanked by machine-gun fire from cunningly-concealed concrete blockhouses, each topped by an observation dome. However, American maps made specially for the attack, show a considerable growth of bushes in the ditch, which should have been cleared by the garrison. Had the Officer Candidate Regiment been there, the story might well have been different.

Learning from previous mistakes, no attempts were made to penetrate into the tunnels. Starting with the troublesome observation posts, two-man squads carrying 34-pound satchel charges ran to the doors of the bunkers, placed the explosive and took cover. After the charge went off, two more men with another charge ran in through the hole and placed it on the stairs leading down to the tunnel system to prevent the enemy from filtering back onto the top of the fort. At one stage a charge was dropped down a ventilator shaft. The resulting explosion was so heavy that it blew a German back up to the surface. At other points, fuel was poured down the ventilators and ignited with a thermite grenade. The problem was that supplies of explosives and fuel were soon exhausted. Everything had had to be hand carried across the river and up to the fort by engineers and infantry already heavily laden with their normal battle equipment, personal weapons, and ammunition. The only way to get supplies across in a hurry was by spotter aircraft, and 500 pounds of explosives were dropped by parachute along the road to the rear of the fort.

During the afternoon, the reserve regiment managed to cross two battalions and by nightfall they had cleared the town of Koenigsmacker. Thus by the end of the first day, the division had eight infantry battalions on the east bank, but the only heavy weapons were a few portable antitank guns. The force was completely cut off, and there was no immediate expectation of a bridge being built. Had the enemy possessed sufficient reserves, the force could well have been annihilated as their only support was from the artillery massed on the west bank. Air missions were impossible, but in spite of this, seven towns and villages had been cleared and the bridgehead was some six miles wide by two miles deep. Efforts to construct a raft at the Malling site had been frustrated when it overturned, dumping its load into the river.

After dark, resupply efforts were started in earnest, cloaked from the inquisitive enemy artillery. An eyewitness described the conditions as terrible: "Crews groped their way across inundated fields. Time and again the craft smashed into submerged fence posts and sank. Fence wire and tangled hedges fouled propellors, rendering motorboats helpless; and out in the stream they were rocked, tossed, and swept off their course.... Once on the other side, the supplies had to be carried through knee-deep mud. Surgical teams operated on the wounded, who were retained as far as possible in the bridgehead— only those whose life was in acute danger without hospital treatment were ferried back. Even perambulators were pressed into service for carrying equipment."[9] There is some evidence that the engineer units responsible for the ferry operation were not quite up to the task. There were cases where boats were abandoned, leaving the infantry to man them themselves, and considerable time was lost on account of this. It would seem that some engineer units were filled up with nonspecialist personnel who were inadequately trained for action under fire.

During 10 November, there was considerable action on the left in the area held by the 359th Regiment. The 3rd Battalion was expelled from Kerling by a spirited German attack, and it was later discovered that the American positions had been pinpointed for the attackers by Frenchmen who sympathized with the Germans.[10] As it was, the regiment was forced to fall back for reorganization and the vital road out of the bridgehead was exposed. Possession of this road was vital if the 10th Armored was to be able to fulfill its mission of moving to the Saar. However, the enemy did not have the reserves to back up the thrust, and backed by massive artillery support, the three battalions advanced again during the morning. By the evening, although Kerling remained in German hands, the Americans held a solid front from Rettel on the river to the high ground north of Kerling and extended south toward Oudrenne in the next valley.

In the center, the 357th moved off to attack the Métrich fort which was their initial objective. The rain had been replaced by fog which hindered movement, but it also made observation difficult for the enemy. It proved impossible to clear the whole area, but by nightfall the works were surrounded and the regiment was firmly established on the vital ridge.

On the right, A and B Companies of 1st Battalion, the 358th were in possession of roughly half the surface of Fort Koenigsmacker. C Company, having repulsed a counterattack against Basse-Ham, then moved up to reinforce the troops on the fort. They approached from the rear, but found themselves faced with a particularly deep portion of the ditch and were forced to move around to the west. Once on top they were able to join the other two companies in repulsing a counterattack by the garrison which erupted from a shelter point in the extreme southeast of the perimeter. The American tactics continued as before, moving from shelter to shelter and destroying them as they went with explosives and fuel, which again had to be dropped by light aircraft. The 2nd and 3rd Battalions, although fired on from the area of the fort and from behind it, managed to slip past during the early morning fog. The latter unit managed to establish themselves on the Elzange ridge, but the former, moving later were pinned down and forced to dig in short of their objective.

After the second full day of fighting, the situation of the troops in the bridgehead was just as precarious. There were still no tanks or tank destroyers on the east bank, so the only support available was from the artillery—"working in mud up their knees and firing round the clock."[11] The infantry were soaked to the skin and half frozen, and it is such conditions that sort out good divisions from bad ones. The 90th kept going. As darkness fell, all attention was diverted to the problems of supply, as by that time, it was taking up to three hours to cross the river. The 1st Battalion of the 359th, the last reserve remaining on the west bank tried to cross, but were forced back by the current. Everything thus depended upon the engineer companies, standing up to the waist in the freezing, swirling water, trying to construct the vital bridges. At midnight, the bare structure of a bridge was in place at Malling, but it was not until the following night that the first vehicles were able to cross. Thus the troops had to simply hang on, depending on the limited supplies ferried over or dropped by the spotter plane pilots.

That was the time for an effective German counterattack, which if pressed home would have caught the Americans unsupported by armor and compressed into a still narrow area and without the eyes provided by air cover. Indeed, the divisional staff were on tenterhooks, apparently unaware of the weakness of the enemy. Purely by chance the 90th Division had hit the boundary between the 416th and 19th VG divisions, which meant that the German corps headquarters had to take over control of the battle.[12]

Early on the morning of 11 November, all three regiments returned to the attack. Their spirit was remarkable in view of the fact that all concerned had had hardly any sleep for 48 hours, were soaked to the skin, and were both cold and hungry. In the north, the 359th Regiment again came under attack just before dawn. The 1st Battalion, which was on the extreme left of the bridgehead was violently shelled and then attacked by a force of some 150 men and three SP assault guns that moved out of the woods to the east of Malling. Luckily the battalion had a number of antitank guns which had been ferried across during the night and were able to knock out two of the German guns. The infantry, however, were put off balance and began to give way. This critical situation was rescued when an understrength platoon of only ten men from A Company charged into the German flank. This was followed up by accurate American artillery fire and another flank attack from a platoon of the reserve battalion, led by Captain Albert Budd. Although seriously wounded, Budd continued to direct his men until the enemy withdrew.

On the right of the regiment, the 3rd Battalion on the high ground to the north of Kerling was also counterattacked by infantry and SP guns, against which their bazookas proved ineffective. In desperation they were forced to call for artillery fire on their own positions. Two of the company commanders were killed as they rallied their men, but the enemy was forced to withdraw owing to lack of reserves to follow up their initial penetration. This sort of action, often fought hand to hand by small isolated groups of men, calls for initiative and great personal courage. Without high morale and thorough training, small units can fall to pieces when their officers are killed and communications break down.

In the center, two battalions of the 357th moved on down the ridge of the Maginot Line, running southeast from the town of Koenigsmacker. The works themselves were manned only by a scratch security detachment of some 250 men, and the forts were more or less inoperative. Specialist troops would have been required to man their complicated power supply and ventilation systems—that particular sector in 1940 had 21 mounted guns and had been garrisoned by 1,400 men. However, disregarding the actual forts, there were a large number of shelters, bunkers, and interval casemates in the so-called Elzange Subsector, in which a determined force could have resisted for days. In accordance with the new tactics for dealing with fortifications, the Americans made no attempt to penetrate into the underground workings. Bunkers that could not easily be taken were simply demolished with explosives, and where opposition was discovered, a few men were dropped off to surround the place. By nightfall, the regiment was on the high ground overlooking Briestroff, well in advance of the units on either flank. This left them with a 4,000-yard carry for supplies across a series of gullies and in broken, wooded country.

On the southern flank of the bridgehead, the 358th Regiment had what the Division After Action Report termed an "exceptional day." During the morning, the 3rd Battalion managed to capture a German relief force of some 150 men who walked into an ambush. They were heading for the fort but their three-man advance party was captured and gave the game away. The 2nd Battalion finally managed to get past the fort to the north, while the 1st Battalion continued the struggle inside, reinforced by G Company. One by one the remaining bunker entrances were blown in, with the result that the garrison was gradually forced back into the underground parts at the southwest corner. The effects of more fuel poured down the ventilators prompted the first surrenders. In the meanwhile, G Company had moved around to the rear of the fort, where they were due to receive a surprise. The Germans in the fort decided that they had had enough and that it was time to retire gracefully. Leading from the rear entrance of the fort was a tunnel that ran some 400 yards north-west toward a well. The Germans filed through the tunnel (apparently about 150 men), and as they emerged from the other end, they ran slap into G Company and were taken prisoner.

In all, the Americans took some 300 prisoners in the Koenigs-macker operation, but the enemy dead were never counted. Their own losses were 111, killed, wounded, and captured. The fort was the only one of the Metz type to be successfully taken by storm, an action which redounds to the credit of the 1st Battalion, 358th Infantry. However, it must be said that they were faced by inferior troops, not to be compared with the Officer Candidate Regiment which so ably defended Driant. Also, the attackers were furnished with adequate plans and were able to surround the fort, thus hindering reinforcement. The area of Koenigsmacker was only half that of Driant and the interior structures were less complicated. This meant that it was possible to occupy the area with the troops available and to isolate the garrison without having to penetrate underground. The new tactics of proceeding systematically to smoke out the defenders had paid off handsomely.

Throughout the day, work had been proceeding on the bridge at Malling. 11 November was Patton's birthday, and Bradley relates an incident when he telephoned his congratulations. Patton told him that the engineers had struggled for two days to build the bridge, and when it was finished, a tank destroyer started across. "As it neared the end, it suddenly veered off the planking and snapped the cable anchoring the bridge to the shore. In an instant the structure snaked and tumbled off downstream. 'The whole damn company sat down in the mud,' Patton said, 'and bawled like babies.' "[13] Another source puts this on 12 November and states that the reason for the collapse was that the bridge was hit by enemy artillery.[14] This version gives the completion of the bridge as 0211 on 11 November, but says that owing to the causeway leading to it being flooded, it could not be used before the morning of the following day. The first vehicles to cross were engineer trucks, on account of their high-chassis construction, and they took with them jeeps, antitank guns, and much-needed ammunition. Finally two tank destroyers made their way over the river, which was slowly beginning to recede, and at this point the bridge was temporarily damaged, causing the loss of the third tank destroyer.

Work on the bridge at the Cattenom site was plagued by difficulties, and the engineers were constantly disturbed by enemy shelling. When one section was ready, it was discovered that the end had settled down on a minefield as the water level dropped. The whole section had to be refloated and the area under it de-mined before it could be placed in position.

However, it is certain that by the early morning of 12 November, there were two tank destroyers in the bridgehead, and that with the flood receding, there was a slight improvement in the supply position—luckily for the 90th Division. For in the meanwhile, there was trouble brewing on the other side of the hill. After the failure of the local counterattacks, the enemy realized that they did not have sufficient forces to disturb the bridgehead, and appealed to OB West for a panzer division. After a day of wrangling with OKW, they were finally allocated the *Kampfgruppe* of the 25th Panzergrenadier Division, which was resting and refitting near Trier. Final permission to use this force was reluctantly given, although it was realized that success by Patton toward the Saar could jeopardize the planned Ardennes operation.[15] However, due to an immediate shortage of fuel, it was not expected that the unit could arrive before 11 November, ready to attack as planned during the afternoon. In fact, the group arrived in dribs and drabs as fuel became available, with the result that the attack was postponed until the following morning.

OB West had ordered that the attack be made due south from

Sierck which lies beside the Moselle, but the plan was changed owing to the unsuitability of the terrain—the force would have had to cross a steep ravine in which a small river called the Montenach flows. Thus at around 0300 on 12 November, the Germans struck the positions of the 359th Infantry, coming in from the east. The force was made up from the 35th Panzer Grenadier Regiment stiffened by ten tanks and assault guns. The first rush drove the 3rd Battalion outposts out of Kerling once again, the vital crossroads on the road leading into the bridgehead. Three hours later the main attack developed along this axis with the obvious intention of penetrating as far as Petite-Hettange and thus directly threatening the Malling bridge. The armor moved along the road with the infantry marching in single file on either side, toward the reserve positions held by the 2nd Battalion—leaving their flank open to attack from the north by the other two battalions, against whom a secondary attack was launched.

First resistance was encountered when the German column ran into an ambush laid by G Company of the 2nd Battalion which was supported by a heavy weapons detachment. The mortars and machine guns of the latter managed to impose a valuable check, and forced the attackers to detach a portion of their forces to deal with the threat. A certain Private Oliver continued to man his machine gun until killed, accounting for 22 German dead. A sergeant in the mortar platoon was so close-pressed by the enemy that he threw away the weapon's bipod and fired it from the hip. Although surrounded, G Company continued to hold out until the Germans were driven off by artillery fired from the west bank of the Moselle.

The rest of the attacking force pressed on down the road toward Petite-Hettange, leaving their flanks more and more exposed. They managed to destroy two antitank guns which had been emplaced at the entrance to the village, but a third gun brought the advance to a temporary halt only a mile from the bridge site. At that moment, the battalion commander, Colonel Booth, had managed to gather a scratch force of service personnel—cooks, drivers, clerks, and the like—at the crossroads just to the southwest of the village. These men poured a hail of bazooka and small-arms fire into the disorganized Germans. The guns of 20 American artillery battalions opened up, and just in the nick of time the only two tank destroyers in the bridgehead rumbled onto the scene in the half-light of dawn.

This nearly provoked a tragedy, however, as the Americans were not expecting any of their own armor. An enthusiastic bazooka team was just about to take a potshot at the vehicles when the men were brought down by a flying tackle executed by Sergeant Land. Just at the last moment he had recognized the American M-10's. The latter, saved from immediate destruction, managed to knock out two German assault guns and damaged a third one.

Faced with such determined opposition and the hail of artillery, the enemy force began to retreat, at first in an orderly manner but leaving some 200 dead behind them. However, as they moved back down the road toward Kerling, E and G Companies tore into their exposed flank in a wild charge, transforming the retreat into a rout. The German attack against the rest of the 359th Regiment to the north was also repulsed after savage hand-to-hand fighting.

In all, this effort had cost the Germans more than 400 killed, some 150 prisoners, 4 valuable tanks, and 5 assault guns. Although the 359th Regiment had been hit hard, by the afternoon they had reorganized and were able to recover most of the lost ground. The Germans had had high hopes for the attack by the 25th Panzer Grenadiers, but the forces employed were far too weak to be able to disturb the buildup of the bridgehead.

In the center during 12 November, the 377th Infantry made further progress along the central ridge, although still hampered by isolated resistance from the Maginot bunkers which dotted the terrain. With some difficulty their reserve battalion had been brought across the river during the preceding night. This was urgently required as the two lead battalions were beginning to feel their losses and the strain of continual combat.

On the right, the 1st Battalion of the 358th Infantry was placed in reserve to recuperate from the attack on Fort Koenigsmacker. The other two battalions managed to clear the villages of Valmestroff and Elzange after bitter street fighting. It was there that a new weapon was encountered for the first time: a mine made from wooden and plastic parts which could not be found by the mine detectors which the Americans used at the time.

Thus by the end of 12 November, it could be stated that the bridgehead was secure, although progress had been far slower than anticipated, and the 10th Armored Division was still not across. The Malling bridge was repaired, and as the waters receded still further, two platoons of tanks and other support vehicles drove across. Construction of a bridge at the Cattenom site was well under way and an efficient smokescreen was in position. All this, however, was little comfort to the troops on the east bank. The personnel strength of some units had been halved, and the men were still largely without blankets, warm food, and dry clothes. German resistance was still not broken, and the further the 90th Division advanced, the more they moved away from the protective umbrella of the massed artillery on the west bank. In the absence of effective air support, it was vital to get the guns across the river before any further advances could be made.

The German commanders were most scathing about the quality of the 19th VG and 416th Divisions. "Little resistance was offered by the two divisions in the area . . . their fighting quality was low and in any case they were stretched out on far too wide a front."[16] However, if one considers how poorly armed they were, they managed to fight pretty well; the 90th Division certainly did not have everything their own way. There were no mass surrenders, and both units managed to maintain a cohesive front of sorts. But by the evening of 12 November, General Balck at Army Group G had given up hope of eradicating the bridgehead north of Thionville. Faced with a further threat from the south of Metz, he ordered his forces in the north onto the defensive, having been told that he could not expect any further reinforcements of any size.

THE 95TH DIVISION CROSSING AT THIONVILLE

We left the 95th Division containing the western perimeter of the Metz fortifications and with one battalion established in the somewhat precarious bridgehead opposite Uckange—a bridgehead which had been planned simply as a diversion. However, on 10 November, faced by the flooded Moselle and the apparent impossibility of bridge building to support the 90th Division effort, General Walker decided upon a subsidiary effort. He needed a bridge for the 10th Armored Division to cross in compliance with his orders. The only spare troops available were the 2nd Battalion of the 378th Infantry, commanded by Lt. Col. Autrey Maroun, who were in division reserve. Like most of the 95th, they had virtually no combat experience, but as events were to prove, this was apparently no disadvantage.

In a letter to the author, Colonel Maroun (now Major General, retired) wrote as follows: "I was called to 95th Division HQ, where the chief of staff, Colonel Harvey Golightly showed me a XX Corps order signed by the G-3, Colonel Snyder. I was to reconnoiter at Thionville for a site for a possible bridge over which the 10th Armored Division (so I believe) could cross. Upon consultation with the division commander [General Twaddle] and upon my recommendation, I was ordered to make a reconnaissance in force. This was at 1515, 10 November. We had no prior warnings as Thionville area was not in the 95th Division's zone."

Colonel Maroun proceeded immediately to Thionville with his S-3, while his engineers were contacted and his executive officer, Major Granzin, was ordered to get the battalion on the move. They were at Batilly, which meant that they had 22 miles to cover in the dark and over unfamiliar narrow and winding roads. The orders specified reconnaissance, and when this had been carried out, it was assumed that the battalion would retire to the west bank.

With the Moselle everywhere flooding its banks, Thionville was a sensible choice; for where the river ran through the town it was contained between high artificial banks. This naturally narrowed the stream, but the disadvantage was that the speed of the current was dramatically increased by the venturi effect. The town itself was split in two by the river, with the Americans on the west bank and the Germans on the east.

The troops arrived at 0330 hours and at 0400, Colonel Maroun issued his orders to the company commanders. There had been no time for a proper survey of the terrain, and as it was dark, he naturally had to accept the advice of the engineers on the spot who were to provide the boats. In the end, a site was chosen at the southern end of the town, which would bring them onto an island largely occupied by the railway station and storage yards. Beyond this was a canal which backed onto Fort Yutz. This was an outdated bastioned fortification built by the French engineer Cormontaigne in the mid-eighteenth century to guard the approaches to the town from the southeast. The official report states wrongly that it was built in 1857,[17] and another source speaks of the guns of the fort "commanding" the Moselle.[18] This gives a false impression of the place because it was retained purely as a historic monument and had no integral artillery of the type found in the later Metz forts. It consisted of a high stone-faced rampart with grassy slopes on top and a wide ditch in front. Its defenders were armed only with the normal infantry weapons but had the advantage of a well-protected position. The fort is still there today and forms an attractive grassy park on the outskirts of an otherwise undistinguished town.

It was decided that E Company, commanded by Lt. James Prendergast, would cross first at 0830 on 11 November, followed by F Company. The first boat was launched on time, and it and the second boat managed to cross without being detected. The third boat was fired on from a pillbox just to the south of the crossing site, and while the men from the first two boats moved off to deal with it, mortars and machine guns opened up.

In spite of this, 150 men of E Company were over the river within an hour and a half. But as the advantage of surprise had been lost, casualties began to mount and further boat trips became hazardous. By dark, only a few men from F Company had crossed.

E Company spent the day clearing part of the island between the river and the canal, while the engineers surveyed for a bridge site. During the morning, however, Maroun's orders were expanded by General Walker. He was ordered to use the whole battalion in order to seize a bridgehead deep enough to deny the enemy the use of small arms and mortars against the bridge site. To achieve this, the high ground to the east around Haute-Yutz had to be captured.

Under the welcome cover of darkness, the rest of F Company was brought over to the island, although several boats were swept away. When more craft were obtained, it proved possible to transport G and H Companies during the early morning. In the meanwhile, patrols from F Company had located two bridges over the canal, one at either end of Fort Yutz. (These were in fact, sluices built in 1746 by Cormontaigne to control the level of the water in the moat of the fort.) F Company decided upon a simultaneous attack on both bridges, supported by a half-hour bombardment by corps artillery. Additional fire cover was provided by tank destroyers emplaced on the west bank, and a reserve company was ready to exploit the first entrance gained.

At 0700 the operation commenced. The 2nd Platoon achieved surprise at the southern bridge, killing eleven of the enemy, and by 0800 was inside part of the fort enclosure. The northern thrust, however, lost the element of surprise as it had to delay to deal with troublesome pillboxes. The men were brought to a halt on the bridge by heavy German fire, and were further hindered by an iron door which had to be blasted open. Elements of the 74th Infantry Regiment from the 19th VG Division were defending the area.

Having already lost 20 men, the officer in charge of the northern attack called a halt for reorganization. Thus the southern thrust was the one to be immediately exploited, with confused fighting in and around the ancient fort supported by a platoon from G Company. The enemy put up a stiff fight, but were finally taken in the rear when the men on the northern bridge succeeded in breaking down the iron door and rushing inside the fort. By the evening the battalion controlled most of the interior, and it was planned to undertake the final clearance the following day.

The whole operation assumed even greater significance while this fighting was in progress. General Walker, influenced by the first counterattacks against the 90th Division and with Patton breathing down his neck to get the armor across, gave orders for the engineers to start work on the Thionville bridge regardless of casualties. During the afternoon, 95th Division issued Operational Instruction No. 5. This required the 2nd Battalion to finish off Fort Yutz, take Basse-Yutz (the suburb around the fort), and finally occupy Haute-Yutz and the Fort d'Illange. This was the first step in a plan to link up with the isolated 1st Battalion, 377th Infantry, in the Uckange bridgehead some six miles to the south. Fort d'Illange was the twin of Fort Koenigsmacker, situated on high ground about a mile and a half south of Thionville and with one (inoperative) battery of four 100-mm turret guns. This was quite a large slice of cake for a single infantry battalion to cope with, lacking in armored support and with no sign of enemy willingness to give up the struggle.

During the night, supplies were ferried across the river and the casualties were evacuated to the west bank. For the following day, 13 November, F Company reinforced by two platoons of G Company was assigned to mop up the remaining enemy pockets in Fort Yutz, a task that was achieved by midmorning. This secured the area for the engineers to start work on their bridge although it was still under mortar and artillery fire, and in accordance with orders, steps were taken to expand the bridgehead. One artillery shell was fired into Basse-Yutz, which produced a fluttering of white sheets. The Germans had departed and the Americans were able to form a defensive perimeter from which patrols were able to establish contact with 90th Division troops.

For operations the following day, Colonel Maroun issued this order: "After an artillery preparation from 0630 to 0645, G Company will attack and seize the town of Haute-Yutz by 0830 . . . E and F Companies will enter Haute-Yutz upon its capture by G Company and will be at the line of departure (the southwestern edge of the town) by 0830 ready to launch an attack on the hill 300 yards southwest of Haute-Yutz. Double envelopment will be used with E Company attacking the hill from the east, and F Company attacking from the north using a covered route . . . upon capture of the objective, all companies will guard against counterattack and will be ready to continue the attack of Fort d'Illange on battalion order."[19]

G Company attacked up the main road leading to Haute-Yutz and despite considerable enemy resistance, were established in the town more or less on schedule. The two follow-up companies then charged up the neighboring hill, firing from the hip. By 0940 they were on the top, having taken 11 prisoners in the process and according to orders, began to re-form for the attack on the fort.

Colonel Maroun then sent Lt. James Billings with an interpreter to the fort, having promoted him for prestige purposes with a spare pair of captain's bars. The reason for this was that a German soldier had displayed a white flag as the Americans approached. The fort was garrisoned by a company of the 74th Regiment. Their commander, a major (some accounts say that he was a captain), received the envoys but declined to discuss terms. "I will fight to the last," he said, in true Hollywood style.

Thus there was no solution but to assault the fort, using the same techniques that had proved successful at Koenigsmacker. The place had to be eliminated if the enemy were to be denied observation of the crossing site, where the engineers were already toiling to construct the vital bridge. A call was put through to corps artillery, who produced a spectacular barrage of 155-mm and 240-mm shells onto the top of the fort—more as a morale booster than with the hope of doing any damage.

E and F Companies then moved off along the small road from Haute-Yutz. The latter moved into the shelter of the Bois d'Illange, where they swiftly silenced some troublesome enemy machine guns. E Company, however, found itself in trouble as soon as the men broke cover. The Germans had emplaced six 120-mm mortars in the fort and these opened fire with devastating effect, forcing the attackers back into the wood. They then made a second attempt to get over the main road leading south past the fort, and again were forced back, this time by machine-gun fire. Having lost 32 men, they retired into the woods and were placed in reserve. F Company, to the north of the fort, progressed slowly uphill under intense mortar fire. As no vehicles had been able to cross the river, they were lacking bangalore torpedos and engineer stores normally required for tackling such forts. Faced by the usual multistrand wire obstacle, they had to cut their way through by hand—in daylight and under heavy fire!

Two gaps were made and two platoons entered the fort, capturing three heavy mortars in the process. To replace the shattered E Company, the bulk of G Company was brought up during the afternoon and also managed to get through the perimeter wire.

Thus, by evening, Colonel Maroun had four platoons on the objective. This was an incredible achievement when one considers that the small force had been in constant action for four days without a pause—their first real experience of combat. During the early afternoon a bridge had been completed, which enabled the battalion rear HQ and medical facilities to move over into Fort Yutz. Of more immediate importance was the fact that two platoons of tank destroyers and a number of antitank guns crossed to the east bank. After that, priority was given to 10th Armored Division traffic which poured across the bridge during the night and the following day. Patton had his bridge, although not in the intended place.

Also during the night, carrying parties from H Company brought up the much needed explosives and demolition equipment, while patrols on top of the fort searched for the enemy strongpoints. Five were definitely located, and at first light, were attacked with heavy charges. Captain Adair, CO of F Company, was in charge, and while the 81-mm mortars kept the defenders busy, two-man squads rushed the doors, carrying beehive charges. When these went off, other squads were ready to throw threaded charges through the resulting holes (10-pound packs of TNT strung together with primer cord). These methods effectively ended resistance in the bunkers. Yet in spite of this, small groups of enemy continued to hold out; although many of them had left during the night, including the garrison commander who was going to fight to the last. One man out of the many who distinguished themselves during the operation, was Sergeant Bussard. He was awarded the Distinguished Service Cross for charging a pillbox alone, although he was wounded in both knees as he approached. He killed four and captured twelve of the occupants, and was again wounded as he tried to return to his platoon.

At 1040, 67 survivors surrendered to Colonel Maroun, who himself had been wounded during the attack, and 74 dead members of the garrison were counted. Maroun had refused to be evacuated, but the final capture of the fort virtually ended the career of "Maroun's Marauders" (as they became known), as a separate command entity. In recognition of their activities, the 2nd Battalion, 378th Infantry, was awarded battle honors by General Twaddle on 23 November. In March 1945, the battalion was given the highest unit award possible—the Distinguished Unit Citation. This stated, "During the five days of this action, the 2nd Battalion, 378th Infantry, engaged in its first offensive operation and, functioning until the last day as a separate command, forced a crossing of the flooded Moselle River, advanced more than three miles against a stubbornly resisting enemy, killed an estimated 300 Germans, captured 215 prisoners, reduced two major fortifications and routed a large enemy force. During this period the battalion suffered more than 200 casualties.

"The desperate determination, great personal courage and outstanding personal skill of the officers and men of the 2nd Battalion, 378th Infantry gained the bridgehead at Thionville, which made possible the successful execution of the XX Corps plan for the capture of Metz. Their example is an inspiration to all members of this command."[20]

Fair words, but hardly exaggerated. It takes a very well trained and officered formation in any army to perform so outstandingly in their first operation. If corps had not been so desperate for a bridge, they would almost certainly never have been given the chance.

That was not the end of the story, however. While the 2nd Battalion was still smoking out the defenders at Fort d'Illange, Colonel Robert Bacon was given command of all the 95th Division forces on the east bank of the river. Bacon, who had previously commanded a regiment in the 90th Division, was one of those men of action who crop up in any war and whose names are always in the forefront when special formations are required. His mission was to gather the 2nd Battalion plus some tanks and tank destroyers, and attack southward to relieve the defenders in the Uckange bridgehead. This achieved, Task Force Bacon was to carry on south and force their way into Metz. As the bulk of his new force was still occupied, Colonel Bacon was forced to start off with the troops that he could scrape together for the drive south, as in the meanwhile, the situation of the 1st Battalion at Uckange had become desperate.

During the morning of 13 November, the last of the rifle companies was finally ferried over the Moselle when it had receded sufficiently. The battalion was then ordered by 95th Division to move off to the north, bypass Bertrange and Immeldange, and capture the town of Illange—where they would link up with Colonel Maroun's men. They took the two former towns without difficulty, but as they regrouped prior to moving off, they were struck by a task force from the 73rd Regiment (part of the 19th VG Division), supported by some antitank guns. The forces in the two towns became separated and went to ground as the Germans roared up and down the long main streets in armored personnel carriers shooting at anything that moved. Communication with their artillery on the west bank broke down.

It was only restored early in the morning of 14 November, with the first sergeant of A Company acting as forward observer. However, in spite of the usually effective American artillery response, the enemy were not easily discouraged. They pressed their attacks all day, supported by light armored vehicles—to such an extent that at 2200, the battalion commander reported that his position was "desperate." One must remember that the 1st Battalion men were armed only with the weapons that they could carry and had been in action nonstop since the evening of 8 November. American troops have often been criticized for being too soft and having no staying power, but this facile judgment is belied by so many of the small-unit actions that combined to make up the story of the battle of Metz.

During the evening, communications again broke down, and on the morning of 15 November, the remainder of the battalion was still holding out in the gutted ruins of the two villages. Bacon's force arrived just in the nick of time, but during his advance, Colonel Maroun was again wounded. This time he was unable to carry on and played no further part in the Metz operation. For his personal leadership and valor, he was awarded the Distinguished Service Cross.

Using his tank destroyers as self-propelled artillery, Colonel Bacon shelled the Germans out of Bertrange and Immeldange, and by 1300, the beleaguered forces were relieved. Their strength, however, had been reduced to a mere handful of officers and men, but instead of being sent into reserve, they immediately became a part of Task Force Bacon. This composite force was made up from the 1st Battalion, 377th Regiment and the 2nd Battalion 378th Regiment, plus the 95th Reconnaissance Troop, the 807th Tank Destroyer Battalion and D Company of the 778th Tank Battalion. Their exploits, however, belong to a later chapter.

THE 10TH ARMORED DIVISION
EXPLOITATION OF THE BRIDGEHEADS

When the main offensive started, the 10th Armored Division was assembled in the Molvange area about five miles northwest of Thionville and far enough away from the Moselle to be free from enemy observation. Its mission was to pass through the 90th Division bridgehead and, when it had broken out, to advance in two main columns. The one on the left was to race for the Saar crossings, while the column on the right was to aim for the important communication center of Bouzonville on the Nied River. There, it would be in a position to help cut rail and road communications with which the Metz garrison could be reinforced.

When discussing the activities of General Walker's only armored force, it must be borne in mind that, as far as the higher echelons of command were concerned, the capture of Metz was only incidental to the greater plan of establishing a bridgehead over the Saar and advancing to the Rhine. Therefore, this formation soon fades from the picture as far as the subject of this book is concerned. Metz remained a problem for the infantry to solve.

As mentioned earlier when discussing the problems faced by Patton in September, the country between the Moselle and the Saar was not particularly suitable for exploitation by armor. The road system was limited, and in view of the terrible weather, armored vehicles would be restricted to using what hard-surface highways were available. We have seen that the ways out of the 90th Division bridgehead were limited, and the only really useful road was the one leading northeast from the crossroads at Kerling—hence the efforts made to retain command of this village.

The division spent a frustrating five days waiting for orders to move, at the mercy of the flooded river and the valiant efforts of the engineers. In the end, it was the Thionville crossing by Maroun's Marauders that opened the way for the 10th Armored. This site was particularly suitable for bridge construction as both ends could be securely anchored on the solid walls of the riverbank, avoiding the problem of flooded approaches faced by the engineers at Malling and Cattenom.

Work at the Thionville site was commenced on 12 November by the 1306th Engineer General Service Regiment, which was ordered by General Walker to get on with the job regardless of casualties. A smoke screen was provided, but when the wind changed the following day, the engineers were cruelly exposed to German shelling and mortar fire. Hence the need for the 2nd Battalion, 378th Infantry, to capture the high ground overlooking the site and to eliminate the heavy mortars emplaced at Fort d'Illange.

Wearing flak suits, the engineers worked all through the day and at 0930 on 14 November, they had completed what was stated to be the longest Bailey bridge in Europe at that time.[21] Support vehicles for the infantry were the first across, but in the afternoon, CCB was given traffic priority. They started to lumber over the bridge and then drove north toward the 90th Division area where they moved in behind the Kerling position held by the 359th Infantry. At the same time, space on the Malling bridge was freed for CCA.

On 15 November, the offensive by the armor got under way, and in spite of some opposition, managed to break through the German crust and fan out over the poor roads. On 17 and 18 November, owing to the limited hard surfaces, they were forced to split into small units, but the weather cleared and enabled their airborne artillery to take to the air. On 19 November, CCA managed to gain a foothold across the Nied river, but by that time the infantry had surrounded Metz. As there were no signs of a German relief force in the offing, the armor was then switched north toward the Saar—leaving Metz to be mopped up by the 5th and 95th Divisions.

THE 5TH DIVISION ATTACK IN THE SOUTH

During the early stages of the Battle of Metz, the spectacular action was in the north, where an assault crossing of the Moselle had to be made. In the south, the 5th Division had already crossed this hurdle back in September, and were poised in their bridgehead to complete the encirclement of the city. Their actions, however, must also be considered in the light of the broader plan for the November campaign. Apart from the XX Corps mission to take Metz and move northeast toward the Saar, this called for XII Corps on the right to attack across the Lorraine plain toward Faulquemont. The 6th Armored Division, which belonged to the latter corps, was to use the 5th Division bridgehead, and there was a certain amount of overlapping on the intercorps boundary. Once the attack got under way, the Germans were convinced that 6th Armored and 10th Armored would meet up in the vicinity of Faulquemont.

Although the operations of XII Corps do not form part of this story, it is interesting to note that their advance from their positions to the east of Nancy was to be over exactly the same ground as the abortive French offensive that opened the war in August 1914. Oddly enough it was a XX Corps, commanded however, by a certain General Foch, which bore the brunt of the fighting and carried out a gallant rear-guard action near Château-Salins. The French were back again in 1918, assisted by six American divisions, but before the offensive toward Faulquemont and the Saar could begin, the enemy obligingly surrendered.

To recapitulate, the 5th Division relieved the 95th Division at the beginning of November and moved back into their old positions. On the right, 2nd Infantry took up positions in the bend of the Seille opposite Cheminot—the village that had barred the advance of the 7th Armored Division in mid-September. In the center, the 10th Infantry Regiment faced the Seille River facing east, and on the left, 11th Infantry Regiment occupied a line between Sillegny and the Moselle at Corney. During their rest period, the regiments had been brought up to strength after losses suffered during the earlier stages of the battle.

The mission assigned to General Irwin was to attack toward the east, parallel with XII Corps on the right, and then to be prepared to move north to meet up with the 90th Division, thus completing the ring around Metz. The attack would skirt to the south of the known outer defenses of the city and then swing around them. This movement was to be carried out by the 2nd and 10th Regiments—the 11th Regiment would hold the rest of the division line initially, and would then move north into the suburbs of Metz to help in the reduction of the city itself.

The division objective was to seize and hold a crossing over the river Nied, about ten miles east of the start line, in the area of Sanry-sur-Nied. When this was achieved, the northward swing could commence. The control of the Nied valley would deny to the enemy the use of the communications that ran along it, including the main railway to Strasbourg and the branch line to Saarbrücken. Neither the Seille nor the Nied was a difficult barrier to cross in normal weather, but the torrential rain that had swollen the Moselle had an identical effect on the smaller streams in the area. The ever-present mud would make vehicle movement difficult and life most unpleasant for the infantry.

The old adversaries of the 5th Division, the 17th SS Panzer Grenadiers, still held most of the line facing General Irwin's men. This was no longer a "panzer" division as such as its armor was virtually nonexistent—it had four Mark IV tanks and six SP assault guns.[22] It did, however, have a fully equipped artillery regiment, and the division as a whole was overstrength. This may have sounded good on paper, but the bulk of the newly-arrived replacements were poorly trained, and the division no longer rated as an "attack" unit. Its right wing was joined to troops from the 462 VG Division, the Metz garrison force; but in the area to the south of the city, they could only muster a number of static machine-gun battalions and low-grade security troops.

The higher German command in the area (XIII SS Corps) was hampered in its tactics by the order to keep contact at all costs with the Metz garrison. When hit by the XII Corps attack, they were forced to wheel back on themselves instead of being able to conduct an orderly fighting retreat toward the Saar and the Westwall.[23]

After settling back in their old positions, the 5th Division regiments busied themselves with active patrolling to feel out the enemy line, and with clearing the minefields that had been laid during the October lull. The inevitable psychological warfare unit also made an appearance, broadcasting loudspeaker appeals to the Germans to give themselves up, with the tempting prospect of hot food and plentiful cigarettes as bait. These operations never seemed to have any spectacular result during the Metz battle, but a trickle of deserters did come over, offering information about the German positions.

The longest stretch of front line was held by the 11th Infantry, forming the pivot around which the other two regiments would wheel.

They had to resort to filling out their ranks with scratch platoons made up from service troops, cooks, and clerks. Although comparisons are invidious, one is always drawn back to the example of the First World War, when an attack on such a front would have been carried out by an entire army, preceded by a bombardment possibly lasting as long as a week. In 1918, the forces assembled for the attack on the front from south of Metz to Dieuze numbered 31 divisions, supported by some 600 batteries of artillery!

During the waiting period, a number of German aircraft were reported over the 5th Division sector. These were only reconnaissance machines, but it did demonstrate the Luftwaffe could still fly. The real enemy, however, just as in the 90th Division zone, was the weather. Foxholes filled with water in the downpour and the few roads were washed out, hampering the movement of stores. The vital Arnaville bridges, which had withstood German artillery in September, were all swept away, so that communication with the rear was seriously impaired. All movement across the river, apart from hazardous ferry trips, had to be made via the bridges at Pont-à-Mousson and Nancy in the XII Corps area. The initial objective, the Seille River, had swollen from its normal 20 yards to a width of 200 yards, in the process washing away the few available bridges and overflowing the fording sites. Thus right from the outset, the general situation was highly unfavorable for an attack with such slender forces.

General Irwin originally had been told that the 5th Division would not start its attack simultaneously with that of XII Corps; but General McBride, commanding the neighboring 80th Division, had apparently not been informed of this.[24] This is odd, as Field Order No. 12 issued by XX Corps specified that the neighboring XII Corps would attack on D-day, whereas 5th Division would move "on Corps order."[25] The original Third Army order specified that on army order, operational control of the 80th Division would pass to XX Corps, but there is no evidence of this having been carried out. Had the order been carried out, the boundary problems would have been considerably eased.[26]

D-day for the Third Army attack was set for 8 November, in spite of the weather and the lack of air support. The XII Corps moved off, including 80th Division, who expected to be joined on their left by 5th Division. As the communications of the two formations were inextricably muddled, this could have led to disaster, but the one-day lead by the 80th Division was to yield a hidden bonus in that it forced the Germans to abandon the line of the Seille.

Throughout the night of 8/9 November, the engineers labored to complete bridges across the river and to mark the approaches for the infantry. At 0600 hours, the 2nd Infantry launched the attack of the "Red Diamond" 5th Division, crossed the swollen river against negligible opposition, and found the key village of Cheminot unoccupied. At the same time, the 10th Infantry crossed on footbridges provided by the engineers, with the 3rd Battalion in the lead. They moved on across the soggy ground, leaving small pockets of enemy resistance to be mopped up later by the 2nd Battalion. When the latter moved across the river about an hour later, they ran into determined opposition centered on Hautonnerie Farm, a group of solid stone buildings about a mile back from the river. In front there was virtually no cover and the fields were strewn with mines—reminiscent of the earlier attacks on Pournoy-là-Chetive by the same formation. In fact it was F Company, virtually reconstructed after having been almost wiped out during the latter operation, which had to bear the brunt of the attack. Being inexperienced, they promptly hit the ground. Pinned down by a hail of small arms, mortar, and artillery fire, the men were rallied by their commanding officer, Captain Kubarek, who ran from group to group encouraging them. Initially in ones and twos and then in small squads, they picked themselves up and straggled after the captain. The squads formed into platoons, and firing from the hip, the company drove the small group of Germans out of the farm. While they consolidated, waves of medium bombers roared overhead to drop their loads on Goin and Pommerieux, villages directly in front of the 10th Infantry line of advance.

This was the first response by the air forces which had been possible, but in spite of the large numbers of aircraft involved that day, results were apparently negligible and were hardly felt by the troops on the ground. (Accounts of the actions of the 90th Division during this period do not mention air activities.) The clouds forced the bombers to drop their loads from upward of 20,000 feet, and although many of the bombs were destined for the Metz forts, most of them seemed to have missed—quantity rather than quality was the result. It was only where breaks in the clouds allowed the pilots to identify their targets that anything significant was achieved. The fighter-bombers, who naturally relied on visual identification, were severely hampered in their efforts, but did manage to delay the movement of enemy reinforcements.

On the first day of the 5th Division advance, casualties were generally light and the bulk of the enemy tended to melt away to the northeast. Two battalions of the 10th Infantry, and all three of the 2nd, had a secure bridgehead over the Seille; and the following day, the 6th Armored Division was committed. They worked closely with the 2nd Infantry, and Task Force Lagrew drove forward to take Vigny which was handed over to the GI's who followed. The armor then moved on to take Buchy, and this operation finally cleared communications along the intercorps boundary. By the evening of 11 November, the armor was across the Nied, having swung across the front of the 2nd Infantry and forced a crossing at Sanry. This spectacular advance enabled American artillery to be brought up within range of the main road from Metz to Saarbrücken which they were able to shell at Courcelles-Chaussy thus hindering movement in and out of the city.

During 12 November, the 5th Division was forced to pause to regroup and reorganize lines of communication. During the advance of the other regiments, 11th Infantry had been able to make small gains, following on the heels of the gradually retiring enemy, and was even able to extend its thin crust to assist the 10th Infantry to concentrate against the Bois de l'Hôpital. It was within this area of woods that the bulk of the German artillery south of Metz was emplaced and the high ground afforded valuable observation. The 2nd Infantry moved into the Nied bridgehead that had been created by 6th Armored, where they defeated a counterattack by elements of the 17th SS Panzer Grenadiers during the night.

The following day, 13 November, engineers bridged the Nied and more troops from the 2nd Infantry reinforced the bridgehead. Rain and even snow brought great discomfort to all concerned, and the foul weather naturally tended to increase the number of nonbattle casualties from such mundane but crippling ailments as trench foot. In spite of general lack of opposition by the enemy, every mile advanced by the 5th Division extended its lines of communication to the overextended front. Enemy efforts were mainly concentrated on eradicating the Neid bridgehead as this lay firmly across one of the escape routes from Metz and controlled the use of the railway to Saarbrücken. The full might of the German artillery was concentrated on Sanry where five companies and a few armored vehicles clung on desperately. During the night a large force tried to force their way into the small town, but were driven off after bitter street fighting. The tanks fired for ricochet effect against the road surfaces and bounced their shells into the Germans who suffered an estimated 200 casualties.

Elsewhere in the 5th Division sector, the 10th Infantry occupied the two disarmed groups of forts (Yser and Aisne) to the south of the Bois de l'Hôpital. The 11th Infantry had the grim satisfaction of reoccupying the area of Pournoy-là-Chetive and Coin-les-Cuvry, which the division had had to abandon in September after so much loss of life. Although resistance was beginning to stiffen, by the evening of 14 November, the regiment had closed up to the south of the Verdun group of forts and had taken Prayelle farm after a hard fight.

During the evening of 13 November, General Irwin was contacted by Walker, who congratulated him on the performance of his men. During the conversation he was given authority to decide whether or not to keep the small force across the Nied or to bring them back in order to concentrate on the northward drive to encircle Metz. As the battalion could be adequately supported by artillery, and its withdrawal would leave his right flank in the air, Irwin decided that they should hang on.

On the following day, the 10th Infantry again made steady progress as they cleared the southern part of the Bois de l'Hôpital, which brought them to within three miles of the suburbs of Metz. Having been told by corps that his division would be able to enter the city, Irwin decided that 10th Infantry was best situated; but if they moved inward, the 2nd Infantry bridgehead could well lose contact. He therefore reversed his earlier decision and requested permission to evacuate the forces back across the Nied. This request, however, was sensibly denied by Patton as it would have meant exposing the flank of the XII Corps.

Thus by the evening of 14 November, six days after the commencement of the offensive, the pincers were gradually closing around Metz, although several routes to the east of the city remained open, albeit subject to harassment by American artillery. Progress had in fact been slower than expected, but taking the weather into consideration and the small number of forces employed, this is hardly surprising. The Germans complained that they did not have any reserves to plug the gaps torn in their front, but in fairness one must state that there were no reserves to back the Americans either. If the Germans had been able to assemble a powerful armored force, they could have torn through the overextended 5th Division lines at one of several places and forced them back to the Moselle. Patton took a gamble by attacking at all with his limited forces, but it was a gamble which paid off in spite of the lack of air cover.

The Closing Jaws

One can really say that the final doom of Metz was determined on 14 November, when the 95th Division, the bulk of which had been guarding the western fortifications, was committed to an active role. In the north, the bridges at Malling and Thionville were in action and the 90th Infantry and 10th Armored were poised to advance toward the Saar. In fact, these two units played little further part in the story of the Battle of Metz, except insofar as their right wing moved southeast toward Boulay and St. Avold, thus closing the jaws finally in conjunction with the 5th Division from the south. From now on we are mainly concerned with the activities of the 95th Division, the 5th Division, and Task Force (TF) Bacon. Again the narrative will be subdivided into sectors of the front for the sake of clarity.

THE 95TH INFANTRY DIVISION ATTACK FROM THE WEST

Although the original mission of the division had been to contain the enemy holed up in the fortifications to the west of Metz, they had not been idle. Patrol activity had been intense as they tried to feel their way toward the German positions, and during the night of 12/13

November, the 378th Infantry Regiment managed to seize a foothold in Amanvillers, a feat which had proved impossible in September.

The original mission assigned to General Twaddle's division was to attack frontally into the city once the pincers had been closed by the 5th and 90th Divisions. This basic plan had been embodied in division Field Order No. 2, which had been issued on 7 November, but this had contained no specific dates or timings. In the meanwhile, however, the situation had altered to the good as far as the 95th was concerned. They had two battalions across the river, instead of the one originally envisaged, and these were in the process of being united as part of TF Bacon. Therefore, on 14 November, Twaddle requested permission from corps to start his attack before the pincers were entirely shut, and instead of the simple attack from the west, to assault astride the river. Although this was a modification of the original corps scheme, permission was granted, and General Twaddle issued Change No. 1 to his field order. This called for regimental attacks to commence on 15 November (377th and 378th, each minus a battalion on the other side of the river) and for the action by the 379th to be continued. Thus, the three regiments and the semi-independent TF Bacon would provide four axes of attack before finally uniting on the drive into the city center. The three regimental combat teams were aligned as follows:

The *379 Infantry* occupied a line running southeast from Gravelotte to Noveant on the Moselle, facing the main forts at Driant and Jeanne d'Arc, plus the so-called Seven Dwarfs and a maze of field-works. This sector was garrisoned by the 1217th VG Regiment.

The *378th Infantry* (2 battalions) were posted on a line running from Gravelotte as far as the end of the Fèves ridge. They were faced by the remaining fortifications, such as the Canrobert works and the Lorraine Group. This area was garrisoned by the 1010th Security Regiment (*Regiment Anton*), a distance of some eight miles.

The *377th Infantry* (2 battalions) held the flood plain to the south of Maizières-les-Metz, between the Fèves ridge and the Moselle. They were faced by the 1215th VG Regiment.

Tactically, the 95th Division was confronted by the same problems that had defeated XX Corps in early September, a lengthy front held by comparatively few troops faced by an enemy in well-fortified positions. There was also the added problem of communication with Task Force Bacon on the far side of the river. Although the quality of the opposition had been reduced, there were no signs of a general collapse. On the plus side, however, the Americans were much better informed about the fortifications and all concerned were agreed that there would be no further frontal attacks. The scheme was to penetrate between the forts and move into the city itself, leaving the isolated garrisons to be starved out.

The mission assigned to the 379th Infantry was to penetrate on both sides of the Jeanne d'Arc group. On their left, the 378th Regiment was to attempt to wheel around to the north of the Fèves ridge and roll up the defenses from the rear. The 377th Infantry and TF Bacon were to advance into the city astride the Moselle.

This plan was well thought out, but it had the inherent risk that, by dividing the forces, they were being exposed to defeat in detail—as very nearly happened. As we shall see, certain elements became cut off and had to be supplied by air drop from light aircraft.

The Operations of the 379th Infantry Regiment[1]

The attack by the 379th had been ordered on 13 November, one day earlier than the main division assault, and was to commence on 14 November by not later than 1430 hours. Support consisted of two field artillery battalions and a company of tank destroyers plus a variety of captured weapons. As the shells from the latter repeatedly fell short, their use was soon discontinued! There is nothing worse for the morale of infantry than to be shelled or strafed by their own side.

The regimental commander, Colonel Chapman, placed his 3rd Battalion in reserve, thinly spread along the whole of the regimental front as a holding force. The mission of the 1st Battalion was to force a way over the infamous Mance ravine and to clear the Seven Dwarfs. The latter had no built-in artillery and were really only a series of irregularly shaped infantry strongpoints, although adequately constructed with concrete shelters for their defenders. The attacking force was well supplied with plans of the works, and individual soldiers were even given three-dimensional exploded drawings of the interior buildings showing such details as where the staircases led and how to find the firing chambers behind the embrasures. On the left, the 2nd Battalion was to move along the road leading between the Jeanne d'Arc group and Fort de Guise.

After a heavy (and predictably useless) bombardment of the forts at dawn, the two assault battalions moved off at around 0600. Although shelled by Fort Driant and the Moselle Battery, the 2nd Battalion managed to make its way around to the north of Jeanne d'Arc and by midday were on their objective, 500 yards to the rear of the fort. There they were counterattacked, probably by troops from the fort, although the fortress commander described the efforts as "feeble."[2] These attacks were beaten off, but the American force (two assault companies) was out on a limb. The attackers had been able to penetrate the line held by the 1217th VG Regiment but could not detach sufficient forces to mop up the enemy holed up in the maze of bunkers and trenches. Thus, the German line closed up again after they had moved through and they found themselves cut off. Their reserve company was unable to get through to them and was forced back by heavy fire.

The assault by the 1st Battalion also enjoyed initial success. Although brought under heavy fire in the ravine, they managed to get across it and by noon were in among the Seven Dwarfs. They captured Forts Jussy North and South but were driven off from Fort Bois la Dame. At this stage they too were cut off and their reserve company also failed to cross the ravine.

General Kittel was informed of the state of affairs at 1200 hours and decided to commit his reserve to stiffen the troops on the spot. He ordered the 462nd Fusilier Battalion under Major Voss to drive the Americans from their foothold in the Seven Dwarfs. A part of this force managed to infiltrate back into the ravine although they suffered heavy casualties in the process. By starting one regiment in advance of the rest of the division, General Twaddle enabled his opponent to shift his meager reserve to deal with a single threat.

The encircled units were supplied during the early part of the evening by spotter aircraft running the gauntlet of enemy fire. They dropped ammunition, radio batteries, and medical supplies. It proved impossible to evacuate the wounded, who had to be cared for on the spot.

During the night, plans were made to relieve the isolated troops, but in spite of several attempts during 15 November, the bulk of the 1st and 2nd Battalions remained cut off, unable to move forward or backward. The following afternoon, there was nothing else to do but to commit the 3rd Battalion and leave the divisional line more or less denuded of its holding force. They launched their attack along the route taken by the 2nd Battalion—the road between Fort de Guise and Jeanne d'Arc. Company I managed to eject the enemy from

Moscou and St. Hubert farms, fortified buildings that had previously hindered the relief attempts. Company K moved against a strongpoint that also barred the way. This consisted of a number of concrete bunkers well blended into the terrain and with a wide field of fire.

However, in view of pressure in the north being exerted by the 378th Infantry, German resistance in the south was beginning to break up. A sergeant and an enlisted man crept forward through a hail of fire to a mound directly in front of the bunkers. There they set up a heavy machine gun and swept the area with a hail of bullets until the enemy stopped firing. The German officer in charge of the strongpoint then surrendered with 46 men, and it later transpired that he had (wrongly) assumed that he was surrounded by a considerable force of Americans.

The elimination of this strongpoint was a great help toward reestablishing contact with the 2nd Battalion, but while forts Driant and Jeanne d'Arc could still fire, movement by road was extremely hazardous. It was intended that at this juncture the 1st Battalion would fight their way northward to join up with the rest of the force, but this had to be postponed for a day. It was not until the morning of 18 November that the regiment managed to link up its scattered formations, but they were through the main fortified line and able to look down on Metz in the valley below. It was only that night, however, that the first supplies could be brought in by road. During daylight, aircraft still had to be used because of accurate fire from the forts, but as landing strips had been cleared, they were able to evacuate the more seriously wounded.

Operations by the 378th Infantry Regiment

Events on the right wing of the division tended to be overshadowed by the activities of the 378th Infantry in the center. It was in this sector that the decisive move in the last phase of the Battle of Metz was carried out. The 378th succeeded where the Prussians had failed in 1870, in that they managed to turn the entire fortified line by moving around the north of the Fèves ridge. In the orders issued on 14 November, the regiment had been ordered to attack at 0800 on the following day. Patrols had shown them the futility of a frontal assault on the ridge, which was guarded by the Canrobert forts. Although only infantry positions, they were fronted along the entire length by a high concrete wall which had previously defeated the 90th Division.

They therefore decided to execute a turning movement around the northern edge of the ridge, through the sector held by the 377th Infantry. As they only had two battalions available, it was necessary to strip the force holding the front opposite the ridge to the bare minimum—without letting the enemy know, naturally. Colonel Metcalf, the regimental commander, entrusted the execution of a daring deception scheme to Captain St. Jacques who commanded the regimental service company. To hold a front of almost 9 miles, Task Force St. Jacques was assigned three rifle platoons, padded out with signallers, drivers, and other HQ personnel. They were armed with a platoon of antitank guns, some heavy machine guns, and a few captured guns of Danish origin. This may sound like a terrible risk, but it was a calculated one. The deception succeeded and the Germans themselves were far too extended to be able to contemplate offensive action.

Preceded by a 15-minute bombardment, the 1st Battalion attacked at 0800 from the assembly positions that they had occupied during the night. Early morning visibility was poor on account of fog and the blanket of smoke that had been laid over the ridge. However, by 1100, Company A had managed to occupy Fort de Fèves, the most northerly of the defensive positions on the heights. Although the company commander was wounded, another injured officer took over, and firing from the hip, the men rushed into the fort. The capture of this relatively weak position may not sound like all that much, but in many ways, it was decisive. First, it meant that a small force was in behind the fortifications and that they had hit the boundary between the 1010th Security Regiment and the 1215th VG Regiment. Second, the enemy had been robbed of a vital observation post. Owing to the lack of optical sighting equipment for the turret guns, the fort was the main fire control center for the whole of the position to the west of Metz, and as soon as it was captured there was a remarkable lessening in the accuracy of the German artillery. The fort was tied into the main fortress communications network, and according to experts who later examined it, it was stuffed with signal equipment.[3]

As can be imagined, this was a bitter blow to the German garrison. General Kittel wrongly dates the attack as having been carried out on 14 November, and goes on to say that the seriousness of the situation only dawned on him at 1300 hours. A local counterattack by around 200 men was defeated by American ground troops and artillery.

On account of the counterattack, the regimental commander decided that a pause should be instituted and the 3rd Battalion be brought up to reinforce the scattered assault force. However, before the orders could be circulated, B Company moved off from the vicinity of Semécourt in the belief that the enemy was still disorganized. They managed to penetrate as far as the Bois de Woippy, and in spite of a counterattack during the evening, established themselves securely there. During the night, the 3rd Battalion moved up, and the following day, cleared out the villages behind the Fèves ridge. From there the terrain sloped steeply down toward the city in the valley—an area with few roads, dotted with small villages, and broken by ravines and gullies. It was totally unsuitable for armored vehicles and could be brought under fire from Forts Lorraine and Plappeville. By all the rules of war, the small attacking force should have been annihilated by a determined garrison sallying out from the forts, but by this stage of the battle, the German command had begun to disintegrate. The problem for the Americans was how to deal with the forts as they did not have sufficient forces to attack them and still continue to advance into the city.

The following day, 17 November, Colonel Metcalf was ordered to start an attack not later than 1300 (later modified to 1400) to capture the Moselle bridges that led into the city center. This was to be part of a concentrated attack by all three regiments plus Task Force Bacon. However, there were will considerable numbers of Germans in among the regimental positions, especially holed up in the Canrobert forts. Today, this whole area is totally overgrown, but at the time of the attack the vegetation would have been limited. Thus the 3rd Battalion was assigned to move toward the city while the 1st Battalion had to be left behind to clear the lines of communication. By the early afternoon, the forts along the ridge had been cleaned out, and at the far end, the Ammanvillers Quarry position was found to be unoccupied. The problem that remained, however, was that from the three companies available to the battalion commander, small numbers constantly had to be detached to guard the captured forts, thus diminishing the force even further.

During this operation, orders were received for the regiment also to advance toward the southwest to help in the relief attempt for the still encircled battalions from the 379th Infantry. In the evening, however, there was a change, as fire from Fort Plappeville had been harassing troops trying to approach the Moselle bridges. The 1st Battalion was ordered to send out patrols to determine the strength of the enemy in the fort, and in the process it was discovered that Fort Lorraine was empty, having been abandoned by its garrison. This was a grave mistake on the part of the Germans, as Lorraine had some of its turret guns operating (a battery of two 100-mm weapons), which would have been well employed firing at the Americans trying to cross into the city.

The following morning, the 1st Battalion was ordered to attack Fort Plappeville. This lay on top of a ridge, and although it was one of the old forts dating from 1868, the whole of the surrounding area was a maze of shelters, bunkers, and trenches. From then on, until relieved by the 359th Infantry on 21 November, the 1st Battalion made vain attempts to dislodge the enemy. At one stage, a company managed to get on top but were soon forced to retire. The only possible solution was for the area to be surrounded, for although they had managed to inflict casualties, the force available was far too small to inflict any serious damage. At one stage, tanks were brought up to fire smoke shells into the ventilators, without any spectacular success.

Operations by the 377th Infantry Regiment

Having cleared the last German opposition from the area of Maizières-les-Metz during an earlier attack, the two battalions of the regiment occupied positions across the flood plain between the Fèves ridge and the Moselle. It was assigned to make the main division effort against the city, starting at 1000 on 15 November. Although one company was still involved in a local scrap around one of the slag heaps to the south of Maizières, the 2nd and 3rd Battalions moved off on time. The former, on the right, advanced down the main road and railway axis toward St. Remy and Metz. On the left, the latter unit advanced parallel to the riverbank. By the evening the 2nd Battalion had cleared St. Remy and had moved into Woippy, a direct suburb of the city and the final springboard for the river crossings. The 3rd Battalion cleared out the opposition between there and the Moselle.

The following day, Woippy was cleaned out in difficult house-to-house fighting. Further advances, however, were held up by two of the older forts, Gambetta and Deroulède. These had no artillery but were supported by guns firing from St. Julian on the other side of the river, which could shoot into the flanks of the 377th Infantry. Late that evening, they were ordered to maintain their positions and to reorganize the following day for an all-out attack on 18 November, by which time Task Force Bacon would have cleared out the troublesome artillery at St. Julian. However, this was modified the next morning, and they started to move toward the river crossings a day early.

Task Force Bacon

Although organically part of the 95th Division, the task force has to be treated as a separate entity. It formed an independent command and was separated from the rest of the division by the Moselle. Its communications ran via the Thionville bridge in the 90th Division zone although it had nothing to do with the latter formation.

All of 15 November was spent in reorganizing and welding together the two somewhat shattered battalions that formed its basic fighting strength, and the force was not able to start its advance from an assembly area around Bertrange until the following morning. Bacon, although an infantryman, used his composite force with all the skill of the born cavalryman. He advanced in two parallel columns, each headed by a few tanks and tank destroyers, with the infantry following on trucks and on foot. When two 155-mm SP guns were added to his force, they too were attached to the armored spearheads. The mobile artillery and the guns of the tanks battered the way through enemy strongpoints which were then mopped up by the following infantry. Well-aimed rounds from tank destroyers were used against individual snipers!

Colonel Bacon's two columns moved south following the course of the Moselle into Metz. On his left, he was separated from the nearest units of the 90th Division by a huge minefield which had been laid by the Germans. The enemy in the sector was the 1216th VG Regiment, which had originally been part of the Metz garrison but had been transferred to the 19th VG Division. The latter, swept away by the advance of the 90th, had become detached from Metz and thus from the 1216th which returned, in fact if not on paper, to the garrison.

The advance started at 0700 with both battalions and the armor advancing together as far as Bousse, where a German rear guard of some 20 men was speedily put to flight. From there, the 2nd Battalion, 378th Infantry moved down the main road toward Ay-sur-Moselle, although without their intrepid commander, as by that time, Colonel Maroun had been evacuated to a hospital. The Germans had mined the road on either side in an attempt to canalize any attack, but the 1st Battalion 377th Infantry moved onto side roads to advance in parallel toward Ennery. When one column was held up, the other could swing in to carry out a flank attack.

Having advanced 4½ miles, Colonel Bacon halted his columns for the night, worried about his open flank as he believed that the 90th Division had not kept pace with his advance. He sent the 95th Reconnaissance Troop off to establish contact and to make sure that no enemy force could infiltrate the gap.

The advance was continued throughout the following day, after a night of intense patrol activity. This has to be seen in perspective by remembering that the infantry component of the task force had by then been in action continuously for between six and eight days with insufficient sleep, no proper hot food, and with limited possibilities of drying their clothing. The 2nd Battalion took Malroy during the afternoon but was then pinned down by massed artillery fire coming from the guns emplaced around Fort St. Julian. Thus the two columns were temporarily halted by the fort, which was the last outpost barring the way into the city, only 3,000 yards away. American reports speak about "the guns of Fort St. Julian" but the fort itself had no integral artillery of its own. Like Plappeville and Queuleu, it was a work dating from just before the Franco-Prussian War, but the bulk of the artillery from the 19th VG Division had been based there during October to support those defending Maizières. It was this mass of guns that had proved such a hindrance to the 377th Infantry as they tried to move toward the river crossings from Woippy.

The German Situation

Before going on to consider the later stages of the attack from the south by the 5th Division, it is worth briefly examining the state of the defenders, both in the city and in the wider sense. In three days the bulk of the 95th Division had penetrated the fortified salient to the west and were poised to commence the final reduction of the city itself. Although there were still considerable numbers of German troops in the area, most of these were locked up in the forts that were still resisting—a factor that meant that a correspondingly large number of Americans were engaged in watching them. In spite of being hampered by lack of transport and heavy weapons, the Germans had not ceased to resist although severely disorganized.

The fate of the Metz garrison was influenced by the general situation facing the whole of Army Group G at the time. During the evening of 16 November General Balck discussed the situation in detail with von Mellenthin, his Chief of Staff,[4] and it is apparent from the postwar report of the latter that the staff were well aware of American troop movements and the identities of the units involved.[5] After a thorough discussion of the position, they came to the conclusion that they could no longer comply with Hitler's orders to maintain contact with the Metz garrison. The only way to save their First Army as a cohesive force was to order a withdrawal to positions along the Nied and to Faulquemont to guard the approaches to the Saar and the Westwall. Orders for this movement were therefore issued and the German First Army informed General Kittel in Metz that from 17 November, he would be on his own. This, however, was only the official confirmation of a state that had existed for some days—the capture of Fort d'Illange on 15 November finally broke the connection between the 19th VG Division and the garrison of the city.[6]

We have seen that General Kittel officially took command in Metz on 14 November, the day the final assault on the city began in earnest. As soon as the American attacks began to develop he used his meager reserves against the 379th Infantry at the Seven Dwarfs and appealed to First Army for help. All that he could be given was the 38th SS PG Regiment, but this unit had been severely mauled in the fighting at Sanry against the 2nd Infantry bridgehead and at the time was engaged in combat around Chesny.[7] From then on, he was reduced to shuffling the few men who could be spared into the gaps which were beginning to appear all over the place.

During 15 November, the few remaining vehicles were concentrated on replenishing the supplies of the major forts that were still resisting, and owing to the danger of interception, telephone communication with First Army was abandoned. Kittel reckoned that his casualties were running at the rate of 15 percent of effective strength daily. The following day there were the first signs that the rats were leaving the sinking ship. The *Kreisleiter* (the local Nazi Party boss) slunk out of the city together with his staff and a number of sympathizers. General Kittel then ordered the Gestapo chief and police president, Anton Dunkern, to depart, but this worthy had received orders from Himmler to stay put. He was therefore placed in charge of the straggler assembly point. By the afternoon, the internal situation had so deteriorated that FFI men were appearing openly in the streets wearing armbands, and French flags were fluttering from some of the houses in expectation of early liberation. As Kittel himself admitted, "The German police no longer controlled the situation."[8] An attempt was made to evacuate the German population, escorted by eight companies of military police specially sent from Darmstadt, but this proved impossible and the police units were disbanded. Surveying the situation during the evening, General Kittel came to the realization that he could no longer hope for a revival, even to a moderate extent. Writing after the war, he said that up to that point he had thought that Metz would be declared an open city at the last moment, but such a generous gesture was far from the mind of Hitler.

The 5th Division to the South of Metz

The main part of 15 November was spent in regrouping for the final move toward Metz and for making contact with 90th Division troops coming down from the north to seal off the escape routes. These were still nominally open although subject to artillery fire from 5th Division guns ranged on the vital crossroads at Courcelles Chaussy.

General Irwin still had the problem that his limited forces were extended over a wide front, with part of the 2nd Infantry holding the Sanry bridgehead over the Nied. When the 10th Infantry moved inward toward Metz, this flank could become uncovered and dangerously exposed. This was emphasized during the afternoon when the Germans made another attempt to dislodge the defenders of Sanry. A battalion of the 38th SS PG Regiment attempted to take them in the rear by moving along the west bank of the Nied, but were dispersed by 2nd Infantry reserves. The Germans retreated back to the north leaving their previous positions unoccupied. The 5th Division history refers to these as the "Sorbey forts," but in fact, the work consisted only of a simple advanced battery position built around 1910 and never armed.

The German forces in the south opposing the 5th Division still consisted mainly of elements of the 17th SS PG Division, which by then had suffered heavy casualties. Pressure on the right from XII Corps had severed their communications with the Metz garrison, leaving only remnants of the 38th SS PG Regiment in contact. On 14 November, this unit was placed at the disposal of General Kittel as a reserve formation, but it spent a whole day refitting after the fruitless attempts to recapture the Sanry bridgehead. The sector of the front facing the 10th and 11th Infantry Regiments was held by static fortress machine-gun battalions, and at about that time, *Obersturmbannführer* (Colonel) von Matzdorf seems to have been appointed to command the motley units concentrated in the southern suburbs of Metz. Kittel does not say how SS officer von Matzdorf got the job, but from his comments, one can infer that this was his status.

The 5th Division recommenced its general advance on 16 November. Leaving its 3rd Battalion to contain a company of the 48th Fortress Machine Gun Battalion who were holed up in the two Verdun forts, the 11th Infantry moved north from Augny, but soon found themselves pinned down by desperate resistance coming from the Frescaty airfield. Already suffering from nonbattle casualties, the regiment lost 4 officers and 118 men, killed and wounded, on that day. Needing a battalion to contain a company may sound extravagant, but the perimeter around the two Verdun forts was some three miles. The regiment could not afford to leave such a German force at large astride their lines of communication, but needed a whole battalion, weakened by losses, to adequately surround the forts to stop the garrison from sallying out.

The nearer the division approached to the city, the more stubbornly the enemy fought. Von Matzdorf set up his headquarters in Fort St. Privat and did his best to organize defense with the limited forces available. He received useful support from the guns of Fort Driant firing across the river from their positions on the high ground above Ars-sur-Moselle.

In the center, 10th Infantry cleared the town of Marly, which was defended by small pockets of enemy troops, and then advanced toward Magny. On the right, 2nd Infantry was ordered to leave one battalion behind in the Sanry bridgehead and to advance with the other two northward to keep pace with the 10th Infantry, which had had to leave its right wing echeloned to the rear.

After the defeat and withdrawal of the 38th SS, German resistance weakened to a certain extent on 17 November, although there was still no sign of a general collapse. The 10th Infantry, with their right flank now secure, pushed into the southeastern suburbs of the city until brought to a halt by Fort Queuleu. This was another of the large old forts of pre-1870 vintage, similar in configuration to Fort St. Julian. During the German occupation it had been used by the local SS as a tiny concentration camp, and today houses a small museum and memorial devoted to the local Resistance movement.

During the day there was a general eastward withdrawal by the rear echelon troops of the 17th SS PG Division. This unit was in process of being pulled out on orders from above, as it was earmarked for the Ardennes offensive. No one, however, informed General Kittel of the fact. As requests for help from the troops defending Fort Queuleu were received at his headquarters, he ordered the 38th SS, which had been assigned to him as a reserve, to go to their aid. As far as he knew, the 38th SS was at Fort Bellecroix to the east of the city; but when he made enquiries, he discovered that the unit had decamped. "It was difficult to know clearly whether the withdrawal of the SS Regiment resulted from their own decision or, as I assumed, was determined by orders from their SS Division."[9] This was surely a declaration of poverty on the part of a German Lieutenant General, but was typical of the relationship between Wehrmacht and SS units—who were often a law unto themselves.

On the American left wing, the two battalions of the 11th Infantry had a hard day. They became involved in a bitter struggle for the possession of Frescaty airfield, which the enemy defended stubbornly. It was not until the evening that they managed to clear the hangar buildings and the nests of bunkers at the northern edge. Further movement was stopped by intense fire directed from Fort St. Privat, which had to be bypassed. The 10th Infantry established themselves around Fort Queuleu and captured Borny, a small town directly to the east of Metz.

On account of reports that the enemy was still pouring out of the city along the open escape routes, General Patton finally gave permission for the remaining battalion to be pulled out of the Sanry bridgehead, which was to be handed over to CCR of the 10th Armored Division. Egged on by Patton and Walker, the bulk of the regiment hurried north through the night. Early in the morning they captured the key rail junction at Courcelles-sur-Nied through which the last rail shipments in and out of Metz had been made the previous day. This left only the road via St. Avold to Saarbrücken available as an escape route. General Irwin then switched the axis of advance of the regiment to the northwest to support the 10th Infantry. During the afternoon of 18 November, they overran the last of the large groups of fortifications to the east of the city, the Marne group, which had earlier served as the headquarters of the 17th SS.

In the early evening, orders were received from corps for the 2nd Infantry to make another change of direction. They were to push north again in order to link up with patrols from the 90th Division. The regimental commander, Colonel Roffe, promptly detached the 1st Battalion and a company of tanks. In the course of a further night march they crossed the main N.3 road to Saarbrücken, and at 1030 the following morning, they made contact with elements of the 90th Division at Pont Marais. This is situated on the N.54 road to Saarlouis, some 8 miles east of Metz. Thus as thin crust of American troops was astride the remaining escape routes and the city was finally encircled, 11 days after the launch of the final combined assault.

In the meanwhile, during 18 November, troops from both the 10th and.11th Infantry entered the city limits of Metz from the south and southwest. Although forts St. Privat and Queuleu continued to resist, the 5th Division men bypassed them and began to mop up the southern suburbs block by block, fighting their way through the maze of railway yards at Sablon.

Although the assault had taken far longer than planned, the Americans were ideally positioned by 19 November to deliver the knockout blow to the defenders of the city, where cohesion was rapidly disappearing.

$$\equiv 11 \equiv$$

The Final Reduction of the City

By the evening of 17 November, American units were poised to enter the city limits from a number of directions. In order to establish the story of the final encirclement of the city, we have followed the operations of some of them up to the morning of 19 November, but this chapter is concerned with the fighting in Metz itself.

Reading counterclockwise from the north, Task Force Bacon was in the area of Fort St. Julian, preparing for an assault on the following day. Across the Moselle to the northwest of the city, the bulk of the 377th and 378th Infantry Regiments had closed up to the Hafen Canal, which at that point ran parallel to the main stream of the river. To the west, the encircled regiments of the 379th Infantry were at last beginning to move forward down the slopes from the fortifications. Directly to the south, the 10th and 11th Infantry from the 5th Division were also in the outer suburbs. All formations were hampered by lack of manpower, both on account of casualties (many of which were of nonbattle origin) and the detachments which had been left behind to mask the forts.

The following forts were still in action and showed no signs of an early surrender: St. Julian, Queuleu, Gambetta, St. Privat, Plappeville, St. Quentin, Jeanne d'Arc, Driant, Verdun, and a couple of the

Seven Dwarfs. Locking troops up inside these works naturally reduced the numbers available to General Kittel to conduct a flexible defense, but also correspondingly weakened the American forces. The latter were further hampered by the moral restrictions on bombing and artillery shelling. They had to restrict their fire to purely military targets on account of the large number of French civilians still present in the city.

The heart of Metz is situated on the east bank of the Moselle, still occupying the space originally enclosed by the eighteenth-century fortifications. This old quarter was surrounded by nineteenth- and twentieth-century suburbs, factories, and railway installations. To the west, the urban area was bounded by the Hafen Canal and to the east, by the Seille which runs into the Moselle. Between the canal and the main stream of the latter are three islands, St. Symphorien, Ile de Saulcy, and Ile Chambière, where the main command post was located in the Mudra barracks. This whole area of river, canal, and islands is crisscrossed by a large number of bridges, most of which were demolished during the evening of 16 November. The rest were blown on the orders of General Kittel late on 17 November, thus finally cutting him off from the troops still on the west bank. As he later generously admitted, he also unwittingly destroyed the telephone link between the command post and the outer fortifications, as the main 40-strand cable ran along one of the main bridges.[1]

Kittel was, however, fully aware that his situation was critical, but had no intention of giving up the fight. He still planned to pin down as many Americans as possible and force them to take the city block by block. On the evening of 17 November, he issued his last set of comprehensive orders to the remaining forces under his command:

The *1215th VG Regiment* was to withdraw toward the Fort St. Quentin position where the regimental staff were to set up their command post. If the front disintegrated, they were to hold out in the fort.

Regiment Anton (1010th Security Regiment) was to remain in the Plappeville area and defend it for as long as possible. If the front broke up, the divisional artillery commander, Colonel Vogel, was to assume command (at this stage, Colonel Anton was missing).

The *1217th VG Regiment* was to hold out in the Driant area, and that evening, the regimental staff under Colonel Richter was to establish itself in the fort.

The *462 Fusilier Battalion* was to continue to engage the Americans in the Seven Dwarfs, and the staff was to withdraw into Fort Jeanne d'Arc which would also be occupied by the staff of the 462nd VG Division.

Combat Group von Matzdorf was to allow itself to be surrounded in Fort St. Privat.

In the city itself, stragglers and various fragmentary forces were distributed around the various barracks and other centers, road-blocks were set up, and food and ammunition were issued. General Kittel decided to stay on and conduct the defense of the city person-ally, rather than retire to the division command post at Fort Jeanne d'Arc. An indication of his intentions regarding the defense of a town can be gained from the order of the day which he issued on taking over the command on 14 November:[2]

It is possible that enemy troops or tanks will break through the outskirts of the city. The troops will be instructed about the following:

a. During the day, the machineguns and the bulk of the troops will occupy the second and third floors of corner buildings. The house entrance must be protected by two guards.

b. The corner house will be manned by no less than a squad.

c. At night, the troops will be on the ground floor.

d. To hang around street corners and then disappear at the first sign of the enemy is forbidden. Every street must give the appearance of emptiness and ambush.

e. The opening of fire in the streets is effective only if the enemy cannot find any cover.

f. Instead of extending in depth, the defense must be linear and should be echeloned in height up to the roofs on street corners and individual streets.

g. *Panzerfaust* (antitank rocket) troops must be on the ground floor. Win-dow open! Ambush!

h. Running about in the streets is forbidden. It is necessary when occupying a house to establish a messenger and supply route not under enemy fire, through the courtyard and garden (by wall break-throughs etc). . . .

ACTION DURING 18 NOVEMBER

The key to an easy entry into the heart of the city lay in capturing any bridges left intact, but this hope was largely frustrated by the wholesale demolitions ordered by General Kittel. Other hopes were pinned on positive action by the FFI, who were estimated to number some 400 combatants. A BBC broadcast ordered the Metz FFI to hinder bridge destruction[3] and this was repeated in a message from XX Corps broadcast in the clear on the morning of 17 November.

On the right of the 95th Division, the three battalions of the 379th Infantry finally established contact with each other behind the fortified line and a supply route by road had at last been opened up. It was decided to attack toward the river valley the following morning with the 1st and 3rd Battalions. Leaving two companies to garrison the Seven Dwarfs, the 1st Battalion moved west across the plateau to where it dipped down into the valley above the suburbs of Jussy and Vaux. They thus managed to cut off the rear communications of Jeanne d'Arc, and by the evening the battalion was on the river at Moulins-les-Metz, where they found the road bridge demolished. During the day, the 3rd Battalion cleared the suburbs to the west of Jeanne d'Arc, thus completely isolating the fortress. As the bridge at Moulins had been blown and as the river there was considered unsuitable for a boat crossing, the regiment was then ordered to contain Driant and Jeanne d'Arc and to mop up the remaining enemy forces and isolated snipers in their area.

In the division center, the 378th Infantry was still gravely short of manpower. With the 2nd Battalion detached to Task Force Bacon, the 1st Battalion was fully occupied in trying to seal off Fort Plappeville. There, Colonel Vogel had been supplied with ammunition and provisions by his neighbor at Fort St. Quentin (Colonel von Stössel). The two forts formed a defended island linked by a causeway on the ridge and were surrounded by steep ridges on all sides except for the front. Von Stössel had his regimental staff, numbering around 25, plus a similar number of engineers. As garrison troops there was Fortress Engineer Battalion 55 and the 2nd Battalion of the 1010th Security Regiment plus various stragglers. This gave him a total of 650 men to defend a large complex, and he based his defense on the four entrances. He stated that there was food for 18 days, but bread, potatoes, salt, and coffee were scarce. There was little ammunition and neither barbed wire nor mines. Apart from personal weapons and a few mortars, firepower consisted of two heavy infantry howitzers—his two 80-mm mortars were without ammunition. The value of the position was that it overlooked the river and canal which the Americans would have to cross, and it could fire into the city. If the Germans had taken steps in time to supply these forts with sufficient weapons and ammunition, the capture of the city would have taken much longer, and the buildings would have been destroyed in the process. In spite of poor radio communication, von Stössel was able to direct the turret guns of Fort Driant and Jeanne d'Arc from time to time. However, "Due to the lack of heavy weapons we could do little to fight the enemy. He keeps himself out of the range of small infantry weapons."[4]

This left the 3rd Battalion of the 378th Infantry as the only unit available to seize the main road bridge running from Longeville across the Ile St. Symphorian. Their 81-mm mortars fired smoke shells to blind the enemy gunners on the ridge containing Fort St. Quentin and Plappeville; and with a few tanks in support, the lead company managed to drive back a small force of Germans guarding the western end. (This was the bridge that Kittel had ordered left intact until the last minute.) A platoon of I Company immediately charged across, but the Germans blew the structure, killing eight men who were still on it. This left three men isolated on the far side; their only course was to take cover. John Kelly, the battalion commander at the time, wrote to me about the courageous action of Lieutenant Crawford, one of I Company's officers. Crawford found a small boat, and under heavy fire, paddled across the river and retrieved the men who had been cut off so suddenly. "Needless to say—*he* was *our* hero of the Battle of Metz." As it was then decided that a crossing would have to be carried out the following day, the rest of the battalion closed up to the river and winkled out the few Germans remaining on the west bank.

The 377th Infantry had the bulk of its two battalions in the suburbs of Sansonnet and Metz Nord. The 2nd Battalion's objective was the bridge over the Hafen Canal to the north, and to reach this, they had to advance down the main N.53 road—known to the Americans as "88 Boulevard." This was on account of accurate fire from one of these dual-purpose guns situated on the island. A short distance from the bridge, the attackers were met by a furious hail of fire from the "88," from machine guns, and 20-mm antiaircraft guns on the island. Most of these were knocked out by the supporting tanks, and it was then discovered that the bridge, although demolished, could still be used. G Company clambered over the wreckage and soon reduced all resistance on the island while engineers managed to repair the bridge sufficiently to permit the passage of jeeps.

During the morning, the 3rd Battalion also managed to cross to the island where some 200 prisoners had been captured. The regiment was then ordered to force their way across the main stream of the Moselle if this could be undertaken without incurring too many casualties. They were told that boats would be made available, but in the meanwhile, the enemy was rallying on the Ile Chambière on the far side. There, General Kittel was organizing the defenders for a last stand around his command post.

The mission for Task Force Bacon was to assault and capture Fort St. Julian on 18 November, planned as follows: The 2nd Battalion, 378th Infantry, was to attack the fort from the rear at 0700, while the 1st Battalion, 377th Infantry, was to bypass the fort and clear the suburb of St. Julian. After this, the battalion was to advance toward Fort Bellecroix and try to cross the Seille. During the morning, the 2nd Battalion moved cautiously around to the rear of the fort where the bulk of the garrison had been distributed among the field fortifications.[5] The attackers were thus delayed by snipers and small groups who had to be flushed out of pillboxes. By early afternoon, however, they had reached the dry ditch that surrounded the work. There was only one way across this, via a causeway and a bridge that led to the main entrance to the interior of the fort. The outer end of the causeway was defended by a courtyard formed of thick walls well supplied with loopholes.

In spite of small-arms fire from all directions, this courtyard was taken by storm while the heavy-weapons section fired at the offending loopholes to keep the defenders busy. Other men had probed their way along the rear of the fort trying to find another way in, but were unsuccessful. Thus the only was was over the bridge and through the heavy metal door at the far end.

Fort St. Julian was designed to cope with methods of attack used during the latter part of the nineteenth century. The rear wall of the fort rose vertically some forty feet from the floor of the ditch, and the main barracks were situated behind this under the rampart. From the barrack casemates, apertures or loopholes were placed to direct fire along the ditch and to cover the bridge. In the center and just to the right of the latter was a projecting building which was also designed to provide flanking fire. Such forts, when fully garrisoned by as many as 1,000 men, could produce such a hail of fire along the rear wall and ditch, that it was virtually impossible to get across without resorting to mining underneath. Siege warfare in those days was a protracted business of lengthy bombardments and a lot of spade work.

The Germans inside were comparatively few in number (362 men commanded by a major). The latter was probably Major Weiler, a battalion commander of the 1215th VG Regiment who had managed to evacuate his men across the river when attacked by the 377th Infantry south of Maizières on 14 November.

The few men in the courtyard were unable to make any impression on the door, so some muscle was called for. Two light tanks were run up into the courtyard (since demolished) and sprayed the surrounding loopholes with their machine guns. Then a tank destroyer was placed in position to fire both armor-piercing and high-explosive shells at the door from a range of fifty yards! All this bombardment accomplished was to make some small holes in the metal. In desperation, Task Force Bacon then produced their ultimate weapon, one of the 155-mm SP guns. This was driven up onto the bridge approach, and from point-blank range, it fired ten rounds at the door—again without success. The target was then switched to the masonry surround, and after a further twenty rounds, the supports finally gave way, leaving the door to collapse inward with a mighty crash. Although a new entrance has since been bulldozed into the fort, one can still see the original gateway and the smashed surround. Had the garrison possessed just one antitank gun, the Americans would not have enjoyed such an undisturbed shoot.

By the time the entrance had been battered down it was dark, so no attempt was made to follow up and penetrate into the interior. In the meanwhile, however, the 1st Battalion, bypassing the fort, tried to push into the town of St. Julian. There it was held up by what the divisional historian refers to as "heavy mortar fire."[6] On the other hand, General Kittel said that he learnt from intercepted radio traffic that the fort was to be bypassed, and that as a result, he sent a heavy antiaircraft battery to take position to the north of Fort Bellecroix "for the purpose of destroying enemy tanks that had broken through."[7]

Headed by the tank destroyers, the battalion managed to move into St. Julian during the early afternoon when opposition slackened, and carried on toward their objective, Fort Bellecroix. This was a huge eighteenth-century work that the Germans (and the French army today) largely used for storage purposes. Company A moved around to the rear, where they took a number of prisoners. However, while C Company was on the road that ran around the northern edge of the fort, there was a tremendous explosion. Company C took the full force of the blast, which had been preceeded by German soldiers rushing out waving white flags. Eight men were killed and 48 were wounded, thus reducing the company to virtually half strength at one stroke. The odd thing is that the few German sources do not mention this event at all. One can only assume that a magazine exploded, either by accident or design. As a result, the battalion pulled back into St. Julian for the night, to reorganize and to care for the wounded.

The other mobile element of Task Force Bacon, the 95th Reconnaissance Troop, spent the day moving west in the direction of Vallières in a vain attempt to establish contact with the 10th Infantry Regiment.

The movements of the 5th Infantry Division were basically described in the previous chapter. By the end of the day, both the 10th and 11th Infantry were in the southern suburbs of Metz, although hampered by resistance for Fort St. Privat and Queuleu. The latter had a considerable garrison probably numbering some 500 men, including the remnants of the southern artillery section, a group of some 200 stragglers, the staff of the 22 Fortress Infantry Regiment, and a few members of the *Volkssturm* (Home Guard). Attempts were made by 10th Infantry to storm the place, but the area of the fort was far too large to be easily dealt with by the limited forces available.

The 11th Infantry were in the southern suburbs of the city, although they had had to detach considerable numbers to watch the Verdun Group and Fort St. Privat, commanded by the energetic von Matzdorf. The regimental history states that German tanks were sighted to the east of the fort, but it is quite clear that the enemy had no armored vehicles in Metz.[8] Karl Clarkson arrived as a replacement in the 1st Battalion, 11th Infantry, as they were surrounding the fort. "We dug a hole and for several days didn't get out as they were firing over our hole. The tanks were firing armor piercing shells at the fort and they would ricochet off and plop into the mud right by us. At night they would try to convince the Germans to give up as they talked to them with a loudspeaker and promised them American chow, oranges, and cigarettes. Every time the Germans wouldn't give up, they fired white phosphorous shells to try and burn them out."[9]

In spite of frustrations caused by the forts, the 10th Infantry did manage to capture one interesting item of booty that day. *Brigade-führer* (SS Brigadier) Anton Dunkern, the former police president of Metz, was found skulking in a brewery by some men from E Company. One can imagine that the men were looking for something other than an SS general in a brewery![10] Dunkern had been around in Metz for some while, and at the time of the first American attacks in September, Erich Kemper, the commandant of the SS Signal School, had the following to say about his activities: "[He] gave us every information with regard to those opposed to Germany and criminal elements in the population, and assisted in the elimination of these enemies."[11]

Robert Allen expands somewhat on the capture of Dunkern, stating that the men who found him mistook him for an army officer in the wine cellar (not brewery). He was taken to Patton as a form of pre-Christmas present; Patton had the pleasure of interrogating him with the aid of a Jewish interpreter. Dunkern was the first high-ranking SS officer to be captured by the Third Army, and being a member of the general SS rather than the military *Waffen SS,* was regarded as a political offender.[12]

Inside the city itself, by the evening of 18 November, General Kittel had ceased "to make plans," and from then on concerned himself purely with the immediate defense of the area around his headquarters on the Ile Chambière.

EVENTS OF 19 NOVEMBER

Task Force Bacon had some unfinished business to complete at Fort St. Julian. At dawn, an officer and an NCO slipped across the bridge at the head of a platoon from F Company of the 378th Infantry. Just inside the tunnel leading back from the blasted doorway, they surprised a German NCO who was placing a squad in firing position. At bayonet point he was forced to take Sergeant Rautmann to the major commanding the garrison, who was persuaded to surrender to him.

The 1st Battalion, which had retired for the night to lick its wounds following the explosion at Fort Bellecroix, moved back into the area. There, somewhat to their surprise, they found that one of the bridges over the Seille at the back of the fort was still in one piece. While forming up, they left a squad to keep an eye on the bridge, and in due course, a group of Germans arrived with a machine gun to set up a defensive position. Initially, the Americans held their fire so as not to alarm the enemy. However, a truck loaded with assault boats arrived unannounced within range of the Germans, who quite naturally opened fire. The American observation squad replied by disabling the machine gun and its crew, putting the rest of the defenders to flight.

At 1130, a rifle company supported by a platoon of tanks crossed the bridge and began to fan out into the old part of the city, constantly harassed by snipers. This area was defended by a motley group of some 700 men from various units, commanded by Colonel Meier who was the city commandant. The latter had his headquarters in a barrack block that was impossible to defend, and during the evening he managed to contact General Kittel on one of the few telephones that was still working (Kittel had ordered the main telephone exchange blown up during the evening of 18 November). Colonel Meier reported that it was impractical to try to evacuate his men to the Ile Chambières and requested permission to attempt to break out. Permission was granted, but he was subsequently taken prisoner.

Advancing steadily, Task Force Bacon managed to gain control of a large part of the city center during the afternoon, and in the evening they were informed that the Gestapo headquarters was still occupied. As it was feared that the staff might escape, two tank destroyers and a few infantry were guided to the building by FFI men, and 20 rounds were fired into it.

The 95th Reconnaissance Troop tried again to make contact with 5th Division to the east of the city, and during a sweep toward Vallières, they met up with elements of the 10th Infantry at 1110 hours—shortly after the pincers had been finally closed across the escape routes by the 2nd Infantry Regiment and the 90th Division Reconnaissance Troop. Later in the day, corps ordered Task Force Bacon to set up another contact point at the railway triangle just south of Fort Bellecroix. Troops were rushed there but on arrival they were met by such a hail of fire from 5th Division artillery, that they beat a prudent retreat.

The 377th Infantry, which had established themselves on the island between the Hafen Canal and the Moselle, were ordered to cross onto the Ile Chambière, where the main enemy resistance was expected. Initially there was confusion as to where the crossing should be made, which resulted in the support bombardment falling in the wrong place. Losses in the first boats were heavy, but by midafternoon a 200-yard foothold had been gained on the far bank where 300 prisoners were taken. By the evening the whole of the 2nd Battalion was across plus one company of the 3rd, and they had managed to enter two of the large barrack complexes on the island.

In the center, the mission of the 3rd Battalion, 378th Infantry, was to cross over the Ile St. Symphorian. Backed by artillery and fire from their supporting armor, two companies paddled across in assault boats during the morning. The support fire disorganized the Germans on the island who were overrun fairly quickly, but when the 3rd Battalion reached the far side, they found that the bridges leading into the city center were down. This meant another boat trip and the job of manhandling the craft from one side of the island to the other, where they had also managed to "liberate" a few rowing boats and canoes.

However, before they could cross into the city, the boundary with 5th Division had to be sorted out. In the last orders concerning boundaries issued by XX Corps on 14 November, the parts of the city to the east of the Moselle Canal had been assigned to the 5th Division, but as the men of the 378th were on the spot and raring to go, a boundary change was agreed—the nearest 5th Division unit, the 11th Infantry, had at that time not been able to clear the area around the railway yards at Sablon. At 1700, the second crossing was made against negligible resistance according to American sources, whereas General Kittel stated that the first assault wave was repulsed by German troops in the Bayern Kaserne (now the Général de Lattre de Tassigny barracks).[13]

Faced by the lack of a suitable crossing site, the 379th Infantry was robbed of the glamor of a storm assault on Metz. The regiment was ordered to clear its rear area and concentrate on buttoning up the main forts. During the morning, contact was made with the 1st Battalion of the 378th who had been attacking Fort Plappeville and the defended ridge between it and Fort St. Quentin. In spite of having a hard nut to crack, the 378th requested a boundary change to give them St. Quentin as well, as it formed with Fort Plappeville, a single defended unit. However, by the afternoon they realized that they had bitten off more than they could chew and requested that the whole complex be turned over to the 379th. At the time, the latter was still busy mopping up its own territory, but during the evening was told to take over responsibility for St. Quentin by the morning.

In the 5th Division sector, the 11th Infantry with two forts in its rear and isolated combat still in progress at the airfield, had only the 3rd

Battalion for the battle around the railway yards, a feature that by its very nature was ideally suited to defense. The bulk of the 10th Infantry was into the eastern and southeastern suburbs, but was still held up by fighting around Fort Queuleu. However, all three infantry divisions were in contact with each other by the morning of 19 November, and the final reduction of the city was purely a matter of time.

That evening, General Kittel noted, "a weird silence prevailed in the city. The previous nightly artillery barrage, which had been very annoying at times, had stopped entirely. The night was clear."[14] With so many of their own troops scattered around the various quarters of the city and with German resistance obviously coming to an end, American artillery was forced to use restraint. Anyway, there was no point in smashing the place up any further. One fact mentioned by Kittel was that attempts were made to air-drop supplies to the encircled forts during the night, although this is not recorded in any of the American sources. He states that, during the night of 19 November, "We failed in our second attempt, by means of three supply planes, to furnish the forts St. Quentin and Plappeville with infantry ammunition. Although the planes were punctually at the arranged spot, the defense troops were not in a position to fire off the required recognition signal because this was the very thing which was lacking." One can only have sympathy for the garrisons as they heard their supply aircraft overhead but could not fire the recognition signal!

EVENTS FROM 20 TO 22 NOVEMBER

This was a somewhat confused period of street fighting as the assault units closed in on the last centers of organized resistance. Aside from the main conflict, the 379th Infantry found that their mission had been greatly extended. Operations Instruction No. 7 was issued; it ordered the regiment to take over responsibility for all the forts still holding out on the west bank. They were required not later than 0730 on 21 November, to launch an attack to contain and then capture Fort Plappeville, the two main bunkers between it and St. Quentin, St. Quentin itself, Jeanne d'Arc, the Seven Dwarfs, and Fort Driant! As much supporting fire as possible was to be employed to effect capture or surrender, but the instruction sensibly stated, "No fortification will be assaulted in the face of heavy enemy fire, or enemy fire that will result in casualties." These orders would appear to be somewhat contradictory as they specified an attack. In practice, however, they meant that as long as the Germans were prepared to make a fight of it, they could only be buttoned down and contained. The proud forts were only worth a regiment to the Americans, who were not going to lose any blood in a prestige attack.

As a preliminary to carrying out these orders, the 3rd Battalion relieved the 378th Infantry in the St. Quentin area, and the following morning, the 1st Battalion took over control of Fort Plappeville. There, they promptly tried an attack, but as artillery was quite ineffective against the fort, they soon desisted in order to avoid casualties. An air strike arranged for 21 November against Plappeville failed to materialize. More subtle forms of persuasion were also tried. The ever-hopeful psychological warfare people were on hand with their loudspeaker trucks, bombarding the encircled Germans with mouthwatering offers of hot food, cigarettes, and other goodies dear to the hearts of soldiers. Colonel Vogel did emerge under a flag of truce and agreed to meet the regimental intelligence officer. He was prepared to negotiate a cease-fire for the evacuation of wounded, but refused to surrender until he was either expelled by force or his food and ammunition ran out.

During this period, the German radio extolled at great length the heroism of the fort garrisons, urging them to do their duty and to continue to resist. Conditions inside the forts, however, must have been pretty grim. With the ventilating and generating systems largely out of order, the wet weather would have produced massive condensation and bitter cold inside the bare concrete chambers. Food was generally in short supply, and even the most fanatical must have realized that the situation was hopeless. It is to their credit as soldiers that they continued to resist until forced to give in from lack of food and water. This latter element was certainly a problem, although the rain had provided a welcome source of supply. It was an irony that one soldier's deluge was another's momentary salvation during the Battle of Metz!

However, other changes were in the offing, and with the Metz battle more or less over, the war had to go on, and the 95th was required for the Saar campaign. Late on 21 November the 379th Infantry was ordered to prepare to hand over their zone to 5th Division troops. The following day the regiment pulled in its outlying detachments, and during the morning of 23 November they were relieved by the 2nd Infantry. The 379th moved to a new staging position around Peltre, a few miles to the southeast of the city, bidding a not too fond farewell to the forts.

The units in the city, having gone to ground for the night, were back in action at dawn on 20 November. The single battalion of the 378th accomplished its final mission when it captured the main railway station, and during the morning, patrols made contact with the neighboring formations. By midday, Task Force Bacon was able to report that resistance had ceased in its sector of the city; and the following day, this composite unit was officially dissolved, the two infantry battalions returning to their parent units. Commanded by a resourceful officer, this task force had provided on a small scale, an able demonstration of cooperation between infantry and armor in the field. In their area the enemy had been prepared to fight against conventional infantry assaults, but by swinging around the flanks and using his armor as mobile artillery, Colonel Bacon had been able to seize the initiative and wage a fluid campaign.

The 5th Infantry Division units managed to clear the southern sector of the city and reported officially that all resistance had ceased at 1200 hours on 21 November, by which time Fort Queuleu had surrendered. Apart from the Verdun Group in the rear, that left Fort St. Privat as an immediate concern for the 11th Infantry. During the afternoon of 20 November, two figures emerged from the fort bearing a white flag. Under the natural assumption that the garrison wished to surrender, the CO of the 1st Battalion and a doctor who spoke German, went forward to meet *Obersturmbannführer* von Matzdorf. All he wanted, however, was to evacuate ten severely-wounded men and then to continue fighting. Major Shell pointed out to him that he might just as well surrender, but von Matzdorf replied that he and his men were prepared to die fighting, "if necessary."[15] Later the same afternoon when news of the surrender of Fort Queuleu was received, Captain Kittstein returned to see von Matzdorf, but the latter still refused to give up. It is probable, however, that he was only speaking for himself and a few devoted followers, for during the night of 22 November, a number of his men deserted and reported that morale inside the fort was low.

On 22 November, the 11th Infantry set up its forward command post in the Hotel Royal, one of the smartest establishments in Metz that had previously been favored by the Nazi hierarchy (including Hitler) when they visited the city. The victors were beginning to enjoy the spoils which they had earned so bitterly.

It fell to the lot of the 377th Infantry to bear the brunt of the fighting for the remainder of the city. By the early morning of 20 November, both battalions were deployed in their narrow foothold on the Ile Chambière, where General Kittel and the last defenders were holed up in the Mudra Caserne and the surrounding buildings. The 2nd Battalion, on the left, was assigned to clear the northern part of the island. Progress was slow as numerous snipers and machine guns were concealed in the solid-stone buildings that had to be ferreted out one by one. Companies F and G were held up by one such block which had a direct field of fire along the street that they were trying to clear. Sergeant Miller of G Company took a bazooka and climbed onto the roof of a neighboring building, from where he was able to knock out the offending machine gun. German medical orderlies then appeared and requested permission to evacuate the wounded. However, Sergeant Miller managed to talk them into surrendering and a long file of men emerged with their hands up. By that evening, the battalion had cleared their portion of the island, and except for mopping up the following day, their part in the battle ended.

The 2nd Battalion had a much harder time of it at the southern end. Fighting from block to block, by the evening they had managed to close in on the Mudra Caserne. There, General Kittel stated that tracer ammunition had set fire to part of the barracks and that the Americans had enfiltrated into the garages. His fear was that they would discover the underground passages with which the whole area was honeycombed. These originated in the eighteenth-century fortifications, but had been modified by succeeding generations of engineers to form a bombproof refuge under the command post. He says that an American patrol who had discovered one of the entrances in the vicinity of the electricity works was driven out by a flamethrower attack.

Early in the morning of 21 November, I Company managed to get into the ground floor of the barracks, but there were still Germans fighting on the two floors above. However, by then the engineers had a bridge capable of bearing armored vehicles over the Moselle, and a tank was brought up. This systematically proceeded to shoot the top floor to pieces, which led to the surrender of the remaining defenders of the command post. A tank was also used to shoot a group of Germans out of a church in which they had barricaded themselves in the center of the island.

It was assumed that when the Mudra barracks fell, General Kittel would be captured. He, however, no longer having any useful command function to perform, had participated in the fighting as an ordinary soldier. At around 1100 hours he was wounded in the knee and taken to the adjacent tobacco factory where the Germans had their aid post. Von Stössel at St. Quentin was notified of the general's incapacity, and the colonel then assumed command of the fortress, such as it was.

Shortly afterward, some men from K Company found an American medical orderly who had managed to escape from the tobacco factory where he had been held prisoner, and he told them that Kittel was there. The company then rushed the building and managed to occupy it without too much trouble. A few determined Germans barricaded themselves in the generating room, but to grenade them out would have robbed the place of power. They were, however, soon talked (or threatened) into surrender.

The fortress commander was found on the operating table, still under anaesthetic. When he came around, he was requested to surrender the garrison, which he quite rightly refused to do. First, he had officially relinquished the command to Colonel von Stössel, and second, the outer forts were still unsubdued. Although they had taken the city of Metz by storm for the first time in some 1,500 years, XX Corps was robbed of the formality of a surrender ceremony with the cameras clicking as General Kittel marched up and handed over his sword and the keys of the fortress. For many, this would have set the seal on the successful outcome of the battle.

All was not quite over, however. The following day, fighting still continued on the Ile Chambière, and the 3rd Battalion of the 377th Infantry had to go through the tunnels flushing out groups of Germans by using phosphorous grenades. At precisely 1435 hours, the regimental commander informed General Twaddle that all resistance in the city had ceased, and three minutes later, this information was logged at XX Corps HQ. The Battle of Metz was officially over, but large numbers of troops were still involved with the outlying forts. It would take another three weeks before the whole area could be reported clear of the enemy and be handed over to the French authorities.

☰ 12 ☰

The Aftermath

After the battle, the euphoria. However, there was little time for celebration as the Battle of Metz was not an isolated event but merely part of the general late autumn campaign all along the Allied front. The Moselle was still just one more river that *had* been crossed and the immediate concern was the Saar—en route to the Rhine. There was a short interval for trumpet blowing while the victors moved into the best quarters in town and were able to lick their wounds.

Mutually congratulatory messages poured in from all sides, full of bombast and, naturally, ignoring all the mistakes that had been made. Those troops not involved in the field were able to celebrate Thanksgiving Day with all the traditional trimmings, by courtesy of services of supply. General Patton's cavalcade roared into Metz with sirens blaring, the general in the pose of a medieval conqueror, where he reviewed the weary men of the 5th Division. Medals were dished out by the score and the usual roistering pep talk was delivered to an enraptured audience. "I am very proud of you. Your country is proud of you. You are magnificent fighting men. Your deeds in the Battle of Metz will fill the pages of history for a thousand years."[1] This was a prophecy that was not fulfilled, otherwise there would have been no need to write this book! The only memorial in the city is a street named after XX Corps.

On 22 November, General Twaddle issued a message to be read to the 95th Division, which ran as follows:

"On 8 November, at the beginning of our offensive against Metz, I told you: 'The road that leads through Metz is the road that will take us into Germany. On it we will earn the title you chose for yourselves—The Victory Division.'

"You were 'green' troops when you heard those words. Now, two weeks later, you are old soldiers. In the hell of fire along the Moselle and around the mighty forts of Metz you proved your courage, your resourcefulness, and your skill.

"Nothing I can say can add to the pride and satisfaction you must feel in your own hearts. Your magnificent performance in this, your first battle, has materially shortened the road that leads to Germany and to Victory."[2]

These plaudits were well deserved, if somewhat flowery. In fact, the 95th got most of the credit for the capture of Metz, which rankled with the 5th Division who had been at it for much longer and whose losses had been considerably greater. The new boys had come in and swept up all the plums. As far as the vanquished were concerned, most of them simply ceased to exist, as the 462nd VG Division and its attached units were written off. The 17th SS PG Division survived as a unit until the end of the war, but seldom as more than a Kampfgruppe (battle group). The same fate befell the 19th VG and 416th Infantry Divisions, who were sucked up in the fighting around the Saar and in the Palatinate.

The "butcher's bill" is impossible to determine with any accuracy. American casualties were computed on a monthly basis and cannot be isolated for any particular period. Statistics make sterile reading matter, but as an example, I will cite the losses suffered by the 5th Division for November, most of which were incurred during the first three weeks of the month: 185 killed, 1,044 wounded, and 147 missing. As these probably include a large proportion of nonbattle casualties, it is impossible to separate the combat losses.[3] The really staggering losses were actually suffered during the early stages of the battle in September, when small units were reduced at times to half strength. As far as the enemy were concerned, General Kittel gives the following figures for the actual battle in the city: 400 killed and 2,200 wounded, but these naturally apply only to his own command and not the neighboring formations. This was probably on the low side, and the XX Corps estimate of 14,368 prisoners, 3,800 killed, and 7,904 wounded, seems rather high. As nobody kept accurate accounts in the heat of battle, we shall never know.[4]

After the fall of the city, the mission of XX Corps was to move its tired troops out of Metz and to resume its place beside XII Corps in the advance to the Saar. The 90th Infantry and 10th Armored Division, who apart from initiating the pincer movement had not been involved in the reduction of the city, were stretched in an arc from the old crossing site at Cattenom, to Bouzonville. General Walker's immediate task was to extricate the 95th Division from Metz and to deploy it to the west for the advance to the Saar—still one more river. This was not so simple, owing to the general devastation in Metz and the lack of bridges. Vehicles were in urgent need of repair, casualties had to be replaced, and equipment overhauled. It was decided that the bulk of the 5th Division should remain behind to finish off the forts, and the relief was carried out in stages between 21 and 23 November. The 95th was to move into the former 5th Division sector and be deployed parallel to the 90th. General Twaddle sensibly asked for four days respite for rehabilitation, which was granted by corps. General Walker had been assigned by Patton the mission of clearing the country as far as the Saar and then of carrying out a number of crossings, following a general offensive to be launched on 25 November. The story of the XX Corps on the Saar and their involvement in the Ardennes campaign, however, belong to another period.

THE FATE OF THE FORTS

When the city of Metz was captured, the following forts were still holding out: the Verdun Group, St. Privat, Driant, Jeanne d'Arc, St. Quentin, and Plappeville, plus some opposition still in the Seven Dwarfs. As before, the 11th Infantry remained in the south and the 10th Infantry were in the St. Quentin sector, while the 2nd Infantry covered the area between Driant and Jeanne d'Arc.

The first to fall was the Verdun Group. The garrison had initiated discussions on 25 November, and at 0800 the following morning, the two forts were surrendered to Major John Acuff, executive officer of the 3rd Battalion. Two officers and 148 men marched out, their food having been exhausted. They were the remnants of the 48th Fortress

Machine Gun Battalion. After the capitulation, the American flag was aptly raised on the forts by K Company, who had fought so gallantly at Dornot as part of the regiment's 2nd Battalion.

Between 24 and 25 November, 2nd Infantry patrols probed the line of the Seven Dwarfs and found them unoccupied, which made it possible to cut communication between Driant and Jeanne d'Arc. There was no intention of wasting valuable ammunition in shelling the forts or of becoming involved in all-out attacks. Therefore, more subtle forms of persuasion were tried, including barrages of leaflets. These informed the garrisons of the fall of the city, and one leaflet ran as follows:

Information for the surrounded German units.

METZ HAS FALLEN!

Among the many German soldiers who are now in safety as American prisoners of war, is Colonel Mayer [Meier], previously the Metz city commandant. [He had tried to break out on the night of 19 November].

Colonel Mayer surrendered because he did not want to burden his conscience with the blood of uselessly murdered civilians.

If Colonel Mayer was with you he would say:

"Comrades!

The main front is already 30 km to the east of Metz.

The last German units in Lorraine are pulling back into the *Westwall* followed by the attacking Americans.

Further resistance in your positions no longer has any tactical value for both the American and the German high commands.

You have done your duty as soldiers.

Your duty now is to save your lives.

The Battle of Metz is lost.

YOU CAN SAVE YOUR LIVES."

STOP PRESS: Lieutenant General Kittel, commander of the 462 Infantry Division (sic) and SS *Brigadeführer* Dunkern are also prisoners.[5]

Some artillery was, however, fired at the forts, and German prisoners later stated that the effects were greatly feared. American small-arms fire was directed at anything that moved during daylight, and after dark, patrols crisscrossed the area to hinder the Germans from sneaking out. Such attempts were certainly made. Colonel von Stössel sent out at least two patrols in an effort to get a message to LXXXII Corps, still his immediate superior authority, but both were captured together with the letters they carried. One of these, as well as giving details of the earlier history of von Stössel's occupation of the fort (St. Quentin), described his efforts to maintain contact with the outside world. Apparently his radio failed on 25 November. He ended by stating that the morale of his troops was good, which may well have been an exaggeration.[6] Prisoners captured stated exactly the opposite.[7] Both, of course, would say what they knew was expected of them.

The second fort to surrender, which freed the 1st Battalion, 11th Infantry, was Fort St. Privat, which had continued to resist in spite of repeated loudspeaker bombardment. On 29 November, Colonel Black, the new regimental commander who had replaced Colonel Yuill on 21 November, held two conferences under flag of truce with von Matzdorf. After the second meeting, the latter agreed to surrender the fort at 1600, and at the time appointed, 22 officers and 488 men emerged, 80 of whom were wounded.

On 27 November, the 2nd Battalion, 11th Infantry, moved out of Metz and relieved the 10th Infantry units in the Plappeville-St. Quentin sector. In the 2nd Infantry area, appeals to Fort Driant were ignored, but a meeting was arranged with Major Voss, commanding at Fort Jeanne d'Arc. Upon being required to surrender unconditionally, the latter termed this "dishonorable and therefore unacceptable."[8] It would seem that some of the German officers were still thinking in terms of the historic usages of war, where the commander of a fortress could capitulate with honor after a token resistence had been made—the garrison would then march out with "flags flying, drums beating, and bayonets fixed" and officers would be permitted to retain their swords. By 1944, the age of chivalry in European warfare was over, alas.

During the last week in November, the 10th Infantry was withdrawn and moved to the east to join up with the 95th Division. The next approach was made on 1 December, to Colonel von Stössel at St. Quentin. Colonel Black, with Captain Kittstein (from a psychological warfare unit) as his interpreter, walked up to the fort with a white flag. Kittstein and an enlisted man actually went inside and arranged a conference to take place between the two respective commanders. At this meeting, terms were discussed but no surrender was agreed. It was not until five days later that a white flag was seen on the fort and a message was received requesting a meeting at 1130, at the bottom of the hill leading up to the western entrance. Colonel Franson was appointed as the American representative, and a surrender was agreed upon which was officially accepted by Franson and Major Russel of the 2nd Battalion, 11th Infantry.[9] The prisoners taken were 22 officers, 124 NCO's, and 458 hungry enlisted men; in addition, there was a large quantity of weapons and military stores.

By then, however, it was time for the 5th Infantry to move on and leave the forts to others. On December 6, the 2nd Battalion was in the process of being relieved by 87th Division troops and getting ready to march to Lauterbach on the German border. However, there were still 5th Division personnel in the area, who on the following day, negotiated the surrender of the neighboring Fort Plappeville. A parley was held outside the fort at 1130; the meeting had been set up by Captain Durst, commanding G Company of the 11th Infantry. After the situation had been explained, Colonel Vogel surrendered unconditionally.

And then there were two—Driant and Jeanne d'Arc. The former was a cause celèbre for the German radio which was still broadcasting morale-boosting appeals to the garrison. Early in the morning on 8 December, the 2nd Infantry Regiment was in the process of being relieved by a unit of the 87th Division. There were, however, headquarters personnel still in the area, when two NCO's from Fort Driant arrived to request a meeting. This was something that the 2nd Infantry had no intention of handing over on a plate to their successors. The capture of Fort Driant was an important battle honor, and apparently General Walker did his best to prolong the relief operation so that the surrender could be taken, justly, by 5th Division troops. At 1500, Colonel Richter, the garrison commander, met Colonel Roffe, commanding the 2nd Infantry, at the base of the hill leading up to the fort. After a parley lasting about half an hour, Colonel Roffe formally accepted the surrender, in spite of claims made by the 87th Division—

which had done nothing to deserve it. Nineteen officers and 592 enlisted men marched away into captivity.

The only fort that the 5th Division had to relinquish to their successors was Jeanne d'Arc, which continued to resist until 13 December, when it surrendered to the 26th Infantry Division. This fort was the largest in area, and we know from General Kittel that it had been reprovisioned just before communications were cut. It also housed the staff of the 462nd VG Division and was commanded by the able Major Voss of the 462 Fusilier Battalion. His garrison amounted to some 500 of all ranks.

The question that remains is, Just what did the Germans holed up in the forts achieve during the twenty-odd days after the fall of Metz on 22 November? In terms of manpower, some 2,650 Germans tied down approximately 9,000 Americans—two infantry regiments plus HQ staffs and support troops, who could have been better employed elsewhere. With an extra division in the line, Walker might well have been able to reach the Saar more quickly. As it was, he had two bridgeheads by mid-December, at Saarlautern and Dilligen, but the latter had to be evacuated as a result of the shift of troops northward to counter the threat in the Ardennes. In the time available, an extra American division would not have produced results sufficiently decisive to hinder German preparations for the offensive. On that basis, one can say that the fort garrisons achieved nothing apart from their nuisance value.

What the Germans did was to let slip a valuable opportunity which could have effected the outcome of their December offensive. It is invidious, of course, for a military historian, seated in a comfortable armchair, to point out the mistakes of his betters, but the following is worthy of consideration, as a historical "might-have-been." Now, there is no such thing as an "impregnable" fort or fortress; all must succumb at some time to starvation even if they cannot be taken by storm or guile. The true purpose of fortification, throughout history, has always been to gain time.

We know that the Ardennes offensive was in Hitler's mind in early September, if not in August, and that anything that would hinder the American advance was welcome. Hence his instructions to Balck in mid-September, to delay Patton as long as possible. During the September battle for Metz, both sides had initially tended to discount the value of the fortifications, and both were surprised that the supposedly outdated works could withstand so much bombardment. Those responsible for the defense of the city and in the higher German headquarters should have realized that they did not have the manpower to hold the Americans indefinitely in Lorraine, and instead of wasting their time trying to construct field works, should have concentrated on the Metz forts. During the October lull, every effort should have been made to get as many as possible of the turrets into working order, which would not have been beyond the bounds of German technical ingenuity. Once that was done, each of the forts should have been stuffed with supplies and ammunition, and garrisoned by small detachments of crack troops, supported by engineers and other specialists.

Well equipped with modern weapons, such troops first could have sallied out and menaced the thin line of Americans containing the salient, thus disturbing the preparations for the November offensive. Second, if that offensive had taken the course that it did, the forts could have successfully hindered attempts to break into the city by firing down on the crossing sites. The Americans might well have found themselves with another Stalingrad on their hands, and the whole of XX Corps would have become involved. A fortification can only fulfill a useful purpose if it forms the base for an *active* defense. But in the end, the Metz forts reacted passively to encirclement. Had they held out for just two weeks longer than the last of them did, Patton would have had his hands so full on the Moselle that he would have been unable to react so flexibly to the Ardennes offensive.

Conclusion

Having studied in some detail the operations of XX Corps in Lorraine during the latter part of 1944, certain basic questions remain to be answered. Throughout the text, I have referred to the wider strategic significance of the fighting along the Moselle and the background of the "great argument" about priority of supply. Patton's champions subsequently claimed, and he himself hinted in his memoirs, that the war could have been finished in 1944—if the Third Army had been given unlimited resources. Sober historical research has disposed of the myth that there was some sort of plot to rob Patton of his just reward; but the fact remains that at the time national sentiments were outraged, and the Third Army imagined that Eisenhower, Montgomery, and Services of Supply had ganged up against them.

Let us now imagine that the Battle of Metz never took place and that during the first week in September, with their tanks full of fuel, Patton's divisions had pursued the fleeing Germans over the Moselle. We know that at that stage little work had been done on the defenses and that the only line where a stand could have been made, was in the inadequate Westwall. Would the Americans have raced to the Rhine?

In dealing with this question I made the point that the main problem, once over the Moselle, was a geographical one. The terrain was vastly different from the plains of central France, and once into hilly Lorraine, armored maneuvers would prove difficult. When the final offensive was launched on 8 November, the two corps involved were between 20 and 40 miles away from the Saar, but were not across this obstacle in any strength until the middle of December, five weeks later. Had the Ardennes offensive not intervened at that point, they would then have been faced by a further advance through difficult country until reaching the Rhine. And then, Where to? All the Allied strategists were in agreement that the prime objective was the Ruhr. Patton, however, with his forces in the Frankfurt-Mannheim area, would have had to turn north and advance up the narrow Rhine valley. Simply advancing blindly into Germany would not have fulfilled any strategic purpose, and unless other Allied units had kept pace, the Third Army would have been out on a limb and liable to have its lines of communication cut. As we know that there were insufficient resources available to maintain an offensive along the whole front, Patton would have been on his own anyway, especially as he claimed the lion's share of supply.

It is also a fact that there were adequate supplies ashore in Normandy and that the problem was to deliver them to the front. Every mile advanced by Patton in September would have proportionately increased his lines of communication, requiring more and more trucks to keep up the flow of stores—trucks that were in desperately short supply. More divisions would have had to be immobilized in order to use their transport, which would have further aggravated the main background problem to the Lorraine campaign—shortage of manpower. In his grandiose dreams, Patton was simply flying in the face of a situation that had to be faced by all the army commanders in northwest Europe at the time.

Even more damning, however, is a statement by the chief of staff of IX Engineer Command, which was responsible for airfield maintenance and construction in the combat zone, quoted by Ladislas Farago. "Had Patton continued through the Saar valley and the Vosges, it must have been without close air support and with a very small contribution in the way of air supply beyond the Reims-Épernay line. We could have fixed up Conflans, Metz, and Nancy-Azelot in time to have done some good, but the next possible fields were at Hagenau and Strasbourg, with no fields except Trier between there and the Cologne-Maastricht Plain. I would not have liked to tackle the job of supplying Patton over the Vosges and through the Palatinate during that October. I don't doubt that we could have carried about two armored and one (motorized) division up to Cologne, But then where? Certainly not across the Rhine. A good task force of *Panzerfaust* (antitank rocket), manned by Hitler Youth, could have finished them off before they reached Kassel."

The foregoing leads one inevitably to the conclusion that Eisenhower's use of the broad-front strategy with the emphasis on clearing Antwerp was the only viable one in the circumstances. One all-out thrust, whether by Montgomery or Patton, would have led to overextended lines of communication which SHAEF could not have supported. It is a prime dictum of military science that the object of a campaign is to destroy the enemy's forces and not to conquer territory. Had Patton advanced to the Rhine, he would have liberated a slice of Germany but would not have contributed significantly to the defeat of the German Army or deprived it of sufficient material resources to make it unable to continue to resist.

The other shadow overhanging the Battle of Metz was that of the Ardennes offensive. If we agree that 1 September was the critical date for the Americans when they ran dry on the Meuse, that same day, Hitler prophesized that "fog, night, and snow" would provide him with a great "opportunity." Had the fighting in Lorraine been conducted differently, would the outcome of the Ardennes operations in December been affected? Throughout this book, we have seen that Third Army was unable to make much progress on account of their lack of manpower to hold such an extensive front, and that they never had anything much in the way of a reserve. This problem, however, applies to the other Allied Armies, and Bradley took the justified risk of holding the Ardennes sector with a minimum number of troops. To strengthen the area, he would have had to take divisions from somewhere else.

The only thing that would have seriously upset Hitler's plans would have been an advance by Patton to the Rhine, thus cutting off his assembly area, or an advance northward up the Moselle valley toward Trier. We have seen that in planning, the Rhine was the goal, to be reached by the shortest and most practicable route. The Moselle valley was rightly considered far too narrow for the movement of an army, and at the start of the September battle, the 90th Division had an open flank toward Luxembourg in the north. There were no divisions available for a strike up the Moselle.

During late September, the 83rd Division was stationed on that flank and was for a time loosely attached to XX Corps, holding the front along the river to the north of Cattenom. In the planning for the November offensive, it was originally intended that the 83rd would launch an attack toward Saarburg in conjunction with the operations of 10th Armored and 90th Infantry Divisions.

While the river crossing was being carried out by the latter, "operational control" by XX Corps was cancelled by General Bradley, and Patton was forced to detach other troops to clear out the Saar-Moselle triangle. He claimed with some justification that Bradley had "welched" on the agreement and that, as a result, he had been stopped from capturing Trier—had he done so the Ardennes offensive would not have taken place. There is some truth in this, as an American division firmly established around Trier would have directly menaced the flanks of the German assembly area.

Having discussed the "might-have-been" elements of the campaign, it is worth considering it from a tactical standpoint. The strategy was determined from above, and although Patton may have privately disagreed, he had in the end to conform to the general policy directives. The Battle of Metz really splits into two separate battles divided by an interim period of stalemate. The September battle, as we have seen, resulted from a whole series of mistakes caused mainly by overoptimism on the part of those responsible for the direction of the campaign. As to what should have been done, General von Mellenthin, whom we have often quoted and who was a most capable staff officer, had the following to say: "The first attacks against Metz were correctly launched by units on the march, without assembling, in an attempt to take the city with one bold stroke. It ought to have been quite clear to the enemy [the Americans] that there was a strong occupying force at Metz, yet it would appear that obvious conclusions were not drawn from this fact. The enemy should have made a systematic reconnaissance and have carefully placed his forces in position for a strong attack on a fortified position. However, in September 1944, the enemy continued the same method of attack. Each attempt was repulsed with heavy losses to the attacker."

In the end, it took several weeks for the high command in Lorraine to realize that the nature of the war had changed—to their disadvantage. The fortifications baffled them and so they continued plugging away without enough troops to do the job properly.

The November offensive was different, as the element of happy improvization had been eliminated. If politics is the "art of the possible," so too is war, and the offensive was well planned within the limits imposed by the available manpower. One cannot blame anybody for the weather, and the salient point is that the troops were able to take it in their stride and still achieve their objectives.

As far as the Germans were concerned, we have seen that their aim was to gain time, and that General Balck was to have few reinforcements. Within the limits opposed from above, one has to admit that the German tactics succeeded beyond their own expectations. They did "stop Patton," although assisted materially by the Americans' supply problems and by the weather.

One thing that the Metz campaign conclusively proved was the fine fighting quality of the American soldier, which has come in for much criticism lately. The battle was fought without the benefit of limitless supplies of ice cream and doughnuts, in often appalling conditions and against a gallant and determined enemy. Whether or not the battle should have taken place at all, is a matter of opinion, since its course was determined by circumstances beyond Patton's control. It is the tactical direction of the fighting that must be criticized, in view of the evident reluctance of those concerned to face up to the realities of the changed situation after the beginning of September. One thing is certain, many lives were senselessly wasted in futile attacks on fortified positions, and with a little more thought, many of those casualties could have been avoided.

Appendix I

The Development of Metz as a Fortress

Metz is an ancient city, deriving its name from that of the Roman city of Mediomatrica. It was first fortified by the Romans as the center of an important network of military roads. Prior to the XX Corps attack in 1944, it had only once before been taken by storm—by the Huns in A.D. 451. During the early Middle Ages, Metz became the seat of an important bishopric, and in 1220, attained the dignity and privileges of an Imperial Free City. In 1552, Metz was occupied peacefully by a French army; work was immediately started on a thorough modification of the medieval fortifications. (The area defended in those days was still the ancient heart of the city, between the Moselle and the Seille, which was surrounded by bastions and ramparts.) Soon afterward Metz was unsuccessfully besieged by the army of the Emperor Charles V, who bombarded it for two and a half months.

Nominally independent, but under French protection, Metz from then on was the basis of the defense of the area; and at the Treaty of Westphalia it was finally ceded to France.

In addition, Metz achieved historic importance as a river-crossing point as well as an important communications center; this was the reason for its successive layers of fortification. Two of the late-medieval city gates can still be seen, although little now remains of the seventeenth- and eighteenth-century defenses. The late seventeenth-century French engineer Vauban undertook radical modifications after 1676; and between 1728 and 1752, one of his successors, Cormontaigne, was at work. The latter built two bridgehead works to guard the crossings over the rivers, and one of these, Fort Bellecroix, figured in the fighting in 1944. Oddly enough, the reason why this one was retained when the rest of the older fortifications were demolished at the beginning of the twentieth century was that the German occupation authorities feared civil commotion—Bellecroix was envisaged as a strongpoint for the city garrison.

As the range of artillery improved during the early part of the nineteenth-century, it became imperative to place the defenses of a town farther out from the center to keep a besieger's guns at bay. As it was clearly impossible to build continuous lines of defenses over such extended perimeters, detached forts came into fashion. These were individual works capable of putting up a stout resistance and which could (in theory) be supported by the fire of their immediate neighbors on either side. In a war situation, they could be rapidly connected by a line of ditch and rampart to be manned by the troops of a field army. Ideally, a ring of such forts would be built on any high ground overlooking the place to be defended.

In 1867, just before the outbreak of the Franco-Prussian War, Séré de Rivières, another well-known French military engineer, started work on four such detached forts at Metz—Plappeville, St. Quentin, St. Julian, and Queuleu. In keeping with French practice at the time, the forts were designed on the already outdated bastion system. They were incomplete at the time of the 1870 siege, and had been overtaken by events in this regard: they were sited between 2 and 3 miles of the city center, whereas the introduction of rifled artillery during the 1860's had increased the range of siege guns to up to 9 miles.

The Germans were content to surround Metz in 1870, and the garrison ultimately surrendered after a few half-hearted attempts to break out. After the war, Metz was ceded to Germany as part of the provinces of Alsace and Lorraine. The new owners immediately set out to complete the four forts and started work on five new ones to finish off the ring around the city—Gambetta, Decaen, Deroulède,

St. Privat, and Des Bordes. (Note that, for the sake of simplicity, I have used the French names for these forts; all the Metz works had German names as well.)

The five new forts were of a more modern polygonal design, which had been pioneered by German engineers earlier in the century. Although they had covered-barrack accommodation, the guns of forts from this period were all mounted in the open on top of the earth ramparts. However, as an indication of the way in which the minds of German engineers were working, the most interesting development during the late 1870s was on the St. Quentin plateau. Fort Girardin was built some 1,000 yards in advance of the earlier Fort St. Quentin, and the two were joined by defensible lines to form a large fortified complex, known as *Feste Friedrich Karl*. This was then connected to Fort Plappeville by further lines, and the whole area was formed into a strong position on the west bank of the Moselle—the supposed direction of a French attack.

Thus by around 1880, in addition to the eighteenth-century defenses of the city itself, there was a ring of forts on the surrounding heights. All might then have stopped if the shell with high-explosive filling had not been invented; it was introduced into most European armies by 1885. The immediate effect of this was that guns and infantry in the open were extremely vulnerable, especially as the symmetrically shaped forts of the period made easy targets. The initial solution to this threat was seen as dispersion—removing the guns from the forts and placing them in between. At Metz, eight batteries were built in the intervals between the works in 1889 and 1898, armed with either 150- or 210-mm guns, in rotating turrets. To protect the garrison, a large number of shelters were also built. This was perhaps the first manifestation of what came to be known as "the battlefield prepared in peacetime" in military literature. At this point, fortification began to concentrate on protection as armies started to burrow deeper and deeper into the ground. Forts began to resemble battleships on land in terms of cost and technical sophistication.

For the Germans, the original strategic importance of Metz was as a barrier against any French attempt to regain Alsace-Lorraine. Together with the fortress of Thionville, the area was formed into the *Mosel Stellung* (Moselle Position) to block the river crossings and the natural avenue of approach. The physical presence of the forts was backed by a network of strategic railways to move the vast conscript army in case of hostilities.

This strategy was essentially passive, but in 1899, the first version of the Schlieffen Plan appeared which involved violation of Belgian neutrality. In this plan, the Moselle Position would form the pivot around which the whole German army would wheel in its movement to take the French in the rear. In the process, Metz would temporarily have to hold the entire might of the French attack and would thus have to be strengthened.

Plans for this were initiated in 1897, and were based on a revolutionary type of fort that had been started two years earlier at Mutzig in Alsace. This work, known as *Feste Kaiser Wilhelm II,* was built on the heights overlooking the main road from Strasbourg through the Vosges. It was the first of a type that became known to specialists as a *Feste,* or fortified group. Previously, forts had been composite structures of regular shape and with the defensive elements grouped together, the artillery for long-range combat and the infantry for close defense.

With the introduction of the *Feste* type, the German forts became areas of defended real estate rather than monolithic buildings. Particularly favorable sites were selected, and on these were grouped together, but separate from each other, the necessary close and distant combat units. Using the shape of the terrain and making the best use of camouflage with natural foliage, such a group would form an independent fortress that could hold out for weeks or even months. Each could support its neighbors with fire from its artillery and could also act as a strongpoint for troops operating in the intervals between the works.

For close defense, a *Feste* consisted of infantry trenches, shell-proof bunkers and guardrooms, and a number of observation posts. For long-range defense, two types of armored battery were provided. First, for hindering an enemy troop concentration and for distant bombardment, 100-mm guns were mounted individually in rotating turrets with all-round fire capability. Second, for counter-battery work and for dispersing attackers, similarly mounted 150-mm howitzers were installed. The batteries were emplaced where possible on reverse slopes. Each mounted between two and four guns and had its own independent barracks; and observation was via armored posts situated well forward. These posts were connected to the batteries and all other parts of the complex by tunnels, and orders were transmitted by telephone and speaking tube.

This subdivision of the defended area was further enhanced by obstacles. Each *Feste* was surrounded by a multistrand barbed-wire entanglement; in some works there were dry ditches, and in places, 10-foot-high iron palisades. Inside the main perimeter, each unit (infantry or artillery) had its own wire surround to make it an independent unit on the surface. Underground, the entire complex was linked by tunnels which could be easily demolished. If an enemy succeeded in penetrating into any unit, it could be isolated and the rest of the *Feste* could continue to resist.

In addition to the combat units, each such work had one or more main barracks to house the bulk of the garrison. These were multi-story blocks equipped with sleeping quarters, bakeries, kitchens, and hospitals. The central power station for generating electricity and providing heating was another separate unit, as was the main command post and telephone exchange. Forced-feed ventilation was installed that could be operated by hand in case of power failure. The German type of turret was hand-operated, which rendered it fairly foolproof in a combat situation.

The weakness of the early (1899-1905) *Festen* was the lack of flank protection and the inability to fire across the intervals. Mainly as a result of lessons learned from the Russo-Japanese War, a number of modifications were made. Extra ditches were excavated, the number of infantry shelters was increased and blockhouses were built to flank the ditches and forward obstacles.

The larger of the *Festen* covered a surprising amount of ground—Driant occupied 355 acres. Well camouflaged, they were virtually impossible to spot from the air, and as each one was different, each posed a different problem to an attacker. Although constructed at various German fortresses, the *Feste* type was mainly associated with Metz and Thionville, where it reached the peak of its development. The 1897 plans called for a line of works along the heights to the west of the city, roughly corresponding to the positions held by the French in 1870. This was a naturally strong position, and work started in 1899 on five forts, Lorraine, de Guise, Jeanne d'Arc, Driant, and the two units of the Verdun Group. At Thionville, Guentrange was built to the west, and while this program was under construction, plans were being made to extend the defenses to the east bank of the river.

The second building period started in 1906, when work was

started on the three on the main east bank, Yser, Aisne, and Marne—plus some smaller infantry works and the two forts at Thionville, Koenigsmacker and d'Illange. These later works had less turret artillery than the earlier ones, and this deficiency was compensated for by a number of advanced batteries for long-range 150-mm field guns, to be armed only on mobilization.

At the same time, attention was again turned to the west bank, where certain defects had become apparent. Lorraine, one of the original works, was found to have insufficient forward observation, and to correct this, the Amanvillers Quarry position was fortified. From there, the line along the Fèves Ridge was occupied by the Canrobert forts, which ended at the Fort de Fèves. Between Lorraine and Jeanne d'Arc, the interval was protected by a number of strong bunkers, and the gap on the other side toward Draint was filled by the so-called Seven Dwarfs.

Several of the later works were unfinished when war broke out in 1914. However, the Moselle Position was immediately garrisoned by 85,000 men armed with 600 guns, 100 of which were under turrets. Although Metz was never attacked during the war, modifications were carried out, and after the German failure at Verdun in 1916, a large number of bunkers were built in advance of the main fortified positions.

In 1914, Metz was probably the strongest fortress in Europe, and when fully garrisoned and supplied, could have held out for months. Had the French broken through in Lorraine, they would have been forced to besiege the place, reducing the works one by one and requiring probably an army of 250,000 men.

The above is just a brief sketch of what is a highly complex and technical subject that is beyond the scope of this book. The interested reader must search in military journals of the 1920s for more detailed information, as there are no books on the pre-1914 German fortifications.

Appendix II

Damage to Fort St. Blaise (Verdun Group)

In the text, much has been said about efforts to neutralize the Metz forts and the comparative lack of success achieved. This failure is particularly striking when one remembers that they were constructed to cope with the demands of warfare at the end of the nineteenth-century, when bombardment from the air had been dreamed of only by writers of science fiction.

Just before the close of the Second World War, the United States Strategic Bombing Survey sent out teams of experts to examine a variety of targets in Europe for the purpose of evaluating the effects of bombing. In view of the stubborn resistance to the ground forces that the Metz forts had provided and the number of bombs expended on them, it was decided that one of the works should be surveyed. Field Team No. 17 went to the area in February 1945 and selected Fort St. Blaise of the Verdun Group as the object of their survey. Their findings are embodied in the U.S.S.B.S. Report, European War, No. 144.

I have decided to summarize the findings as an appendix, rather than include them in the text, because St. Blaise was just one of a number of forts subjected to similar attacks. As it was the only one officially inspected, the findings are not really representative; but since constructional details are similar, it can be taken as average.

At different times the target was attacked by ground troops using artillery of calibers up to 250-mm, and by fighter-bombers dropping 250- to 1,000-pound bombs. Of these operations, the report stated that "no structural damage was apparent from these attacks." On 8 October 1944, 17 B-26's of 9th Air Force dropped 33 2,000-pound bombs on the target from an altitude of 12,000 feet. The report deals with the 28 of these bombs which could be accounted for, six of which were direct hits, and four of which were near misses. The rest impacted between 500 and 1,500 feet of the target, which consisted of the three casemate blocks in the center of the fort. Two of these were single-story batteries; the third was a three-story barrack block.

St. Blaise was built between 1899 and 1905, forming part of the first program of construction of the *Feste*-type fort at Metz. The rear (exposed) walls of the blocks were of soft sandstone some 2-feet thick. Some of the other forts were later modified in that the stone was cased in concrete, but this was not carried out at the Verdun Group. The report states that the unreinforced concrete of the roofs and the interior was of poor quality, a statement that is borne out by early twentieth-century comments by French and German engineers. The interior vaults were supported by walls between 4- and 6-feet thick, and the minimum roof thickness was 10 feet, covered with 15 feet of earth fill. According to the survey, the only modifications that had been carried out were that certain window and door openings had been filled with concrete and three 20-mm antiaircraft emplacements had been added. Thus, the field team (perhaps unwittingly) chose one of the weakest of the Metz forts: those constructed during the later programs were largely of reinforced and special concrete, and one can assume that their resistance to bombardment would have been that much greater.

The armor plating of the German turrets was in two parts: the cupola-shaped turret itself and the surround, or apron. The turret was a one-piece cast construction 16 cm thick and lined with 4 cm of mild steel. The surrounds were made up of a number of segments embedded in a solid concrete block, the thickness of the metal varying between 20 and 30 cm.

Block No. 1 was a battery of four 15-cm howitzers with an armored observation post at each end. It received three direct hits, two of which penetrated through the roof, while the third went through into a tunnel leading to the neighboring block. All three bombs exploded, blowing holes in the roof and damaging the immediate internal area. However, except for dismounting one turret, no severe structural damage was caused.

Block No. 2 also received three hits, one of which malfunctioned, causing only cracking of the concrete; the second went through the roof, resulting in purely local damage; the third struck the curved surface where the concrete roof blended into the rear masonry wall. A section of the concrete cracked off but no evidence of damage could be observed inside the casemate.

Block No. 3 suffered only minor external damage from a near miss.

The surveyors discovered that the whole area was churned up by shell craters, none of which had caused any significant damage. The craters, identified as having resulted from the smaller bombs dropped by the fighter-bombers, showed no evidence of penetration, and displacement of earth was the only result. Despite the report's statement that "on the whole, these structures appeared to be slightly below the average in strength that would normally be expected in this type of construction," it was clear that no significant damage had been suffered—certainly not enough to cause the place to be evacuated. Although one gun was dismounted in the howitzer battery, two 100-mm guns in Block No. 3 were in operation in early November and continued to fire until shortly before the fort surrendered on 26 November.

The inspectors summarized their findings as follows: "It is the opinion of this team that penetration must be obtained before the bomb functions if any damage to forts of this nature is to be obtained, and even when penetration is gained before detonation, too great an area of damage cannot be expected due to the stability resulting from the mass weight of this type of construction."

I have already contended that the forts could have been eliminated by low-level precision attacks by the 617th Squadron, Royal Air Force, using the "Tallboy" and "Grand Slam" bombs specially developed for use against the German submarine pens. As 2,000-pound bombs did penetrate, however, real saturation attacks by the strategic bombing force could well have succeeded, provided that accuracy could have been obtained. During the Metz operation, in addition to the poor weather conditions, the heavy bombers were far too busy elsewhere, and Patton's priority was far too low.

During the Second World War, none of the Allied armies went in for superheavy siege artillery—the aim was to avoid, at all costs, a 1914-18 static-warfare situation. The heaviest guns available to the American field armies were 240-mm, and 8-inch howitzers. Had they possessed such a weapon as the 420-mm (Big Bertha) howitzer used by the Germans against the Belgian forts in 1914 and the French forts at Verdun in 1916, it is probable that the works at Metz could have been destroyed.

What does emerge from the foregoing is that the Metz forts were able to withstand a tremendous amount of punishment, including air bombardment, that was not envisaged by the engineers who designed them. The author has explored many of the forts, and the only serious damage that can be seen is demolition subsequently carried out by engineers. For example, all that remains of Battery Moselle at Driant is some massive lumps of collapsed concrete. Otherwise the structures are all sound in spite of surface chipping caused by shells and small-arms fire. The only turrets destroyed are on the batteries at Guentrange to the west of Thionville, and these were blown up in 1944 by American engineers. The very solidity of the forts must have done wonders for the morale of the German troops who fought in them.

Note on Sources

There are no books about the Battle of Metz except for the detailed account in the official history, *The Lorraine Campaign*. Although excellent, this work is not generally available outside specialist libraries, and its very size would daunt the general reader. In addition to this work, of which I have unashamedly availed myself, the conduct of operations by the American forces is well documented. I have of course made use of the various After Action Reports of the units involved, although they vary in quality and many were compiled several months after the campaign ended—dates tend to become confused. Operational reports, intelligence summaries, and telephone logs were also consulted. Regarding secondary sources, most of the unit histories produced after the war are of poor quality, but exceptions are those for the 5th and 95th Divisions. Few personal memoirs were written; those that I could discover are cited in the Bibliography. The higher ranks involved in the campaign in Europe tended to gloss over the subject of Metz in their postwar offerings.

Most of the records of the German formations below Army Group level have either been lost or were never compiled. A general view of affairs on the German side can be gained from the war diaries and telephone logs of Army Group G and OB West, but for detail I have used the series of manuscripts compiled by captured generals for the Historical Division, Dept. of the Army (auth., Cole, p. 617). Although written after the events described, and often without access to documents, these lucid accounts are invaluable to the historian. To my knowledge, there is no German account of the battle, but one or two histories and memoirs refer to it in general terms. The only unit history compiled deals with the 17th SS Panzergrenadier Division.

Bibliography

The brevity of this bibliography is an indication of the scarcity of secondary sources on the Metz operation: compare this list for scope with those on such battles as Alamein or Arnhem. I have included only books or articles that have proved their worth, omitting a number of dubious unit histories published just after the war.

BOOKS

Abrams, Joe. *A History of the 90th Division in World War II.* Baton Rouge, 1946.

Allan, Robert. *Lucky Forward.* Macfadden, 1965.

Anonymous. *The Attack on Fort Koenigsmacker.* Mayot Enterprises, Eagle Lake, Minn., 1977.

Anonymous. *The XX Corps: Its History and Service in World War II.* Osaka, Japan, 1951.

Anonymous. *The Fifth Infantry Division in the European Theatre of Operations.* Albert Love Enterprises, Atlanta, 1945.

Anonymous. *The Reduction of Fortress Metz—XX Corps Operational Report,* 1 September-6 December 1944. No date or place of publication.

Anonymous. *11th Infantry Regiment History*. Baton Rouge, 1947.

Bradley, Omar. *A Soldier's Story*. Eyre and Spottiswoode, 1951.

Cole, H. M. *The Lorraine Campaign*. Government Printing Office, Washington, 1950.

Eisenhower, Dwight. *Crusade in Europe*. Heinemann, 1948.

Essame, H. *Patton: A study in Command*. Scribner, 1974.

Farago, Ladislas. *Patton: Ordeal and Triumph*. Arthur Barker, 1966.

Fuermann, G., and Cranz, F. *95th Infantry Division History 1919-46*. Albert Love Enterprises, Atlanta, 1947.

Howard, Michael. *The Franco-Prussian War*. Hart-Davis, 1960. New York: Macmillan; Collier Books (Macmillan) paperback.

Hubatsch, Walther. *Hitler's Weisungen für die Kriegführung 1939-1945*. Bernhard and Graefe, Frankfurt/Main, 1962.

Koch, O. W. *G-2 Intelligence for Patton*. Army Times/Whitmore, 1971.

McConahey, William. *Battalion Surgeon*. Privately printed, Rochester, Minn., 1966.

MacDonald, C., and Mathews, S. *Three Battles—Arnaville, Altuzzo and Schmidt*, Government Printing Office, Washington, 1952.

Mellenthin, F. W. *Panzer Battles*. University of Oklahoma Press, 1956.

Patton, G. S. *War as I Knew It*. Houghton Mifflin, 1947.

Pogue, Forrest. *The Supreme Command*. Government Printing Office, Washington 1954.

Spiwoks W., and Stöber H. *Endkampf zwischen Mosel und Inn*. Munin Verlag, Osnabrück, n.d.

Stöber, Hans. *Die Sturmflut und das Ende*. Munin Verlag, Osnabruck, n.d.

Warlimont, Walther. *Erinnerungen*. Frankfurt/Main, 1962.

Westphal, Siegfried. *The German Army in the West*. Cassell, 1953.

Weaver, William. *Yankee Doodle Went to Town*. Privately printed, 1959.

Wilmot, Chester. *The Struggle for Europe*. Collins, 1952.

ARTICLES

Andersen, O. "Kempene om Fort Driant." *Dansk Artilleri Tidsskrift*, Feb., 1978.

Anonymous. "A Little Bit of Metz (Uckange Bridgehead)." *95th Division Journal,* Vol. 27, No. 2, June 1977.

Anonymous. "Le 20 C.A.U.S. Libère Metz." *Revue Historique de l'Armée,* March 1953.

Colin, Général J. "Les Combats du Fort Driant." *Mémoires de l'Académie Nationale de Metz,* Vol. VII, 1962.

Cottingham, L. "Smoke over the Moselle." *The Infantry Journal,* August 1948.

Kemp, Anthony. "Metz 1944." *Warfare Monthly,* No. 46, October 1977.

Kemp, Anthony. "The Maginot Line." *Warfare Monthly,* No. 52, March 1978.

Turner-Jones, C. la T. "Verdun and Metz—A Comparative Study of the Fortifications." *The Royal Engineers Journal,* Vol. XXXIV, 1921.

Notes

(See Bibliography for full references.) The abbreviation MS followed by a number and a name in these notes refers to the series of manuscripts prepared by captured senior German officers after the war, for the Historical Division of the Department of the Army.

CHAPTER 1

1. Pogue, *The Supreme Command,* 53.
2. Eisenhower, *Crusade,* map. 258-59.
3. Montgomery B. L., *Memoirs,* Fontana edition, 274.
4. Quoted by Wilmot, *Struggle for Europe,* 458.
5. Montgomery, op. cit., 274.
6. Ibid., 276.
7. Wilmot, op. cit., 473.
8. Ibid., 434 (quoting General Blumentritt).
9. MS B-308 (Zimmermann).

CHAPTER 3

1. Wilmot, *Struggle for Europe,* 472.
2. Bradley, *A Soldier's Story,* 401.
3. Farago, *Patton,* 206.
4. Bradley, op. cit., 406
5. Ibid., 405.
6. Ibid., 403.
7. Bradley, op. cit., 402.
8. Farago, op. cit., 354.
9. Cole, *The Lorraine Campaign,* 117.
10. Wilmot, op. cit. 473.
11. Quoted by Cole, op. cit., 118.
12. Ibid., 120.
13. Patton, *War As I Knew It,* 120.
14. Howard, *The Franco-Prussian War,* 448.
15. Wilmot, op. cit. 347.
16. Hubatsch, *Hitler's Weisungen,* 286
17. *Führer Conferences,* Fragment 43, 1 Sept. 1944.
18. Cole, op. cit., 48.
19. Hubatsch, op. cit., 272.
20. MS D-222 (Knobelsdorf).
21. Spiwoks/Stöber, *Endkampf,* 25.
22. Hubatsch, op. cit., 243.
23. MS B-042 (Krause).
24. Hubatsch, op. cit., 275.

CHAPTER 4

1. Essame, *Patton,* 202.
2. Ryan, Cornelius, *A Bridge Too Far,* 1974, n. 53.
3. Cole, *The Lorraine Campaign,* n. 121.
4. Third Army, After Action Report (AAR), 5 Sept. 1944.
5. Quoted by Cole, op. cit. 121.
6. Letter from Lt. Col. Howard Clark to Col. T. D. Stamps, U.S.M.A. (West Point), 3 June 1945 (copy in my possession).
7. Cole, op. cit., n. 131.

8. MacDonald and Mathews, Three Battles, Government Printing Office, 1952.

9. Ibid., 25.

10. Ibid., 38.

11. MS B-412 (Einem).

12. MacDonald and Mathews, op. cit., n. 47.

13. Ibid., 55.

14. L. Cottingham, article, "Smoke Over the Moselle."

15. Cole, op. cit., 152.

16. Anonymous, *The 5th Infantry Division,* unpaged.

17. Quoted by Cole, op. cit., 154.

18. Ibid., 153.

19. MS B-042 (Krause), 5.

20. Wilmot, op. cit., 478.

21. Spiwoks/Stöber, op. cit., 37.

22. Farago, *Patton,* 377.

23. Army Group G "War Diary" (KTB), 9 Sept. 1944.

CHAPTER 5

1. Wilmot, *Struggle for Europe,* 492.

2. Pogue, *Supreme Command,* 284.

3. Quoted by Farago, *Patton,* 379.

4. Pogue, op. cit., 290, and Wilmot, 493.

5. Hubatsch, *Hitler's Weisungen,* 243.

6. Cole, *Lorraine Campaign,* 165.

7. MS D-222 (Knobelsdorf).

8. MS B-042 (Krause).

9. Quoted by Cole, op. cit., 166.

10. MS B-412 (Einem).

11. Cole, op. cit., 170.

12. Ibid., 180.

13. McConahey, *Battalion Surgeon,* 87-88.

14. *Vorläufige Gefechtsbericht der 462 VGD über die Kämpfe um den Brückenkopf Metz.* In the Federal Military Archive, Freiburg, West Germany. Index No. III H 293.

15. Third Army AAR, 19 Sept. 1944.

16. Ibid., 17 Sept. 1944.
17. Quoted by Cole, op. cit., 257.
18. 12th Army Group, Letter of Instruction No. 9, 25 Sept. 1944.
19. Third Army, Letter of Instruction No. 4.
20. Mellenthin, *Panzer Battles,* 320.

CHAPTER 6

1. Benoit, Général, "Etude Comparative des Fortifications de Verdun et de Metz," *Rev. de Génie,* 1921.
2. XX Corps G-3 Journal, 17 Sept. 1944.
3. Quoted by Cole, *Lorraine Campaign,* 263.
4. Cole, op. cit., n. 266.
5. Letter from Col. Clark, op. cit., and interview with Général
   Robert Nicolas.
6. *History of XX Corps Artillery,* date and publisher unknown,
   23-24.
7. Cole, op. cit., n. 269.
8. 5th Division AAR, Sept. 1944.
9. This account from *5th Infantry Division* and *11th Infantry Regiment.*
10. Third Army, "Diary," 4 Oct. 1944.
11. TF Warnock Journal, 5 Oct. 1944.
12. *History of XX Corps Artillery,* op. cit., 23. For details of methods
    of artillery observation, see *11th Infantry Regiment.*
13. *5th Infantry Division,* op. cit., unpaged.
14. The dates here are confused. Cole gives the date as 9 Oct. and the
    5th Infantry Division history as 10 Oct. The former, however,
    agrees with TF Warnock Journal. The task force was formed on
    the night of 5-6 Oct. and not 9 Oct. as stated in the Third Army
    AAR.
15. *Wehrmachts Bericht,* 19 Oct.
16. Bradley, *A Soldier's Story,* 427.

CHAPTER 7

1. 5th Infantry Division, unpaged.

2. Cole, *Lorraine Campaign,* n. 305.

3. Mellenthin, *Panzer Battles,* 312.

4. Ibid., 322 and 324. See also MS A-999 (Mellenthin). Plan 17 was the basis for the French attack in 1914 in an attempt to regain Lorraine. The French, commanded by General Castelnau, were defeated by the Bavarian army under Crown Prince Rupprecht.

5. MS A-999 (Mellenthin).

6. OKW order 1835/44 dated 24 Oct. 1944.

7. *Vorläufige Gefechtsbericht,* op. cit. Signature illegible, but the author was adjutant of the 1217th VG Regiment.

8. 462 VG Division, *Besondere Anordnung für die Versorgung,* Federal Military Archive.

9. *History of XX Corps Artillery,* 24.

10. Koch, *G-2 Intelligence.* 69.

11. Hubatsch, *Hitler's Weisungen,* 272.

12. McConahey, *Battalion Surgeon,* 90.

13. XX Corps Operational Report, Appendix 8, 51.

14. Ms A-999 (Mellenthin).

15. Third Army AAR, 13 Oct. 1944.

16. Weaver, *Yankee Doodle,* 154.

CHAPTER 8

1. Cole, *Lorraine Campaign,* 299.

2. Bradley, *Soldier's Story,* 435.

3. Wilmot, *Struggle for Europe,* 563.

4. Third Army AAR, 22 Oct. 1944.

5. Farago, *Patton,* 411.

6. Third Army AAR, 3 Nov. 1944.

7. Quoted in full in XX Corps Operational Report, 62.

8. Army Group G, Telephone log, 300.

9. MS B-412 (Einem).

10. MS A-000 (Mellenthin).

11. Mellenthin, *Panzer Battles,* 324-5.

12. Army Group G, Telephone log, 29 Oct. 1944.

13. Ibid., 25 Oct.

14. MS B-079 (Kittel).

CHAPTER 9

1. 95th Division Journal, June 1977.
2. MS A-000 (Mellenthin), 31.
3. L. Claudel, *La Ligne Maginot, conception—réalisation.* Privately published, Lavey, Switzerland, 1974.
4. McConahey, *Battalion Surgeon,* 93.
5. Abrams, *History of the 90th Division,* 32.
6. McConahey, op. cit., 94.
7. Personal letter to author from Charles Bryan.
8. 358th Infantry AAR, November 1944.
9. Weaver, *Yankee Doodle,* 264.
10. Ibid., 265.
11. Cole, *Lorraine Campaign,* 392.
12. MS A-000 (Mellenthin), 44.
13. Bradley, *Soldier's Story,* 438.
14. Weaver, op. cit., 264.
15. MS A-000 (Mellenthin), 45.
16. Mellenthin, *Panzer Battles,* 327.
17. XX Corps operational report, Appendix 11, 57.
18. Feuermann and Cranz, *95th Division History,* unpaged.
19. Ibid.
20. Ibid.
21. Article by Col. Hall in *The Military Engineer,* April 1948.
22. MS B-412 (Einem).
23. Ibid.
24. Cole, op. cit., 425.
25. XX Corps operational report, 62-63.
26. Third Army AAR, 3 Nov.

CHAPTER 10

1. The account of this action is based on Feuermann and Cranz, op. cit., and regimental AAR's for November.
2. MS B-079 (Kittel).
3. Fuermann and Cranz, op. cit., unpaged.
4. Mellenthin, *Panzer Battles,* 329.
5. MS A-000 (Mellenthin), 65.

6. Cole, *Lorraine Campaign,* n. 406.
7. MS B-079 (Kittel), 36.
8. Ibid., 46.
9. Ibid., 49.

CHAPTER 11

1. MA B-079 (Kittel), 54.
2. Text quoted in full by Feuermann and Cranz, op. cit.
3. Cole, *Lorraine Campaign,* n. 438.
4. Details in a letter dated 2 Dec. 1944, quoted by Fuermann and Cranz.
5. MS B-079 (Kittel), 56.
6. Fuermann & Cranz, op. cit.
7. MS B-079 (Kittel), 56-57.
8. *11th Infantry Regiment,* 38.
9. Letter to the author.
10. 5th Infantry Division.
11. Spiwoks/Stöber, *Endkampf,* 27.
12. Allan, *Lucky Forward,* 138.
13. MS B-079 (Kittel), 61.
14. Ibid., 63.
15. *11th Infantry Regiment,* 39.

CHAPTER 12

1. Farago, *Patton,* 420.
2. Fuermann and Cranz, op. cit.
3. 5th Infantry Division AAR.
4. Cole, *Lorraine Campaign,* n. 447.
5. Translated from original in possession of the author.
6. Text quoted by Fuermann and Cranz, op. cit.
7. *11th Infantry Regiment,* 46.
8. *5th Infantry Division,* op. cit.
9. *11th Infantry Regiment.* 46.

Index